William W. Ireland

Through the Ivory Gate

Studies in psychology and history

William W. Ireland

Through the Ivory Gate
Studies in psychology and history

ISBN/EAN: 9783744758482

Printed in Europe, USA, Canada, Australia, Japan

Cover: Foto ©ninafisch / pixelio.de

More available books at **www.hansebooks.com**

THROUGH THE IVORY GATE:

STUDIES IN PSYCHOLOGY AND HISTORY.

BY

WILLIAM W. IRELAND, M.D. Edin.;

FORMERLY OF H.M. INDIAN ARMY; CORRESPONDING MEMBER OF THE PSYCHIATRIC SOCIETY OF ST. PETERSBURG, AND OF THE NEW YORK MEDICO-LEGAL SOCIETY.

"Prosequitur dictis, portaque emittit eburna."
VIRGIL.

EDINBURGH:
BELL & BRADFUTE, 12 BANK STREET.
LONDON: SIMPKIN, MARSHALL & CO., AND
HAMILTON, ADAMS & CO.

MDCCCLXXXIX.

PREFACE.

THIS book is written in prosecution of the views stated in "The Blot on the Brain." The historical and psychological studies may be considered as a continuation of the papers in that book on Mohammed, Joan of Arc, Mohammed Toghlak, and others. All the characters described in the present work, in my opinion, suffered from some mental derangement. They were led away by delusions or uncontrollable passions from the right comprehension of things, or the right line of conduct. In figurative language, they were visited by spectres which passed through the Ivory Gate. For those unlearned in Greek and Latin it may not be superfluous to observe that the earliest allusion to this fancy occurs in Book XIX. of the Odyssey, line 562, which is thus translated by Pope:—

> "Immured within the silent bower of sleep,
>   Two portals firm the various phantoms keep:
>   Of ivory one; whence flit to mock the brain,
>   Of winged lies a light fantastic train:
>   The gate opposed pellucid valves adorn,
>   And columns fair incased with polished horn,
>   Where images of truth for passage wait,
>   With visions manifest of future fate."

VIRGIL, who delights to reproduce Homer's fine passages, makes Æneas pass from the Elysian fields out of the Ivory Gate (ÆNEIDOS, vi. l. 894):—

> "Sleep gives his name to portals twain,
>   One all of horn, they say,
> Through which authentic spectres gain
>   Quick exit into day,
> And one which bright with ivory gleams,
>   Whence Pluto sends delusive dreams."
>
> *Conington's Translation.*

HORACE (CARMINUM, iii. Ode 27) makes Europa say: "Do I, in the waking state, deplore the baseness of my fault, or does some vain image, fleeing from the Ivory Gate, delude me innocent of any misdeed?"

Amongst those who have furnished me with valuable information, or kindly supplied me with documents and other aids toward the composition of this book, I have to record my heartfelt thanks to Mr. CLARK BELL, New York; Dr. D. CLARK, Toronto; Dr. C. K. CLARKE of Kingston, Ontario; Dr. T. S. CLOUSTON; Mr. GEORGE R. R. COCKBURN, M.P., Toronto; Doctors J. L. ERSKINE, Deputy Surgeon-General; I. KERLIN of Elwyn, Pa.; H. KURELLA; M. LOVELL of Kingston, Ontario; J. A. SEWELL; W. PUGIN THORNTON of Canterbury; and HACK TUKE. In the course of the book, I take occasion to acknowledge information derived from other kind friends.

WILLIAM W. IRELAND.

SCHOOL FOR WEAK-MINDED CHILDREN,
PRESTON LODGE, PRESTONPANS, EAST LOTHIAN,
  20th September, 1889.

CONTENTS.

PAGE

EMANUEL SWEDENBORG—

CHAPTER I.—His Father—Bishop Jesper Swedberg—His Education—Swedenborg's First Visit to England, Holland, and France—Returns to Sweden—Charles XII. back from Turkey, . . . 1

CHAPTER II.—Conversations with Charles XII.—Swedenborg's Experiments in Mechanics—Assessor of Mines—and Member of the House of Nobles—An Ingenuous Confession—Publishes his Philosophical and Scientific Works—Studies Anatomy, 10

CHAPTER III.—Back to Holland—His Treatises on Anatomy—His Philosophical Views on the Nature of the Soul, and on the Correspondences of Nature, . . 23

CHAPTER IV.—His Views on the Connection between the Soul and the Brain—His Theories on the Function of the Brain—The Chemical Laboratory of the Brain—How much Swedenborg Anticipated of Later Discoveries, ... 30

CHAPTER V.—Swedenborg's Merits as a Scientific Man—His Mental Culture—First Signs of Derangement—His Book of Dreams, ... 36

CHAPTER VI.—What befell Swedenborg in London—His Introduction into the Spiritual World—Resigns his Assessorship—The Nature of Delusional Insanity—His Theological Works—Cuno's Account of Swedenborg—Familiar Spirits—Accounts by Robsahm and Harrison—Nature of his Ecstasies—His Trials and Temptations—Peculiarity of his Respiration, . . . 52

CHAPTER VII.—Summary of His Theology—The Spiritual World—Faith and Charity—The Formation of Character—He sees the Spirits of Luther, Melancthon, Calvin, St. Paul, David, and Mohammed—The State of the Soul after Death—The Interior Memory—All Good

		PAGE
	Actions are from God—Swedenborg's Descriptions of the World of Spirits, Heaven, and Hell, ...	76
CHAPTER VIII.—	The Language of Spirits—Their Ideas of Space—The Doctrine of Correspondence in Nature—The Inner Sense of the Bible—He offers to Interpret the Hieroglyphics, . . .	93
CHAPTER IX.—	Swedenborg collects Information about the Planets and their Inhabitants—His Clairvoyance—Story of the Fire at Stockholm—The Queen of Sweden—The De Marteville Receipt, . .	106
CHAPTER X.—	The Last Judgment—The New Church—Swedenborg's House in Stockholm—His Book on "Conjugial Love"—Letter to Hartley—The True Christian Religion—Letter to Wesley—His Last Illness—Dying Declaration—His Death—Remarks on the Nature of his Neurosis, ...	113

WILLIAM BLAKE, ... 130

THE INSANITY OF KING LOUIS II. OF BAVARIA, . . . 135

CHARLES J. GUITEAU—

CHAPTER I.—	The Assassination of President Garfield—The Guiteau Family—Charles Guiteau as a Child—His Upbringing—Joins the Oneida Community—Leaves the Community—His Quarrels with the Perfectionists—Becomes an Attorney—Gets Married and Divorced—Takes to Religious Lecturing—Takes to Politics—Reasons Assigned by him for the Murder, .	160
CHAPTER II.—	The Assassin in Washington Jail—His Hopes of Assistance—The Trial—The Counsel on Both Sides—The Medical Experts—Theory of the Prosecution—Guiteau's Behaviour in Court—Appears as Witness—His Written Plea—Scoville's Singular Method of Defence—Guiteau Addresses the Jury—Mr. Porter's Speech—The Charge to the Jury—The Verdict and Sentence, ...	181
CHAPTER III.—	Guiteau's Behaviour at his Execution—The Autopsy—The Question of his Insanity—Its Character—Was he responsible?—Felton and Bellingham, ...	203

CONTENTS.

LOUIS RIEL—

 CHAPTER I.—The North-West—The Hudson's Bay Company—Manitoba Transferred to Canada—Riel drives back the New Governor, and seizes upon Fort Garry—His Prisoners—The Red River Expedition—Riel is sent to Parliament—Is committed to an Asylum—His Religious Delusions—Is called from Montana to the Saskatchewan River, ... 229

 CHAPTER II.—Appearance and Character of Riel—The Grievances of the Metis—Riel Offers to Withdraw—His Artful Policy—His Religious Delusions—Leads the Metis into Rebellion—Defeated and made Prisoner—His Trial—Evidence about his Sanity—Sentence, ... 238

 CHAPTER III.—Variance about Riel's Sentence—The Question of Insanity—The Medical Reports—Riel's Execution and Burial—Debate in the Canadian Parliament about the Death Sentence—The Degree of the Responsibility of the Insane, . 254

GABRIEL MALAGRIDA, . 265

THEODORE OF ABYSSINIA, . . 277

THEBAW, KING OF BURMA, . 302

EMANUEL SWEDENBORG.

CHAPTER I.

His Father—Bishop Jesper Swedberg—His Education—Swedenborg's First Visit to England, Holland, and France—Returns to Sweden—Charles XII. back from Turkey.

IN this sketch of the life of Emanuel Swedenborg my principal aim is to give an explanation of his claim to supernatural knowledge and intercourse with the dead, on the principles already explained in my book, "The Blot upon the Brain."* There is no obscurity about the ordinary details of Swedenborg's life. Born in 1688, he lived till 1772. He was thus a contemporary of the French Encyclopedists. Voltaire was born six years after Swedenborg and died six years later. Thus Swedenborg's pretensions to supernatural knowledge were made in the full light of a most sceptical time, the

---

* In that work I contented myself with a page and a-half about Swedenborg in the course of a paper on the hallucinations of Mohammed and Luther which was originally published in the *Journal of Mental Science*. I referred the reader to the articles about Swedenborg in the same journal by Dr. Maudsley (July and October, 1869).

In a review of "The Blot on the Brain" which also appeared in the *Journal of Mental Science* (January, 1886), a friendly critic took occasion to regret that I did not give more careful consideration to the most remarkable case of hallucinations on record, and advised me to devote more attention to the subject of Swedenborg.

Those who wish to read a life of the sage, written by an admirer and disciple, should get "Emanuel Swedenborg, a Biographical Sketch," by James John Garth Wilkinson, London, 1886, an admirable biography, and "Emanuel Swedenborg: His Life and Writings," by William White, in two volumes, London, 1867. Mr. White is described by Mr. Wilkinson as not an opponent of Swedenborg, but a free lance in some alliance with him.

B

latter half of the eighteenth century. They were advanced in the clearest and most matter of fact way, indeed with much repetition in his numerous books, in his letters, and in his recorded conversations. A slight study of the subject ought to convince one, that either Swedenborg was subject to delusions and hallucinations, or that his pretensions to commune with the dead and his claim to announce a new revelation were really founded on truth. To admit the latter view would entail the admission of the truth of a new religion, for though Swedenborg recognises the Divine origin of Christianity, the system which he teaches is different from any of the great Christian Churches in essential points of the creed. If any one, dissatisfied with these explanations, wishes for a third one, I, for my part, have no idea what it may be. Whether the curious reader will refuse or accept a rationalistic explanation mainly depends upon his mental tone, his previous education, and his preconceived ideas.

Emanuel Swedberg, or Swedenborg, was the third child and second son of Jesper Swedberg, chaplain of the Royal Horse Guards, and of Sara, daughter of Albrecht Behm, assessor of the Royal College of Mines. He was born at Stockholm on the 29th of January, 1688. In 1692 his father was appointed Professor of Theology at Upsala.

Emanuel was brought up in the University Square of that little town, in the ecclesiastical and religious atmosphere which surrounded his father, who was at the same time Dean of the Cathedral of Upsala, Professor of Theology, a zealous preacher, and a busy writer on religious and other subjects.

Mr. White is a spiritualist, and thus allows of other communions with the departed. While professing his belief in the claims of Swedenborg he thinks that the wonderful Swede has fallen into some errors in his descriptions of the unseen world, as a traveller visiting an entirely new country might allow himself to be led astray by his prejudices or his conjectures. This independent and critical spirit is viewed with hostility by Dr. R. L. Tafel, who is an orthodox Swedenborgian. This learned gentleman deserves our gratitude by giving to the world the "Documents concerning the Life and Character of Emanuel Swedenborg," collected, translated, and annotated by R. L. Tafel, A.M., Ph.D., published by the Swedenborg Society, 36 Bloomsbury Street, London, 1875. To this exhaustive work I shall have frequent occasion to refer.

He was the first who wrote a Swedish Grammar and compiled a Swedish Dictionary. Though deeply religious Jesper Swedberg was a stirring and ambitious man, who could be both generous and selfseeking. After being ten years at Upsala, he left the university town to become Bishop of Skara.

Some bodily and mental gifts that go by inheritance descended to the son, his father's vigorous health, his longevity, his love of writing, his unconquerable self-sufficiency, and what is most noteworthy, his gift of seeing spirits. Jesper Swedberg was profoundly convinced that he had a guardian angel.[*] He used to tell that when a student of theology at Upsala an angel appeared to him and said, "What do you read?"

Swedberg mentioned the Bible and some religious works, on which the angel kindly recommended some more books, apparently commentaries.

Swedberg said, "Some of these books I have; the rest I shall get." The angel then left after quoting some passages from Scripture and blessing Swedberg, who thanked him humbly.

The bishop also claimed to have cured one of his servants of a dreadful pain in her elbows. The woman came into his room, and prayed that, for the sake of Christ, he would take away her pain or she must go and kill herself. "I rose, touched her arm, and commanded the pain, in the name of Jesus Christ, to depart, and in a minute the one arm was well as the other. Glory to God alone!"

Swedberg claims to have delivered, through his prayers, a servant girl called Kerstin from some mental trouble. Three years after she entered into his service. The bishop tells us[†] that one day another girl quarrelled with Kerstin, when she became so embittered that she threatened to go and destroy herself. She went into the drying kiln for the purpose of suffocating herself:—

"Towards two o'clock," Swedberg says, "a feeling of anxiety came over me while I was sitting in my study and writing. My feeling of anxiety for this Kerstin increased more and more, when yet there was no cause for such an apprehension, inasmuch as I did not know what

---

[*] TAFEL, "Documents," vol. i. p. 146.
[†] *Ibid.*, vol. i. p. 148.

had happened to her. I became suddenly troubled about her as if a fire had been kindled in me. I asked where Kerstin was? They answered, that no one had seen her, and that she must be in the drying kiln. The door was locked, and the smoke was issuing from every hole and chink. After the door had been forced, Kerstin was found lying on the drying bench with her face downwards, and in the thickest smoke, so that we were almost suffocated. Her arms and legs were stretched out. I called, I shrieked. No motion, no sound. We laid her upon the bed like a stock. Then I sobbed and called out with a loud voice :—'Kerstin; wake up and arise, in the name of Jesus Christ!' Immediately she became conscious, received life, raised herself up and began to talk. Afterwards I strengthened her with God's Word, and gave her a good draught of Rhenish wine; whereupon she went and followed her occupation."

The bishop was accused of heresy on account of an inscription on the tomb of his first wife which showed a faith in the prayers of the dead for those they left behind. His restless and somewhat aggressive spirit several times got the good bishop into trouble at Court and elsewhere, but his energy always carried him through.

Thus, both by hereditary predisposition and paternal precept and example, the young Emanuel received an early strain of piety of no formal kind.

When above eighty Swedenborg thus writes to a friend about his youth* :—

"From my sixth to my twelfth year I used to delight in conversing with clergymen about faith, saying that the life of faith is love, and that the love which imparts life is love to the neighbour; also that God gives faith to every one, but that these only receive it who practise that love. I know of no other faith at that time than that God is the Creator and Preserver of nature, that He imparts understanding and a good disposition to men, and several other things that follow thence. I knew nothing at that time of that learned faith which teaches that God the Father imputes the righteousness of His Son to whomsoever, and at such times, as He chooses, even to those who have not repented and have not reformed their lives. And had I heard of such a faith, it would have been then, as it is now, above my comprehension."

---

* Letter to Dr. Beyer, "Document," 243. "Life of Swedenborg," by W. White, vol. i. p. 16. *Vera Christiana Religio*, No. 16.

Writing about the same time in his book on the true Christian religion when treating of the Trinity he says:—
"From my earliest years I could never admit into my mind the idea of more gods than one, and I have always received, and do still retain, the idea of one God alone." Thus, for the son of a Lutheran bishop, his early deviations from orthodoxy were pretty wide. Naturally the education of this precious boy was carried out at the University of Upsala. When a student there, Swedberg lived with Eric Benzelius, who had married his sister Anna. Benzelius was then librarian to the university. He afterwards became professor of theology; and then he rose to be Archbishop of Upsala. Swedberg, who did not keep on the best terms with all his kindred, said that he loved Benzelius better than his own brothers, and even loved and revered him as he did his father.

Many years after, Swedberg wrote of his brother-in-law:—
"He was proud outwardly, but inwardly he was good. He was very learned, but all his knowledge consisted in memory."

In 1709 Emanuel Swedberg took the degree of Doctor in Philosophy, a few months before his warlike sovereign, Charles XII., lost his army at Pultowa, and had to take refuge in Turkey. Swedberg's thesis was on some texts of Seneca and Publius Syrus, with moral reflections of his own. When he left the university he had learned some mathematics and could write Latin fluently. He now devoted much attention to mechanics, and made the acquaintance of Polhem, "the Swedish Archimedes," under whose roof he lived for some time. In the year 1710 he set out on his travels, sailing from Gottenburg to London. On the way to London he tells us:—

"I was four times in danger of my life:—1. From a sandbank on the English coast in a dense fog, when all considered themselves lost, the keel of the vessel being within a quarter of a fathom of the bank. 2. From the crew of a privateer who came on board declaring themselves to be French, while we thought they were Danes. 3. From an English guardship on the following evening, which on the strength of a report mistook us in the darkness for the privateer, wherefore it fired a whole broadside into us, but without doing us any serious damage. 4. In London I was soon after exposed to a still greater danger, for some Swedes, who had approached our ship in a yacht, persuaded me to sail with them to town, when all on board had been commanded to remain there for six weeks, the news having already spread that the plague had broken out in Sweden. As I did not observe the quarantine, an inquiry was made, yet I was saved from the halter, with the declaration, however, that no one who ventured to do this in future would escape his doom."

We doubt whether any one was hanged in England at that time for breaking quarantine, but young travellers are apt to be imposed upon.

This was in the days of Queen Anne, when Marlborough was at the height of his glory, and Pope, Swift, Addison, and De Foe were the favourite writers; but to these clever users of words the young Swedish doctor of philosophy paid no attention. He notices in one of his letters to his brother-in-law, Benzelius, that the magnificent church of St. Paul had been lately finished in all its parts. Apparently the only thing which excites his veneration in Westminster Abbey is the tomb of Casaubon, a great scholar, the marbles of whose tomb are never kissed by any one now.

Writing on the 13th October, 1710, he says :—

"I study Newton daily, and am very anxious to see and hear him. I have provided myself with a small stock of books for the study of mathematics, and also with a certain number of instruments, which are both a help and an ornament in the study of science—such as an astronomical tube, quadrants of several kinds, prisms, microscopes, artificial scales, and camera-obscura, by William Hunt and Thomas Everard, which I admire, and which you too will admire. I hope that, after settling my accounts, I may have sufficient money left to purchase an air-pump."

With what English he could muster, Swedberg went to see John Flamsteed, Astronomer-Royal, at Greenwich, and noted all his instruments with scrutinising eye, and how he used them all, which information was sent by letter to a learned society newly formed at Upsala. This society, of which Benzelius is secretary, sends commissions to Emanuel Swedberg to buy instruments, telescopes, microscopes, globes, quadrants, works on astronomy and the higher mathematics, and the Transactions of the Royal Society.

Here is an extract from a letter preserved by Benzelius:—

"You encourage me to go on with my studies, but I think that I ought rather to be discouraged, as I have such an immoderate desire for them, especially for astronomy and mechanics. I also turn my lodgings to some use, and change them often. At first I was at a watchmaker's, afterwards at a cabinetmaker's, and now I am at a mathematical instrument-maker's. From them I steal their trades, which some day will be of use to me. I have recently computed for my own pleasure several useful tables for the latitude of Upsala, and all the solar and lunar eclipses which will take place between 1712 and 1721. I am willing to communicate them if it be desired. In undertaking in astronomy to facilitate the calculation of eclipses, and of the motion of the moon outside those of the syzygies, and also in undertaking to correct the tables, so as to agree with the new observations, I shall have enough to do."

There is no record that the enthusiastic young Swede ever had an interview with Newton, but he made the acquaintance of Edmund Halley, then Savilian Professor of Geometry at Oxford, with whom he had some conversations about a method of finding the longitude by means of the moon. The English Government had in 1704 offered rewards of £10,000, £15,000, and £26,000 to any one who would show a leading method of determining the longitude within sixty, forty, and thirty miles.

Towards the end of 1711, in the postscript of a letter to Eric Benzelius, the following complaint comes out in a postscript, perhaps in the hopes that it should be repeated to the bishop:—

"I have longed very much to see the Bodleian Library since I saw the little one at Sion College, but I am kept back here on account of 'want of money.' I wonder my father does not show greater care for me than to have let me live, now for more than sixteen months, upon 200 rix-dollars, well knowing that I promised in a letter not to incommode him by drawing for money, and yet none has been forthcoming for the last three or four months. It is hard to live without food or drink like some poor drudge in Schonen."

Two hundred rix-dollars make but forty-five pounds, and even allowing for the depreciation of money, the young Swede must have been very careful, and could hardly have saved enough to buy his air-pump. On the 15th of August, 1712, he writes from London, amongst other things, that not finding great encouragement among this civil and proud people, he was going to submit his project about taking the longitude to a French mathematician. He further observes:—

"As my speculations made me for a time not so sociable as is serviceable and useful for one, and as my spirits are somewhat exhausted, I have taken refuge for a short time in the study of poetry, that I might be somewhat recreated by it. I intend to gain a little reputation by this study, on some occasion or other during this year, and I hope I may have advanced in it as much as may be expected from me, but time and others will perhaps judge of this. Still, after a time, I intend to take mathematics up again, although at present I am doing nothing in them; and if I am encouraged I intend to make more discoveries in them than any one else in the present age, but without encouragement this would be sheer trouble, and it would be like *non profecturis litora bubus arare*—ploughing the ground with stubborn steers."

Soon after this he went to Holland, where he visited most of the cities; he was present at Utrecht during the Congress of Ambassadors, when the treaty was signed which ended the War of Succession. Swedberg was in great favour with Palmquist, the Swedish Ambassador, "who," he writes, "had me every day at his house; every day also I had discussions on algebra with him. He is a good mathematician and a great algebraist. At Leyden he learned glass-grinding, and procured all the instruments and utensils for that purpose. From Holland he went to France, and stayed about a year in Paris and Versailles. As usual he sought the company of mathematicians, making the acquaintance of the Abbe Bignon, De Lahire, and Pierre Varrignon. Leaving France he went by post to Hamburg, whence he found his way to Pomerania. He stayed some time at Greifswalde, which he describes in a letter to his father as quite a paltry university. About the same time Charles XII. leaving Turkey, where he had spent five inactive years, made his way through Germany by devious routes, and reached his fortress of Stralsund one winter night in very sorry condition with but one attendant. With difficulty he gets in at the gates, and makes the governor aware that his royal master is really back. The whole town awakes; all the windows are illuminated. The king's feet are so swelled that his boots have to be cut off, he not having been in bed for sixteen days. Charles lies down and sleeps for a few hours. Next morning he is up to review the garrison, survey the fortifications, and make preparations to attack his enemies, the Danes, the Prussians, the Saxons, the Poles, the Hanoverians, the Russians, with the English behind ready to help against the terrible Swede. After all he was but one man, and could make little way without the brave army he had left behind him in Russia and elsewhere. Emanuel's younger brother Eliezer had been with the army in Pomerania; but our learned Doctor of Philosophy never carried military enthusiasm beyond writing Latin poems in praise of Charles XII. and Stenbock, the general who, with a few regular troops and the militia, drove an invading army of Danes out of Sweden, and for a season revived the proud hopes of the country. Ere the enemy gathered round Stralsund, Emanuel Swedenborg got away in a yacht, and returned to Sweden after an absence of four years. Charles himself escaped from the town after it was half in the possession of the besiegers, in a boat with shattered mast, and two men killed by round shot from one of the enemy's batteries.

CHAPTER II.

Conversations with Charles XII.—Swedenborg's Experiments in Mechanics—Assessor of Mines—and Member of the House of Nobles—An Ingenuous Confession—Publishes his Philosophical and Scientific Works—Studies Anatomy.

The old bishop had now an opportunity of introducing his son, Emanuel Swedberg, to the king, back to Sweden after an absence of fifteen years. Christopher Polhem, the great engineer, brought young Swedberg with him to Charles, at Lund. They had frequent conversations with the king, who had a great taste for mathematics. Swedberg records that Charles thought it a misfortune that ten had been made the foundation of our numbers. This was, no doubt, done because men had ten fingers; but ten is an inconvenient number to work in arithmetic, because, by halving it, we at once get to an odd number, which, being halved, brings us to a fraction. Moreover, it contains neither a square nor a cube of four, and cannot be halved by equal numbers down to one. The king took the trouble to devise names for single numbers up to sixty-four, and thence by double numbers up to $64 \times 64 = 4096$.

This scheme, which the king worked out and put into Swedberg's hands next day, struck him with admiration. He observes,[*] in a letter to Nordberg, who was writing his " Life of Charles XII." :—

" The compendious mode of His Majesty in the discovery of characters and names, and the easy method in which they could be changed, so that, by means of certain marks, they could be varied by each new number, as well as his project for multiplication, considering the short

---

[*] Tafel, " Document," 199.

time he devoted to it, could not fail to excite my astonishment; and I am compelled, therefore, to regard him as a man of deeper thought and more subtle penetration than could or can be supposed by any other man. I am forced also to admit that, if he had chosen, he could have been for all times the foremost among his subjects even in this particular; at least he could have obtained, as easily as any one else, the laurel which is sought for by the learned.

"I was also led to think and to believe that in the other matters, too, of which you will leave to posterity a complete record, he must have had a deeper understanding than he showed outwardly."

Swedberg now occupied his mind principally with mechanics and mining. The most northerly country in Europe, Scandinavia, has little to give in the products of her soil. The riches of Sweden are derived from her minerals. For ages past, the Swedes have been skilful in mining, metallurgy, and chemistry.

It was therefore natural that Swedberg, now back to the house of his stirring father, should turn his attention to those subjects, by which riches and fame should be gained. Through the reckless wars of Charles XII., Sweden was drained of its wealth and manhood. Swedberg himself wrote about this time that his country was in her death-agony. It was no time for a man to sit down to study abstract science, but there was little chance of such a mind remaining long content simply to work in the furrows of the useful. He enumerates fourteen new inventions with which his mind had been occupied—improvements in syphons, sluices, air-guns, aquatic clocks, all savouring of the bold and striking. The first in the list is the construction of a sort of ship, in which a man can go below the surface of the sea and do great damage to the fleet of an enemy; a flying chariot, or the possibility of floating in the air and moving through it; a method of discovering the desires and affections of the minds of men by analysis. To perfect such devices does not seem beyond human attainment. Men are still at work upon some such projects; but in those days it might be said that the young mathematician had mistaken the limits of the possible, and was really wasting his time in sterile efforts. For two years—1716-1718—he published in irregular numbers a periodical called "The Dædalus Hyperboreus," describing various inventions. He was appointed to assist Polhem at the construction of the docks at Carlskrona, and the sluices connecting Lake Wiener with Gottenburg. By Charles's order he was appointed Assessor in the College of Mines. The king, himself insensible to female charms, so far interested himself in Swedberg's affairs that he wished to promote a marriage between Swedberg and one of Polhem's daughters. Writing to Eric Benzelius on 14th September, 1718, Swedberg says: "Polhem's eldest daughter is betrothed to a chamberlain of the king, Manderström by name. I wonder what people will say to this, inasmuch as she was intended for me. His second daughter is in my opinion much prettier." It would thus appear that Swedberg was not sorry to turn his hopes upon the younger sister, who was at that time about fifteen years of age. Not being willing, as a biographer* tells us, to accept Swedberg's overtures, "she did not suffer herself to be betrothed. Her father, however, had a great affection for him, and gave him the lady in a written agreement, hoping that in future years his daughter would be more favourably disposed. This bond his daughter, from filial obedience, signed. Great was her depression of mind after thus binding herself to one to whom she felt no attachment; and her brother, in compassion, abstracted the document secretly from Swedberg, who used to read it over day after day, and soon missed it. When Swedberg found what anguish he had caused to the object of his affections, he freely relinquished all claim to her hand, and took his departure from her father's house." Whether or not this was the way in which the engagement ended, it is certain that Swedberg deeply resented it, and broke off all connection with the family, so that three letters, which Polhem wrote to Swedberg, were returned to him unopened; wherefore Polhem wrote to Benzelius† :—"As I understand that he is probably now at Upsala,

---

* WILKINSON, p. 14.
† TAFEL, vol. i. p. 636. We also learn from Tafel that Emerentia Polhem "had a literary taste, and was known in her time for a work on Swedish Rhyme. In 1723 she was married to Rückersköld, Councillor of the Court of Appeals, to whom she bore nine children. She died in 1760."

I must beg you to offer him my greeting, or else to send it him by letter wherever he may be at present, and also to ask him to favour me with one of his welcome letters, which are so much the more acceptable in our house, as he has given us sufficient cause to love him as our own son."

Charles made use of his talents as an engineer in transporting on rollers two galleys and five large boats and a sloop fourteen miles overland to the Iddefjord. These he used for his pontoons to transport his large cannon to be used at the siege of Fredericshall. The reason why he could not take the vessels round by the open sea was that he was not strong enough to face the Danish and English warships, which might have disputed their passage. With some difficulty Swedberg managed to save his attendance at the siege of Fredericshall, where Charles met the death which he had braved so often (14th December, 1718). Sweden was then allowed the peace which she so sorely needed.

The year after, the old bishop, Jesper Swedberg, and his sons were ennobled by Queen Ulrika Eleanora, the successor of Charles. As it was usual for Swedes, on being subjected to the ennobling process, to make some change in their name, they now assumed that of Swedenborg. Emanuel now enjoyed the privilege of sitting in the House of Nobles, whose power was augmented at the expense of that of the Crown after the death of Charles XII. His duties as assessor required daily attendance at the College of Mines. Apparently this college gave permission to private enterprise to commence mining, decided on all disputes connected therewith, and looked after those mines in which the State claimed an interest.

Supported by the influence of his father, and connected by the marriage of his sisters and other relatives with some learned and important personages in the State, Swedenborg's position and prospects were probably thought to be happy. Nevertheless, he was not contented. Perfectly aware of his own eminent abilities, he thought that in another country they might be better appreciated. In December, 1719, he thus writes to Eric Benzelius:—

"MOST HONOURED AND DEAREST BROTHER,—I send you herewith the little work which I mentioned in my last respecting a decimal system in our coinage and measures. This is the last that I will publish myself, because *quotidiana et domestica vilescunt* (i.e., because things that have reference to domestic and every-day affairs are considered of no account), and because I have already worked myself poor by them. I have been singing long enough; let us see whether any one will come forward, and hand me some bread in return."

After mentioning some of his plans with a view to publish his discoveries about fire and stoves, he goes on:—

"I intend to spend all my remaining time upon what may promote everything that concerns mining, and, on the basis which has already been laid, in collecting as much information as possible. *Thirdly*, if fortune so favours me, that I shall be provided with all the means that are required, and if meanwhile, by the above preparations and communications, I shall have gained some credit abroad, I should prefer by all means to go abroad, and seek my fortune in my calling, which consists in promoting everything that concerns the administration and the working of mines. For he is nothing short of a fool, who is independent and at liberty to do as he pleases, and sees an opportunity for himself abroad, and yet remains at home in darkness and cold, where the Furies, Envy, and Pluto have taken up their abode, and dispose the rewards, and where labours such as I have performed are rewarded with misery. The only thing I would desire until that time come, is *bene latere* (i.e., to find a sequestered place where I can live secluded from the world). I think I may find such a corner in the end; either at Starbo or at Skin[skatte]berg."

He ends by saying that it will be four or five years before he can carry out this plan.

And so he went on in the meantime with his pamphlets and papers, and the transactions of learned societies. In the spring of 1721 he gets leave of absence from the College of Mines to go to Amsterdam to get a heap of manuscripts printed.*

---

* We here give Mr. Wilkinson's list of these publications, as some imperfect proof of the extraordinary range and activity of his mind, and the course and succession of his studies. He published the following little works at Amsterdam:—1. "Some Specimens of a Work on the Principles of Natural Philosophy, comprising New Attempts to explain the Phenomena of Chemistry and Physics by Geometry." 2. "New Observations and Discoveries respecting Iron and Fire, and particularly respecting the Elemental Nature of Fire; together with a new Construction of Stoves." 3. "A New

This could not well be done in Sweden, and in those days it was impossible to get the sheets properly corrected without the personal oversight of the author. Swedenborg had found a patron in Louis Rudolf, Duke of Brunswick, who helped him to defray the expenses of his journey. To him Swedenborg dedicated the fourth part of his " Miscellaneous Observations," published at Leipzig in 1722. He was absent from Sweden fifteen months, during which he visited the mines and smelting works near Aix-la-Chapelle, Liège, and Cologne.

In 1724 he was offered the Professorship of Mathematics in the University of Upsala, which he would not have. " My own business," he writes to Benzelius, " has been geometry, metallurgy, and chemistry, and there is a great difference between them and astronomy. It would be inexcusable for me to give up a profession in which I think I can be of good use ; further, I have not the *donum docendi* (*i.e.*, the gift of teaching) ; you know my natural difficulty in speaking." Swedenborg was now in easy circumstances. He had inherited a good deal of property, principally in mines, from his stepmother, who died in 1720. She was with difficulty dissuaded by his father from leaving everything to Emanuel, whom she favoured above all her other step-children. In 1735 he derived further property by the death of the old Bishop, who passed away at the venerable age of eighty-two.

The records of the College of Mines attest that he was assiduous in his duties, and the important books which he planned and wrote show that he spent most of his leisure in study. He attended the Sittings in the House of Nobles, and occasionally spoke. He was in favour of the limitations in the power of the Kings of Sweden, which were introduced

---

Method of finding the Longitude of Places on Land or at Sea, by Lunar Observations." 4. " A New Mechanical Plan of Constructing Docks and Dykes." 5. " A Mode of Discovering the Powers of Vessels by the Application of Mechanical Principles."

In 1722 he published at Leipzig " Miscellaneous Observations connected with the Physical Sciences," parts i. and iii. ; and at Hamburg in the same year, part iv., principally on Minerals, Iron, and the Stalactites in Baumann's Cavern. These works have been translated by C. E. Strutt, and published by the Swedenborg Association.

on the death of Charles XII., and approved of the sentence on Count Brahe and Baron Horn, who, with eight others, were beheaded for conspiring to restore a despotic government (1756).

Swedenborg's Memorial to the Secret Committee of the House of Nobles on the impolicy of declaring war against Russia in 1734, is a document worthy of a great statesman. The justice of his anticipations as to the probable consequences of a contest with Russia was confirmed in the dear school of experience, when war was actually declared in 1741, for the Swedes were unable to make head against Russia, and lost a great part of Finland.

About the details of the assessor's private life during this period almost nothing has been recorded. Robsahm, an admirer and disciple of his later years, says :—

"It is well known that Swedenborg in his youth had a mistress, whom he left because she was false to him. Besides this there cannot be found in his life any traces of a disorderly love." *

General Tuxen when entertaining Swedenborg, now old and lost in religious ecstasies, jocosely asked him :—

"Whether he had ever been married, or desirous of marrying? He answered, 'No; but that once in his youth he had been on the road to matrimony, King Charles XII. having recommended the famous Polhem to give him his daughter.' On my asking what obstacle had prevented it, he replied, 'She would not have me, as she had promised herself to another person, to whom she was more attached.' I then craved his pardon if I had been too inquisitive. He answered, 'Ask whatever question you please, I shall answer in truth.' I then inquired whether in his youth he could keep free from temptations with regard to the sex? He replied, 'Not altogether; in my youth I had a mistress in Italy.' After some little pause, he cast his eye on a harpsicord, &c."

On this subject,† Mr. White observes :—

---

* See WHITE, vol. i. p. 122 ; and TAFEL, vol. ii. p. 437 ; and vol. i. p. 628.

† Dr. Tafel objects to Robsahm's statement that it was made on hearsay ; but Robsahm was a respectable man, Director of the Bank of Stockholm,

"No doubt Robsahm refers to his life in Stockholm and not in Italy. It may have been that Swedenborg was misunderstood by General Tuxen, and that (Italy) was supplied by his imagination. Yet there is fair cause for belief in both mistresses. The confession to Tuxen was not exhaustive, and Robsahm did not know everything. Moreover the Italian mistress is more credible after the Stockholm one, even as the chances of marriage are greater with widowers than bachelors."

Swedenborg was fifty years old before he ever reached Italy. A man of eighty-two may perhaps, looking back thirty-two years, talk of fifty as a time of youth, but hardly as an excuse for the case in point. Swedenborg says, elsewhere, that an inclination for women had been his chief passion, and in his book, "De Amore Conjugiali," he allows the keeping of a mistress to be venial, under certain conditions.

There is still extant, a letter dated 1729, from Jonas Unge,* who married Swedenborg's sister, Catherine, in the course of which he asks Swedenborg why he lets all chances of a good marriage slip away, and recommends a desirable match. Whatever the reason was, Swedenborg lived his life alone.

The most prominent events in Swedenborg's life are the publications of his books. They mark the evolution of his mind, and Swedenborg's biography is only interesting as the strange history of a great mind. After 1722, we hear of

---

and a friend of Swedenborg: we may fairly conclude that he would not lightly make such a statement. Dr. Tafel thinks it incredible that Tuxen would have asked such an indelicate question of Swedenborg, before his own wife and daughters. This was stated to be done in the last century, when conversation before ladies was much freer on some points. Tafel also objects that we have not the original Danish of Tuxen's account. It was first published in 1790, translated into English by Augustus Nordensköld, "whose unchaste conduct during his stay in Manchester was such as no New Churchman could overlook," and whose own brother testified that "he (Augustus N.) had lost the interior discernment of what is good and true." Therefore Tafel holds that he invented this scandal about Swedenborg, and interpolated it into Tuxen's account, the fraud being published during Tuxen's life. If it had not been for respect to Dr. Tafel's careful researches, I should never have thought the question needed discussing.

* TAFEL, vol. ii. p. 148.

neither book nor pamphlet for above ten years, and then he obtains leave to go to Leipzig to get printed a great pile of manuscript, the product of his enormous mental force. He leaves Stockholm on the 10th May, 1733, with a party of Swedish gentlemen. Their first visits were to Stralsund and other scenes of the last war. Then he travels through Germany and Bohemia, visiting and observing everything noteworthy, especially recording what he saw at mines and smelting houses. At Leipzig and Dresden he got printed three folio volumes, "Opera Philosophica et Mineralia." The first volume is entitled "Principia Rerum Naturalium, sive Novorum Tentaminum Phænomena Mundi Elementaris Philosophice Explicandi." "The Principles of Natural Things, being New Attempts towards explaining the Phenomena of the Elemental World." The second tome is on iron; the third on copper, brass, and zinc, what these metals are, how to find them, how to extract, smelt, and assay them, in short, all about them. He has now finally dropped writing in Swedish and writes in Latin, no doubt because he does not wish his readers to be confined to one country. Though he overcame the difficulty of composing in a strange language, Swedenborg never fairly acquired the art of writing. His volumes remind one of a scroll or commonplace book from which a finished work might be elaborated; but which no man, with the artistic talent an author should possess, would dream of sending to the printer. The three folio volumes are now published, at the expense of the Duke Rudolph of Brunswick, in a handsome form, with copper-plate engravings. Swedenborg's works are full of repetitions and superfluous sentences; here and there are passages which strike us with their weight and truth, and sometimes the power of expression is added to the power of thought; now-a-days, they are only interesting as showing the development of the mind of the writer. His studies were pursued in the natural manner, in the same series indeed in which Comte has arranged the sciences, on the principle of decreasing generality, from the general and simple to the complex and particular. From mathematics he passed to physics; from physics, to chemistry and mineralogy; from chemistry, to anatomy; from anatomy, to physiology;

from physiology, to psychology. Here an ordinary scientific mind would have stopped; but we can see all through his scientific writings the impetus which pushed him on to speculate, and then to dogmatise, on the nature of the soul and its condition after death, and to seek in God the final cause of all things. To use his own words, "The end of the senses is that God may be seen."

In the "Principia Rerum Naturalium," now published at Dresden in 1734, he tries to explain the origin of the world on principles taken from geometry. Nature, according to this work, originated in a geometrical point which lies between the finite and the infinite, and shares the nature of both. Nature exists in leasts; from observing given portions of matter we may infer what takes place with the smallest particles or rise to the largest planetary masses. The same laws govern all. The geometrical point has inherent in it the potentiality of all motion. The primeval planetary masses were made of points in perpetual spiral motion or undulation round the vortex of the sun. An outer area of ether was first formed, then it broke, when by the action of magnetic forces it was condensed into planetary masses. Then the chaotic elements of the planets condensed into air; then into water; then around the globules of water grew crusts from which came crystals of salts, from which the mineral kingdom was formed. From this, by a series of changes, a fit soil for vegetables was formed, after which animals appeared.

The "Principia" shows the tendency in Swedenborg's mind to give a realistic form to mere fancies, and the extreme patience with which his reason would work under the command of the imagination. At a later period of his life Swedenborg came to the conclusion that these geometrical points, not being predicated of any substance, were nothing beyond conceptions of the human mind. Even at the time when he wrote the "Principia" Swedenborg was not quite sure of the foundation of his theory. He observes :—

"Since the point is of such a nature that it must necessarily be contemplated as proceeding from the infinite, and yet, existing before any finite, and so must be considered as non-geometrical, inasmuch as the finite is produced by it, like always begetting its like; I could wish that some other person capable of the task would favour us with a better or more just view of the subject. For my own part, I would willingly give up the further consideration of this first ens to which something of infinity adheres, and proceed to the finites.

"This was hard; his point he was bound to make clear: yet after much ado he ends in taking it for granted."*

It may check our disrespect of this folio full of solemn trifling to recall a similar conception, broached by a more practical investigator. Faraday † had a brooding impression that particles are only centres of force; that the force or forces constitute the matter; that therefore there is no space between the particles distinct from the particles of matter; that they touch each other just as much in gases as in liquids or solids; and that they are materially penetrable, probably even to their very centres.

But, as Dr. Mayo remarked in a letter to Faraday, "your mathematical point is either a simple negation, as having neither magnitude nor parts, or is itself, after all, a material atom."

The atom of Epicurus, the existence of which is argued by Lucretius in his wonderful poem, is a real particle occupying space and having divers shapes. The atom of chemistry, though too small to be seen, is also regarded as a real body, out of whose placements and displacements all chemical compounds are built up. The existence of such atoms, though scarcely a pure assumption, cannot be proved; but at any rate an arrangement of chemistry has been made out of it by which its facts can be stated in a way which gives clearness to their conception by the mind. Faraday observes that the fundamental and main facts of chemistry are expressed by the term "definite proportion;" the rest, including the atomic notion, is assumption, but without the experimental skill of Dalton and Berzelius, showing the reality of combining proportions, that is, that certain substances form chemical combinations with one another in given proportions by weight

---

* WHITE, vol. i. p. 93.
† "Life and Letters of Faraday," by Dr. Bence Jones; London, 1870; vol. ii. p. 178.

and volume, the atomic theory would have remained a vapid hypothesis. The facts support the theory, and the theory gives an explanation to the facts. The theory may become insufficient, but it has served a good purpose in the building up of modern chemistry, and there is as yet no other theory to take its place. Swedenborg's geometrical dream had no such framework of facts upon which it could take form, and was of no use even as a provisional hypothesis.

About this time Swedenborg formed a friendship with Christian Wolff, Professor of Mathematics and Philosophy, at Marburg. Wolff was a metaphysician of the School of Leibnitz. In many of his ideas he agreed with Swedenborg, and by his writings and correspondence had an enduring influence on the mind of the learned Swede. That indefatigable philosopher before he left Germany published at Dresden a book on "The Infinite and the Final Cause of Creation and the Mechanism of the Intercourse between Mind and Body." Having shown by reasoning that the universe must be finite since it is composed of parts, he leads the reader back to a first cause uncaused and infinite. This he considered an *à priori* proof of the existence of God. He now asks how can the infinite have a connection with the finite. As Epicurus said, nothing but matter can move matter: How can the finite subsist without the continual contact of the infinite, and how is this contact made? In this difficulty he has recourse to revelation. He finds the connection between the infinite and the finite in the only begotten Son of God, through whom the first finites are connected with the last, and both with God.

Swedenborg returned to Stockholm in July, 1734.

His inquiring mind now turned to the study of anatomy. Very few men indeed have studied this science to any purpose save as an entry to the healing art. Swedenborg was led to it through philosophic curiosity. Mr. Wilkinson tells us that his principal attention was directed to the study of the human frame for eleven years up to 1744.

"We do not know," observes his learned biographer and translator, "to what extent he was a practical anatomist. He informs us that he had made use of the dissecting room, and it is said that he attended the instructions of Boerhaave at the same time as the elder Monro, the authority for which is, however, only traditional. Be this as it may, it is plain that Swedenborg derived his knowledge of the body chiefly from plates and books, though assuredly he was one who lost no opportunity of pursuing his subject in the best way."

CHAPTER III.

BACK TO HOLLAND—HIS TREATISES ON ANATOMY—HIS PHILOSOPHICAL VIEWS ON THE NATURE OF THE SOUL, AND ON THE CORRESPONDENCES OF NATURE.

IN 1736, Swedenborg again obtained leave from the king to go abroad for the space of three or four years, that he might compose and publish some literary work. He gave up one-half of his salary to his substitute. He set out on the 10th July from Copenhagen to Hamburg, thence to Holland.

We find in his diary the following strange reflections on the Dutch nation :—

"I have considered why it was that it has pleased our Lord to bless such an uncouth and avaricious people with such a splendid country; why He has preserved them from all misfortunes; has caused them to surpass all other nations in commerce and enterprise; and made their country a place whither most of the riches, not only of Europe, but also of other places flow. The principal cause seems to me to have been that it is a republic, wherein the Lord delights more than in monarchical countries; as appears also from Rome. The result is, that no one deems himself obliged and in duty bound to accord honour and veneration to any human being, but considers the low as well as the high to be of the same worth and consequence as a king and emperor; as is also shown by the native bent and disposition of every one in Holland. The only one for whom they entertain a feeling of veneration is the Lord, putting no trust in flesh; and when the Highest is revered most, and no human being in His place, it is most pleasing to the Lord. Besides, each enjoys his own free will, and from this his worship of God flows; for each is, as it were, his own king, and rules under the government of the Highest; and from this it follows again that they do not, out of fear, timidity, and excess of caution, lose their courage and their independent rational thought; but in full freedom, and without being borne down, they are able to fix their souls upon, and elevate them to, the honour of the Highest, who is unwilling to share His worship with any other. At all events, those minds that are borne down by a sovereign power are brought up in flattery and falsity; they learn how to speak and act differently from what they think; and when this condition has become inrooted by habit, it engenders a sort of second nature, so that, even in the worship of God, such persons speak differently from what they think, and extend their flattering ways to the Lord Himself, which must be highly displeasing to Him."

From Holland he passed through Belgium to France, where he remained for a year and a-half. In April, 1738, Swedenborg crossed the Alps into Italy, and spent about a year in that country, principally in Venice and Rome. Some notes of his travels have been published. They show his usual desire to see everything, but throw no fresh light upon his character or state of mind. In 1740, he published, at Amsterdam, "Œconomia Regni Animalis;" and in November, 1740, he was again back to Stockholm.

Swedenborg published two large treatises on Anatomy,* and left an enormous manuscript on "The Brain," which has only recently been given to the world. From these we may learn what his views were on Psychology. It is easy to see the importance of the question. Were his ideas on the nature of the soul which he accepted or discovered by unaided reason, the same or similar to those which he professed to derive from the instruction of the angels? It was, he tells us, a restless curiosity to learn something of the nature of the soul which impelled him to study the anatomy and physiology of the body.

---

* The praiseworthy diligence of his followers has given us excellent translations, with learned notes, of Swedenborg's scientific works. The English titles of the books cited above are—"The Economy of the Animal Kingdom, Considered Anatomically, Physically, and Philosophically." Amsterdam, 1741.

"The Animal Kingdom, Considered Anatomically, Physically, and Philosophically." This was published in three parts, two of which appeared at the Hague in 1744, the third at London in 1745.

"The Brain, Considered Anatomically, Physiologically, and Philosophically," by Emanuel Swedenborg, edited, translated, and annotated by R. L. Tafel, A.M., Ph.D., in four volumes. One of these volumes was given to the world in 1882, the second in 1887.

The large work on "The Animal Kingdom" gives us what was then known of anatomy and physiology; and even in those days the naked eye anatomy of the human body was pretty well worked up. In the Prologue to "The Animal Kingdom," Swedenborg tells us that he means to examine thoroughly the whole world or microscosm which the soul inhabits, for it is in vain to seek her anywhere but in her own kingdom.

The following is a *resumé* of Swedenborg's views at this time on the relation of the soul to the body, expressed, as far as brevity permits, in his own words.

The soul forms the body before the mind is awakened by sensory impressions. By means of the senses the soul is aware of what takes place in the extremes of the body in order that it may keep all things under its auspices, and dispose them according to contingencies. The soul is a more subtile substance than the body, but has exactly the same form and appearance. At death it divests itself of the corporeal world in which it has lived, and betakes itself to its own sphere. The materials which the soul has borrowed to form the body are now dispersed in the earth and air. It never again unites with a corporeal frame. Thus, even in 1734, Swedenborg had entirely got rid of the notion of the resurrection. At first Swedenborg seems to have found the soul in the doctrine of the animal spirits common amongst physiologists of the time; but this view he afterwards gave up. The question, Whether the soul is not material? he adroitly parries by asking, What is matter? If it be defined as extension endued with inertia, the soul is not natural, for inertia only belongs to the last things of nature, such as water and minerals. On the other hand, he believes the soul, like everything created, to be extended, and hence it may be called material.

In the "Animal Kingdom" he refers to the fanciful doctrine of representation and correspondences. He finds a perpetual symbolical representation of spiritual life in the corporeal life, as likewise a perpetual typical representation of the soul in the body. He promises to treat of*—

"Both these symbolical and typical representations, and of the

---

* "The Animal Kingdom," vol. i. p. 451.

astonishing things which occur, I will not say in the living body only, but throughout nature, and which correspond so entirely to supreme and spiritual things, that one would swear that the physical world was purely symbolical of the spiritual world; insomuch that, if we chose to express any natural truth in physical and definite vocal terms, we shall by this means elicit a spiritual truth or theological dogma, in place of the physical truth or precept; although no mortal would have predicted that anything of the kind could possibly arise by bare literal transposition, inasmuch as the one precept, considered separately from the other, appears to have absolutely no relation to it. I intend hereafter to communicate a number of examples of such correspondences, together with a vocabulary containing the terms of spiritual things, as well as of the physical things for which they are to be substituted. This symbolism pervades the living body; and I have chosen simply to indicate it here for the purpose of pointing out the spiritual meaning of *searching the reins.*"

In the vain chase of these fanciful analogies between mental affections and physical structure, Swedenborg never came in sight of the wonderful correspondences of transcendental anatomy and the analogous development of the embryo, which attracted the imaginative mind of Goethe. It was left for a later generation of anatomists to show that all the bones are modifications of the vertebræ, that the ribs and limbs are moveable vertebral processes, and that the head itself is composed of a series of vertebræ, the central cavity of which is widened to enclose the brain, which is a continuation of the spinal cord, folded forwards and backwards to occupy less space. The fact is, Swedenborg approached the study of anatomy on the wrong side. For merely surgical purposes one may go to examine and dissect the human body at once; but to do so scientifically one should commence the study of vertebrate animals in their simplest forms, and pass step by step upwards to man, who has the most complex structure of all. Swedenborg's acquaintance with zoology and botany was trifling compared with his knowledge of human anatomy. It is singular that, though a contemporary of Linnæus, he never seems to have met with his great fellow-countryman. Swedenborg actually denied the sexes of plants, asserting that all plants were male, and that the soil stood to the seeds in the relation of the mother, but this was after his mind had been opened by converse with the spiritual world.

In another place* Swedenborg writes :—

"To discover the soul there are two ways; one by bare reasoning, the other by the anatomy of the body. On making the attempt I found myself as far from my object as ever. No sooner did I feel the soul within my grasp than I found it eluding me, though it never wholly disappeared from my view. Thus my hopes were not destroyed, but deferred, and I have frequently reproached myself with stupidity for being ignorant of that, which was yet everywhere most really present to me; since by reason of the soul we hear, see, feel, perceive, remember, imagine, think, desire, will, and by the soul we move and live. The soul it is by cause of which, and out of which, the visible corporeal kingdom chiefly exists, and to the soul we are to ascribe whatever excites our wonder in the body, for the body is constructed after the image of the soul. Thus did I seem to see, and yet not to see, the very object with the desire of knowing which I was never at rest. At length I awoke as from a deep sleep and discovered, that nothing is further removed from the understanding than what is present to it, that nothing is more present to the understanding than what is universal, prior and superior, than what is indeed itself. What is more omnipresent than the Deity—in Him we live, and are, and move—and yet, What is more remote from the operation of the understanding?"

The following passage is noteworthy as containing views identical with those which he afterwards published as revealed to him through his converse with the spiritual world.†

"There are no innate laws in the mind. Conscience is generated from instruction adopted by free choice scrutinised by the reason, and passed by the judgment into the will. When the conflict of life is over, conscience is discovered either killed, wounded, or victorious. If killed, it is a sign that the mind has given up all love and fear of higher things, and has resigned itself to the rule of the lower forces. If wounded, it is driven about from hope to despair, at one moment laying down its arms in exhaustion, and at another renewing the combat, or else seeking solace in the doctrine of predestination, or of

---

* WHITE, vol. i. p. 142. "Economy of the Animal Kingdom," part ii. No. 208.

† "Economy of the Animal Kingdom," part ii. Nos. 358-363.

universal grace bestowed without any effort to deserve it, or sometimes it attacks and impugns the truth, although the conscience that does this is well nigh dead of its wound. If victorious, it overflows with transporting joys.

"In the light into which the soul enters at death the conscience pronounces its own sentence. If good, it rejoices in the light; if evil, it hastes away in pain, even as an injured eye shrinks into darkness, though all the while the light is excellent and blameless."

The likeness between the views about the soul and the future life given by Swedenborg in his "Anatomical Treatises," and the doctrine promulgated at a later period as the outcome of supernatural revelation is admitted by Dr. Wilkinson in the following noteworthy passage*:—

"The doctrines which they (the 'Œconomia Regni Animalis' and the 'Regnum Animale') set forth respecting the human body are reiterated with scarcely an omission in his 'Theological Treatises,' and particularly in his 'Arcana Cœlestia,' where they serve as the ground-work of his stupendous descriptions of the life of man after death, when he is associated with his like, according to the laws of order and degrees; and, if he is capable of it, becomes a part of the grand human form of heaven. It is therefore at once edifying and delightful to examine the scientific evolution of those doctrines in the 'Animal Kingdom,' and to observe how wonderfully coherent they are, and how firm they stand in nature. At the same time, far be it from us to admit that Swedenborg's theology was the outgrowth of his science. This has been stated to be the case, and it is an assertion easily made, a proposition which the sceptic will be too ready to conceive. But we give it a direct negative; it is the off-spring of a double ignorance—an ignorance of both the premises. Those who are best acquainted with the writings of Swedenborg know full well that it has not a glimmer of probability to support it."

Without pretending to a knowledge of Swedenborg's writings at all approaching that of Dr. Wilkinson, one may surely hold that if Swedenborg had through his studies in the natural world anticipated the general drift of the revelations made to him several years later, this constitutes some ground for believing that his fancied revelations came from no deeper

---

* "The Animal Kingdom," vol. ii., introductory remarks by the Translator, p. 62.

source than the depths of his own mind. Towards the end of the prologue to the "Animal Kingdom,"[*] Swedenborg writes :—

"Whoso believes revelation implicitly, without consulting the intellect, is the happiest of mortals, the nearest to heaven, and at once a native of both worlds. But these pages of mine are written with a view to those only, who never believe anything but what they can receive with the intellect, consequently who boldly invalidate, and are fain to deny the existence of all supereminent things, sublimer than themselves, as the soul itself, and what follows therefrom—its life immortality, heaven. Consequently they honour and worship nature, the world, and themselves, in other respects they compare themselves to brutes, and think that they shall die in the same manner as brutes, and their souls exhale and evaporate; thus they rush fearlessly into wickedness. For these persons only I am anxious."

Nevertheless Swedenborg had already parted with many doctrines deemed essential to the Lutheran creed of his country, especially the Trinity, justification by faith without works, and the resurrection of the body. In his "Principia" Swedenborg had quite ignored the cosmogony of Genesis, which was then received by the churches in the literal sense. It was probably on this account that the book was put in the "Index Expurgatorius" by the Pope. It was one of his early heresies that he lost faith in hell fire; writing to Benzelius in 1719 Swedenborg combats his theory that the sun is the abode of the damned. "The nearer the sun," he argues "the finer are the elements. Hence the sun ought to be the abode of the blest. It would be absurd to imagine that the sun's heat is used to torment the bodies of the damned. In the nature of things, there is no pain without destruction. When fire burns our flesh it dissolves and destroys the flesh, and with its destruction ends the possibility of sensation, and therefore of pain."

---

[*] See Translation by J. J. Garth Wilkinson, vol. i. p. 14.

CHAPTER IV.

His Views on the Connection between the Soul and the Brain—His Theories on the Function of the Brain—The Chemical Laboratory of the Brain—How much Swedenborg Anticipated of later Discoveries.

Here is a sketch of Swedenborg's views on the nature of the soul and its relation to the nervous system as contained in his work on "The Brain," recently translated and given to the world for the first time by Dr. Tafel, in two volumes, filling about 1500 pages octavo, which are to be succeeded by two more volumes. The original MSS. appears to have been written between 1741 and 1743.

The soul is like the Deity of the microcosm which it weaves and forms into its own image in accordance with its own essential form,* and works in harmony with the end which it beholds in itself. By virtue of its presence in the body the soul becomes cognisant of things around. Thus the soul is endowed with, and enjoys, a certain kind of omnipresence, omniscience, omnipotence, and providence in its own little world. To the soul is adjoined a queen which administers a part of the empire, not so much from nature and the necessity of love and justice flowing thence, as from the understanding of truth and the affection of good, nay even from a certain voluntary choice. This is called the rational mind which properly belongs to us and is human. Yet as the body is related to its soul, so the soul is related to the God of the universe, to whom alone belongs without limit Omni-

---

* This is precisely the same doctrine as is revealed in Swedenborg's treatise on "Heaven and Hell," published in 1758. "The corporeal form is adapted to the spirit according to the form of the latter, and not conversely, for the spirit is clothed with a body according to its own form," N. 453, p. 215.

potence, Omniscience, Providence, Esse, Doing, Living; for from Him the soul has acquired its essence, power, force, and life. The soul is the universal essence of its body. Each soul is peculiar and proper to each body. The soul of one person cannot belong to or be transferred to the body of another. From the beginning the soul presides over the formation of the body. The body represents the soul in a visible image. "If therefore, you abstract from the blood these elementary and terrestrial parts, and if you abstract from the animal spirit its purer parts of the same kind, what then remains is nothing but a form derived from the determination of the soul, or the veriest being of the body, presented under a similar form to that which is seized by the senses when it is found combined with terrestrial elements; but which form is purified of its really corporeal parts." This means that if the grosser parts of the body, such as the skin, muscles, bone, and blood were all withdrawn, the soul would still remain, presenting the same outline and appearance, composed of rarer or subtler elements. In short, a man's ghost or spirit is composed of some thin ethereal substance and keeps the shape of the man which it actually held during life while it was conjoined with the grosser parts of the body. In the living frame there are several essences, the highest of these is the soul, the middle is the animal spirits, and the lowest is the blood. The soul, the highest essence, imparts being, life, and the power of acting to the middle essence, the animal spirit imparts powers in like manner to the lowest, the lowest consequently exists and subsists by means of the middle.

The intercourse between the soul and the body is established and maintained through the brain, especially through the frontal portion of the gray matter of the cerebrum. From the brain, as a centre, the soul, which comprises the mind, looks around on all things on the circumference of the body so that it is able to embrace and keep all things under its auspices and intuition. The soul, from the gray or cortical substance of the brain, produces the fibres which, passing through the central and medullary portion of the brain and through the medulla oblongata and spinal cord, are distributed to those organs which are subject to the behests of the will.

The cerebrum sends also fibres to the organs of the senses so that it becomes aware of the contact and pulse of the outer elements and forces of nature. The cerebellum, on the other hand, sends nerves to form and preside over the organs of the abdomen and chest. Swedenborg regards the eighth pair of nerves and the great sympathetic as coming from the cerebellum, which, of course, is a mistake. He observes that it is generally acknowledged that the cerebrum is the common sensory as well as the general motor organ, but it is not so well known that it is also the laboratory of the animal spirit and of the blood, and therefore most abundantly furnished with organs and a chemical apparatus. This notion of the animal spirit, now never heard of, was familiar to the anatomists of those times, and plays an important part in Swedenborg's physiology. He regards the brain as a gland for the elaboration of the animal spirits. He was aware of the gray matter of the brain being principally composed of cells or spherules as he calls them; each cell has a nerve of fibre which apparently he regarded as a permeable tube, agreeably to Malpighi's maxim, "Nature exists entire in leasts."

He observes that each cell is at once a minute brain, a minute sensory organ, a minute eye of interior sight, a minute motor organ, a minute heart or gland, or a minute laboratory for the elaboration of animal spirits. This animal spirit which is prepared in the nerve cell is poured or propelled into the nerve fibre and from thence passes into the blood. It is, however, too volatile to be poured into the blood unless mixed with lymph, and this lymph percolates from the minute arteries under the dura mater and passes into the lacteal vessels of the brain. The motor fibres proceeding from the anterior or frontal portions of the cerebrum which are destined for the muscles, subject to the will, pass through the corpora striata. This is quite in accordance with the physiology of our day. Swedenborg held that the fibres of the middle and back part of the hemispheres go toward the corpus callosum and through that organ into the body of the former. Thus, though Swedenborg correctly indicated that the corpus callosum received the converging fibres from the circumference of the brain, he thought that this was to convey the animal spirit to the fornix lying below. Here was what he called the great chemical laboratory of the brain consisting of the corpus callosum, the fornix, the three ventricles, the choroid plexus, the pituitary gland, &c.

Changing his form of expression, Swedenborg calls the cerebrum a large conglomerate gland, and the pituitary body a corresponding conglobate gland. The cerebellum also is a laboratory to prepare a chyle which passes into the blood. "There are also," he remarks, "several other laboratories of the purer lymph, but the principal supply comes from the cerebrum, the other sources being like smaller brooks or streams. The lymph charged with the animal spirit is carried down by the jugular vein, where it meets with the chyle conveyed by the thoracic duct into the subclavian vein, so that these two fluids meet together to produce that noble offspring —the blood."

The nerve fibres sent by the cerebrum to excite the blood-vessels, being rolled up into vascular forms, serve to the blood as means of conveyance, and receive from the arteries the purest elements for the elaboration of the animal spirit, which they conduct back to the brain. In fact, Swedenborg seems to regard the inner coating of the arteries as a nervous element, and some of the capillaries as at once nervous and vascular. The brain, like the heart, is a circulatory organ. It undergoes a constant motion of expansion and construction; this force, originally derived from the soul, commences in the gray substance of the brain; each single nerve cell dilates so that the whole mass of the brain is expanded from all its depth. This expansile and contractile motion is also shared by the dura mater. The lateral ventricles at the same time contract and lengthen out, and then return to their former shape. The corpora striata and medulla oblongata swell out and then contract. By this apparatus the fluid of the lateral ventricles, containing animal spirit mixed with serum, is pumped downwards. Swedenborg described a posterior opening from the lateral to the third ventricle, in addition to the anterior one now called the foramen of Monro. The existence of this posterior opening denied by later anatomists was rediscovered by Mierzejewsky in 1872.* On the lateral ventricles again dilating, the fluid, or some of it at least, went back through the foramen of Monro.

How much of this fanciful theory of the laboratory for the animal spirits was elaborated by Swedenborg himself is not known to me. To criticise it would be like mutilating the dead. His enthusiastic editor, Dr. Tafel, points out how many of his views are still maintained by modern physiologists, and claims for Swedenborg a number of discoveries in the anatomy of the brain, which have been confirmed by other observers working with later experience and on more precise methods. As the scale of this work does not allow us to dwell much longer on this subject,† all that can be here done is simply to indicate those observations of Swedenborg which appear to have originated from him, passing over those claims made by Dr. Tafel, which seem to be illfounded or insufficiently supported. Dr. Tafel by his able and learned notes and commentaries has himself contributed to render this task much easier than it would have otherwise been. Swedenborg held that sleep was induced by the brain collapsing through the contraction of the little rifts and clefts which intersect its substance. Whether such spaces exist is perhaps not yet decided, but it is now generally held that the brain has less blood in it during sleep than in the waking condition,—the blood probably passing into the venous sinuses. Swedenborg held that the humours which collect in the interstices of the brain tissue pass through the intervening spongy bones into the nostrils, and Dr. Tafel informs us that such open passages have been demonstrated by Key and Retzius in the rabbit, and what is more to the purpose, that injections have been occasionally passed from the brain to the nasal passages in human beings. Observations in disease have led physicians to suppose that there may be some oozing of fluid between the brain and the nasal passages. Swedenborg never arrived at the idea that the skull being a closed vessel the total

---

* "The Brain," vol. i. p. 755.

† The reader in quest of further information may consult two able reviews of Dr. Tafel's Translation written by Dr. A. Rabagliati in "Brain," vol. vi. p. 404, and vol. x. p. 512.

amount of fluid in it must by the laws of gravitation always be the same. Some hold that when the blood in the brain is increased a corresponding amount of serum is expelled downwards into the cavity of the spinal cord.

Swedenborg asserted that the will had its seat in the cerebellum, and some modern physiologists have defined the cerebellum as a regulator of the will in muscular motions. Swedenborg's views of the functions of the corpus striata agree very closely with those of some modern physiologists. He says the corpora striata initiate motions which at first originated with the cerebrum, and were voluntary, for it is a well known fact that voluntary acts by daily habit become spontaneous, or that habit is like second nature.

Swedenborg's guess from analogy, that the spherules or nerve-cells of the brain cluster round the vessels like grapes or currants on the stalk, agree with the delicate microscopic observations of Dr. Bevan Lewis.

Swedenborg describes the cerebro-spinal fluid twenty-seven years before the publication of the treatise of the Italian anatomist Cotugno, to whom the credit of this discovery has been assigned.

Lastly, Swedenborg describes at much length the motion communicated to the brain by the act of respiration, and also how this motion was imparted to the whole body. Swedenborg had a peculiarity in his own breathing, which led him to pay especial attention to the relation of respiration to thought. Of this more will be said later on.

CHAPTER V.

SWEDENBORG'S MERITS AS A SCIENTIFIC MAN—HIS MENTAL CULTURE—FIRST SIGNS OF DERANGEMENT—HIS BOOK OF DREAMS—HIS FIRST REVELATIONS.

SWEDENBORG had now reached his fifty-fifth year, an age when the forces of life have begun to decline and when a man's best work is generally done. He tells us that he was content with his lot, and apparently he had reason to be so. He held an office of dignity and importance, and though the salary was small he had inherited enough to be in easy circumstances. He associated with men of rank and learning and was received even at court, a distinction of which he was evidently proud. He had abundant leisure to pursue his favourite studies, and his books, though they never became popular, had given him a wide reputation in learned circles. Few men living could claim to be his equals in breadth of knowledge. His comprehensiveness of view disposed him rather to arrange acquired facts than to grope after new ones. The tendency of his mind was to endeavour to grasp the universal plan of nature, not to journey along a by-way of science and follow out some central idea by observation and experiment. Swedenborg was a maker of systems, and when he came to a stop he would try and overleap it by a theory rather than endeavour to resolve it by laborious investigations.

In science men give the palm not to those who know most or write best, but to those who lead us a little deeper into the secrets of nature, who tell us something we did not know before. What his claims were as a direct investigator of nature it would require a good deal of reading in old scientific works to determine. Emerson, amongst a deal of striking statements rarely answering exactly to the realities, shoots into utter legend when he tells us:—" It seems that he anticipated much science of the nineteenth century; anticipated in astronomy the discovery of the seventh planet, but unhappily, not also of the eighth; anticipated the views of modern astronomy in regard to the generation of earths by the sun; in magnetism, some important experiments and conclusions of later students; in chemistry, the atomic theory, in anatomy, the discoveries of Schlichting, Monro and Wilson, and first demonstrated the office of the lungs."*

Mr. Kingsley also informs us that Swedenborg was " a sound and severe scientific labourer to whom our modern physical science is most deeply indebted."

His reputation as a scientific man amongst scientific men would mainly depend upon his works on mineralogy and metallurgy. Dr. Wilkinson informs us that the chapters on the conversion of iron into steel were reprinted at Strasburg in 1737; and the treatise on iron was translated into French by Bouchu, and published at Paris in 1762 in the magnificent "Descriptions des Arts et Metiers." Cramer says of the work in his "Elements of the Art of Assaying," that Swedenborg has "given the best accounts, not only of the methods and newest improvement in metallic works in all places beyond seas, but also of those in England and the American Colonies."

Swedenborg made some observations on the deposition of stratified rocks by the sea, and the gradual rising of the Swedish coast from the Baltic, useful contributions to the growth of geology. He is also said† to have anticipated Herschel in the place of our sun towards the milky way, and the theory of Lagrange on the periodicity of the deviations in the course of the planets.

At this time a great region lay open to the scientific explorer; a man of Swedenborg's mental power and training had but to march in and make discoveries. Geology was

---

* Emerson's " Representative Men," Swedenborg or the Mystic.
† "Nouvelle Biographie Générale," Paris, 1865, Swedenborg.

waiting for Hutton, now approaching manhood. Chemistry was waiting for Black, Cavendish, Priestley, and Scheele. Lavoisier, the greatest of them all, had now entered the shores of light. Swedenborg, more anxious to appease his thirst for knowledge than to resolve this or that scientific question, pushed eagerly forward to study anatomy that he might find out the nature of the soul.

After all what we have to consider is the cultivation Swedenborg's mind had received through the life of intense study he had led, through the researches he had made, the learned books he had written, his travels and stay in foreign countries and his great opportunities for the study of human nature. All his life he had been a searcher for truth; in his own words he had been "a spiritual fisherman, a person who investigates and teaches natural truths and afterwards spiritual truths in a rational manner." With an Eastern sage he might have said, "I have read all the histories, and learned all the sciences, and solved every riddle save the riddle of death."

About his deeper religious life during all those years we know little save that he had reflected much on the problems of the universe, and on moral and religious truth. His disciples believed that this long period of life, passed in science and study, was but a preparation for his religious mission. "It would seem," writes Dr. Wilkinson, "that he expected the kingdom of God to come upon him in the shape of clear principles deduced from all human knowledge; a scientific religion resting upon nature and revelation, interpreted by analysis and synthesis, from the ground of a pure habit and a holy life. His expectations were fulfilled, not simply, but marvellously."

That such a writer as Dr. Wilkinson should remain so little known[*] is but another sign of the times in which

---

[*] Dr. Wilkinson had to wait thirty-six years before his admirable "Biography of Swedenborg" came to a second edition. In the preface to this edition he says, the only public notice I recollect of the following little work was a generous review in the Unitarian organ, *The Inquirer*, then (1849), edited by Mr. Lalor.

literature is getting wider, but ever shallower and shallower.

With his accomplished biographer I have gone so far in agreement, but here our paths diverge. Our interpretation of facts is different. He assumes the reality of Swedenborg's celestial mission, while I seek to interpret the wanderings of a great intellect. One or other of these explanations must be true. There is no third way of getting out of the difficulty, nor are we entitled, from the obscurity of the facts, to stay in uncertainty. Had Swedenborg lived in an earlier age, had he not been so fond of recording in writing his thoughts and feelings, the process of his mental derangement might have remained in mystery. As it is, there are signs enough left to guide those acquainted with nervous diseases to a rational explanation of what followed.

The reader should here recall that Swedenborg had a hereditary tendency to hallucinations. The approach to the neurotic condition was, no doubt, a state of cerebral excitement and hyperæsthesia of the senses; flashes of light appeared before his eyes, what mental pathologists call simple or elementary hallucinations of vision. These were seen even when his eyes were closed. Voices were heard on waking after sleep, one of the most favourable times for hallucinations. The following description of the excitement of his senses and the exaltation of his mind have been collected by a learned editor of Swedenborg's writings, from confessions scattered through the voluminous works of the master.

In the "Animal Kingdom," Swedenborg tells of being commanded to write, and of admonitions heard of wonderful things which happened to him during the night; and in another place he says that he saw a representation of a certain golden key that he was to carry, to open the doors of the spiritual kingdom.

Dr. Tafel observes[*]:—

"The nature of Swedenborg's spiritual states, before the light of the spiritual world had perceptibly dawned upon him, he describes

---

[*] Vol. ii. part 1, p. 145.

most clearly in the following passage written on the 27th of August, 1748: 'Before my mind was opened, so that I could converse with spirits, and thus be persuaded by living experience, there existed with me for several years such evidences, that I now wonder I could remain all the while unconvinced of the Lord's government by means of spirits. *During several years, not only had I dreams by which I was informed concerning the things on which I was writing* [see Note 161]; but I experienced also, while writing, changes of state, there being a certain extraordinary light in the things which were written. Afterwards I had many visions with closed eyes, and light was given me in a miraculous manner. There was also an influx from spirits, as manifest to the sense as if it had been into the senses of the body; there were infestations in various ways by evil spirits, when I was in temptations; and afterwards when writing anything to which the spirits had an aversion I was almost possessed by them, so as to feel something like a tremor. Fiery lights were seen,* and conversations heard in the early morning, besides many other things; until at last a spirit spoke a few words to me, when I was greatly astonished at his perceiving my thoughts. I was afterwards, when my mind was opened, greatly astonished that I could converse with spirits; as the spirits were that I should wonder. From this it may be concluded how difficult it is for man to believe that he is governed by the Lord through spirits; and how difficult it is for him to give up the opinion that he lives his own life of himself without the agency of spirits' (Spiritual Diary, No. 2951). [See Note 162.] An additional reference to those dreams which Swedenborg had before

---

* This appearance of fiery lights Swedenborg describes more particularly in his "Adversaria," vol. iii., No. 7012, in these words: "Flames signify confirmation; such a flame has, by the Divine mercy of God-Messiah, appeared to me many times, and indeed of various sizes, and of different colours and lustre; so that while I was writing a certain little work, scarcely a day passed, for several months, without a flame appearing to me as bright as a chimney fire; this was at the time a sign of approbation, and it was before the time when spirits began to speak with me in an audible voice."

An allusion to this sign of approbation will be found in the photo-lithographic edition of Swedenborg's Manuscripts, vol. vi., page 318, where he treats in a compendious form of the "Corpuscular Philosophy" (*Philosophia corpuscularis in Compendio*), and where, at the bottom of the page, he asserts the truth of his article in this form: "These things are true, because I have [received] the sign" (*Hæc vera sunt, quia signum habeo*).

he was fully introduced as to his spirit into the spiritual world, was made by him in the beginning of 1746, in the 'Adversaria.' After speaking of dreams, visions, and representations, in a general way, he says there: 'That these things are so I can attest; and their being so ought the less to be doubted, because, by the Divine mercy of God-Messiah, they have happened so frequently, that they have become quite familiar to me. I learned them partly by dreams which I had at first during a number of years, *when I learned something of their real signification*, and partly by the other revelations [*i.e.*, visions and representations]; and also by additional revelations, as, for instance, when the very letters appeared written before my eyes, and were read to me, &c., &c. But I am not yet permitted to say more concerning these' (vol. ii., No. 183).

"Another description of the degree in which his spiritual sight was opened during that time is given by him in the 'Spiritual Diary,' under the date of 31st August, 1747, in these words: 'For nearly three years [about the middle of 1744], I was allowed to perceive and notice the operation of spirits, not by a sort of internal sight, but by a sensation which is associated with a sort of obscure sight, by which I noticed their presence, which was various, their approach and departure, besides many other things' (No. 192).

"If now we take a retrospective view of Swedenborg's spiritual experiences before he was admitted consciously into the spiritual world, we find that his first spiritual manifestations were no doubt in the form of dreams."

In 1859, Klemming, the Royal Librarian at Stockholm, bought from the heirs of Professor R. Scheringsson, who died in 1849, aged ninety, an old parchment-bound MS. diary in the Swedish tongue, and in Swedenborg's handwriting. It was found to be a relation of the dreams and visions which disturbed his repose during the time when he received his first celestial communications. Of this manuscript Klemming got printed a hundred copies, under the title of "Swedenborg's Drömmar," "Swedenborg's Dreams."* It is not a matter of wonder that the authenticity of this diary has been disputed by Swedenborgians; for it must ever be a most embarrassing document to the apologists of the New Church. Nevertheless,

---

* TAFEL, vol. ii. part i. p. 145. See also WHITE, vol. i. pp. 195, 196. A translation of "The Dreams," is given in TAFEL's "Documents."

it is admitted to be genuine by Dr. Wilkinson, Mr. White,* and Dr. Tafel, who are all believers in the reality of Swedenborg's claim to supernatural revelation.

In 1743, the assessor got leave to set out for Holland, in order to get printed the MS. of the "Regnum Animale." The Diary commences on the 21st July, when he left Stockholm. On the 20th of August he is at Harlingen, on his way to Amsterdam, which he is known to have reached on the 11th of September. On the 11th of December he was at the Hague, where the book was being printed. In the Diary there are a few entries without dates. The whole Diary is worthy of attention as bearing upon his mental condition.

The Diary, as printed in Tafel's "Documents," fills seventy-three pages octavo. It begins with an entry of the 21st July, 1743, when Swedenborg left Stockholm. A few notes of travel bring us up to 20th August, after which we have nothing till we come to some general observations, written in December, on a great change which he himself had noticed in his state of mind and health. Then follows a record of his dreams with his interpretations of them, commencing with the night of 24 × 25th March. From a note in the Diary this peculiar state of health had lasted from the middle of October, 1743. The latest entry in the Diary is for 26 × 27th October, 1744. During this period Swedenborg was in a very disturbed state of health, perhaps owing to overwork in the preparation of his anatomical treatise. His nervous system was at once exhausted and excitable. In his first entry he notices that his inclination towards women, which had been strong, had ceased. His eyesight was weakened. He had long sleeps mingled with dreams, terrible, vivid, and impressive. These dreams seemed to have recurred well-nigh every night; for it is noted as remarkable that in the night of 3 × 4th April he had no dreams. Sometimes he was in a state of ecstasy even while

---

* Mr. White says, "The Diary has been examined by the best experts in Swedenborgian literature, and all confess that its authorship is incontestable. The handwriting, the style of thought and of diction, are plainly and inimitably Swedenborg's. Many, with every desire to discredit its genuineness, are unable to find ground for the least exception."

awake; luminous spiritual writing appeared before his eyes, and a dull sound was heard in his ears. He records again and again that he could not govern his thoughts. Wicked thoughts crowded into his mind. Cold sweats sometimes broke out upon him, and he had frequently nervous tremors. He speaks of his usual tremors, and that they pervaded every limb. As he was conscious of these affections, they could scarcely have been epileptic. He writes:—"April 24 × 25, in Amsterdam. During the whole night, for about eleven hours, I lay in a strange trance. [I know not] whether I was asleep or awake. I knew all that I dreamed, but my thoughts were kept bound, which at times produced perspiration. I cannot describe the nature of the sleep during which my double [conflicting] thoughts were as it were severed, or rent apart." He describes himself as having on one occasion a swoon, on which he fell on his face.

Some of the dreams he describes were distressing and baffling. He felt himself falling into an abyss. He tried to ascend to a high place by means of a rope, but some one below pulled against him. He was driven in a carriage into a lake, a figure ran at him with a naked sword, and seeking to draw his own sword to defend himself, he found nothing but a broken sheath. He fought with a dragon and wounded it in the mouth. He was attacked by bulls, and harassed and bitten by dogs and horses. The corpse of his brother Eliezer was seen lying between two boars, who ate the head off. An executioner, a tall woman, with a little girl, who laughed at her work, cut off a number of heads, and then roasted them, and put them into an empty stove, which never filled. Many of the dreams are of a highly erotic character, but it must be borne in mind these were written only for himself to read. In his interpretations he thinks that women represent truths, and he writes that he is their devoted servant, but these words were afterwards struck out. He dreams also of the anatomical work on which he was engaged. He dreams of his father and brothers and sisters, of his friends, and his old patron, Charles XII. He saw the king sitting in a dark room; another time Swedenborg tried to understand his broken French; another time he saw him in battle covered with blood. Several times his dreams seem to have passed into visions in the waking and half waking states.

Virgil represents amongst the terrible and dismal figures at the gates of Tartarus :—

> " In medio ramos, annosaque brachia, pandit
> Ulmus opaca, ingens; quam sedem Somnia volgo
> Vana tenere ferunt, foliis sub omnibus haerent."
>
> " Æneidos," vi. l. 283.

> " Full in the midst of this infernal road,
> An elm displays her dusky arms abroad :
> The god of sleep there hides his heavy head,
> And empty dreams on every leaf are spread."
>
> Dryden's " Translation," l. 394.

Long before Virgil's time wise men had learned to disregard these figments of their drowsy fancy. One would scarcely have expected that a philosopher like Swedenborg, at the very time he was engaged in writing about the anatomy and physiology of the organs of the senses and of the brain, should keep a written record of his dreams. It appears that he had commenced to do so now and then as early as 1736. What is more remarkable still is the attitude of his mind towards the dreams recorded in the Diary. Swedenborg knew that, to use his own words, " dreams are suggested by the blood and past thoughts;" and no doubt he would have applied this axiom to any one else, but for himself his mental attitude was pronounced. He accepts these disordered and incongruous dreams as having all a meaning—in fact, as having a message from heaven in an emblematic form. This is the drift of his interpretations. Some of his solutions are whimsical and far fetched. We can see that he is working out a system of interpretation; we can discern in his reflections throughout the Diary many of the views afterwards given to the world in the books which record his intercourse with spirits. In these later treatises he taught that dreams come either directly from God, or from angels, or from the spirits.[*] They, if bad spirits, might deceive and

---

[*] See Tafel's note on Swedenborg's " Philosophy of Dreams," vol. ii. part 2, p. 1070.

mislead. The following will give an idea of the kind of explanations with which his mind seems satisfied. He appeared in his sleep before the Queen of Sweden negligently dressed and without his wig. He excused himself, when she said that it did not matter. The queen was offered jewels, but, on being told that she had not been offered the best, she threw the gems away. The meaning of this is, Swedenborg writes, that—

"I should then write and commence the epilogue of the second volume, to which I wanted to write a preface, that was not, however, required. I acted on this instruction. What she said about the jewels had reference to the truths which had indeed been discovered, but which were withdrawn again, because she was indignant at not receiving all.

"I saw a boy running off with one of my shirts, and I ran after him. It means probably that I had neglected to wash my feet."

He dreamt of his aunt and her two grandchildren; this signified his work on the internal senses and the brain. He adds—

"My being conveyed in a costly carriage to Count Horn, who was the President of the College of Chancery and Prime Minister, and thence to another town, means perhaps that my work will be prolonged to the soul.

"Afterwards something holy was dictated to me during the whole night. The concluding words were *sacrarium et sanctuarium*, when I found myself in company with a woman whom I loved. This signifies extreme affection for what is holy, for all love derives thence its origin.

"Afterwards I slept a little, and it appeared to me as if a quantity of oil mixed with mustard was floating about. This probably denotes the state of my life in future, that there will be joy in it mixed with adversity, or perhaps it means a medicine intended for me."

The soles of his feet being white, signified that his sins had been forgiven, the foot typifying the natural state. A naked woman, whose skin was smooth and bright, and who had on her thumb a miniature painting, was sitting at his left hand. She came round and sat at his right, and turned over the leaves of a book when the drawings came out. This apparently signifies that, with God's help, I shall execute many handsome designs in my work, and that henceforth speculation, which has hitherto been *à posteriori*, will change into *à priori*, this seemed to be signified by the change of position.

A yellow man striking a woman meant the philosophy of the day, striking at what he Swedenborg had written. Sometimes he is not satisfied with one interpretation, and suggests two or three. Now and then he seems to abandon one correspondence for another, as when he has a vision of two loaves of fine bread offered to him, which he thinks means the Lord's Supper. On two other occasions he receives fine bread on a plate, which he regards as a prediction that the Lord would instruct him as soon as he attained a state of simplicity when he should know nothing.

The following passage is taken from the first general description of his condition in December, 1743:—

"How my inclination (*hogen*) for women, which had been my chief passion (*hufwudpassion*), suddenly ceased.

"How during the whole time I slept extremely well at night which was more than favourable.

"About my ecstasies before and after sleep.

"My clear thoughts about matters and things.

"How I resisted the power of the Holy Spirit; and what took place afterwards. About the hideous spectres which I saw, without life; they were terrible; although bound, they kept moving in their bands. They were in company with an animal, by which I, and not the child, was attacked.

"It seemed to me as if I were lying on a mountain, below which was an abyss; knots were on it. I was lying there trying to help myself up, holding on to a knot; without foot-hold, and an abyss underneath.—This signifies that I desire to rescue myself from the abyss, which yet is not possible."

"How a woman lay down by my side; it seemed to me as if I were in a state of wakefulness. I desired to find out who she was. She spoke in a low voice; but said that she was pure, while I had a bad odour. She was, I believe, my guardian-angel, for temptation then began."

After this passage the Diary begins to be kept more regularly. The following is the first entry:—

"1. March 24 × 25.* I was standing [in my dream] beside a machine which was set in motion by a wheel; I became more and more involved in its spokes (*stängar*), and was carried up, so that I could not escape: when I awoke.—This means either that I ought to be kept longer in straits, or it describes the state of the lungs [with the embryo] in the womb, on which subject I wrote immediately afterwards.† It had reference to both."

He has dreadful trials and searchings and temptations and cries to the Lord about his impurity and worthlessness. Towards the end he feels himself purified. He notes October 13 × 14. "Among other things I was told that during the last two weeks I have begun to improve in my looks, and to appear like an angel. May God grant that this be so. May God aid me in this, and not take away from me His grace."

As early as the 5th of the previous April he had supernatural manifestations. He writes afterwards:—

"I awoke and slept again many times; and all (I dreamt) was in answer to my thoughts, yet so that in everything there was such life and glory that I can give no description of it, for it was all heavenly; clear to me at the time, but afterwards inexpressible. In short, I was in heaven, and heard a language, which no human tongue can utter, with its inherent life, nor the glory and inmost delight resulting from it."

The following note, April 6 × 7, appears to record the first clear revelation which he received:—

"At ten o'clock I went to bed, and in little more than half-an-hour afterwards I heard a noise under my head. I then thought that the Tempter was gone. Immediately afterwards a tremor came over me, powerfully affecting me from the head over the whole body, accom-

---

* The mark × between two dates signifies the intermediate night.

† At the time when Swedenborg began writing his spiritual experience of 1744, he had prepared for the press the manuscript of the "Regnum Animale" as far as Vol. i., No. 272 (p. 331 of the Latin Edition, and p. 398 of the English Edition); for the allusion which he makes in No. 1 to "the state of the lungs in the womb," is one of the subjects discussed in that paragraph.

panied by some sound; this was repeated several times. I felt that something holy had come over me. I then fell asleep, and about twelve, one, or two o'clock at night a most powerful tremor seized me from head to foot, with a sound like the concourse of many winds. By this sound, which was indescribable, I was shaken, and thrown [from the bed] on my face. While at the moment I was thus thrown down, I became wide awake, and I then saw that I had been prostrated. I wondered what all this meant, and then spoke, as if I were awake. I noticed, however, that these words were put into my mouth: 'O Thou Almighty Jesus Christ, who of Thy great mercy deignest to come to so great a sinner, make me worthy of this grace!' I lifted up my hands, and prayed, when a hand came and strongly pressed my hands; I then continued my prayer, and said, 'O Thou, who has promised to receive in mercy all sinners, Thou canst not otherwise than keep this Thy word!' I lay on his bosom (*sköte*), and looked at Him face to face. It was a countenance with a holy expression, and so that it cannot be described; it was also smiling, and I really believe that His countenance was such during His life upon earth. He addressed me and asked, if I had a certificate of my health (*om jag har sundhets pass*)? I answered, 'O Lord, Thou knowest this better than I;' when He said, 'Do it then!'—This, as I perceived in my mind, signified, 'Love me really, or do what thou hast promised.' O God, impart to me grace for this! I perceived that I could not do this by my own strength. *I now awoke in a tremor.* I again came into such a state that, whether asleep or awake, I was in a train of thought. I thought, What can this mean? Has it been Christ, the Son of God whom, I have seen? But it is sinful in me to doubt this.' As we are, however, commanded to try the spirits, I reflected on everything; and from what had happened the previous night I preceived, that during the whole of that night I had been purified and encompassed and preserved by the Holy Spirit, and thus had been prepared for this purpose."

Swedenborg judged it best to keep silent about this heavenly vision. We find the following entry dated April 7 × 8 :—

"46. All the while I was in society constantly as before, and no one could [observe] the least change in me; this was of God's grace. . . . I was not allowed to mention the large measure of grace which had fallen to my lot; for I perceived that on the one hand it could serve no other purpose than to set people thinking about me, either favourably or unfavourably, according to their disposition towards me; and, on the other hand, it would not be productive of any use, if the glorification of God's grace [served to encourage] my own self-love.*

"47. The best comparison I could make of myself was with a peasant elevated to power as a prince or king, so that he could have whatever his heart desired; and yet there was something in him which desired to teach him that he himself knew nothing."

In the following passage we have traces of some lingering doubts or misgivings :—

"110. April 21 × 22. Afterwards, because it seemed to me I was so far separated from God that I could not yet think of Him in a sufficiently vivid manner (så lefvande), I came into a state of doubt whether I should not direct my journey homewards; a crowd of involved reasons [then] came, and my body was seized with a tremor. Yet I gathered courage, and perceived that I had come [to Holland] to do that which was best of all, and that I had received a talent for the promotion of God's glory; I saw that all had helped together to this end; that the Spirit had been with me from my youth for this very purpose; wherefore I considered myself unworthy of life, unless I followed the straight direction. I then smiled at the other seducing thoughts; and thus at luxury, riches, and distinction, which I had pursued. All these I saw to be vain; and I discovered that he who is without them, and is contented, is happier than he who possesses them. I therefore smiled at all arguments by which I might be confirmed: and with God's help made a resolution. May God grant His help."

Swedenborg left the Hague on 13th May, and arrived in England on the 16th, new style.

The Diary is continued in London. The following is the last entry :—

"26 × 27th October. In the morning, on awaking, I fell into a swoon or fainting fit, similar to that which I experienced about six or seven years ago at Amsterdam, when I entered upon the 'Œconomia

---

* This paragraph, according to a statement of the Swedish editor, is crossed out in the original, the pen having been drawn through each line. After a good deal of trouble a portion of the writing has been deciphered by him. The words in brackets have been supplied by the translator.

Regni Animalis;' but it was much more subtle, so that I was almost dead. It came upon me as soon as I saw the light. I threw myself upon my face, when it gradually passed off. In the mean time short interrupted slumber took possession of me. So that this swoon or *deliquium* was more interior and deeper; but I soon got over it.— This signifies that my head is being cleared, and is really being cleansed of all that would obstruct these thoughts—as was also the case last time—because it gave me penetration, especially whilst writing. This was also represented to me now, in that I appeared to write a fine hand."

It is evident that the belief that he was intrusted with a message from heaven dawned slowly on Swedenborg's mind. It is, therefore, not surprising that there is a difficulty in making out when he first became fully possessed with the consciousness of his Divine mission. He seems himself to have assigned different dates,—in 1743, 1744 and 1745.

The vision described below must have been either in May, 1744, or in April, 1745.

His friend Robsahm once took an opportunity to ask Swedenborg "How it was granted him to see and to hear what takes place in the world of spirits, in heaven, and in hell?" Whereupon Swedenborg answered as follows:—

"I was in London, and dined rather late at the inn where I was in the habit of dining, and where I had my own room. My thoughts were engaged on the subjects we have been discussing. I was hungry, and ate with a good appetite. Towards the close of the meal I noticed a sort of dimness before my eyes; this became denser, and I then saw the floor covered with the most horrid crawling reptiles, such as snakes, frogs, and similar creatures. I was amazed—for I was perfectly conscious—and my thoughts were clear. At last the darkness increased still more; but it disappeared all at once, and I then saw a man sitting in a corner of the room; as I was then alone, I was very much frightened at his words, for he said, 'Eat not so much.' All became black again before my eyes, but immediately it cleared away, and I found myself alone in the room.

"I went home; and during the night the same man revealed himself to me again, but I was not frightened now. He then said that He was the Lord God, the Creator of the world, and the Redeemer, and that He had chosen me to explain to men the spiritual sense of the Scripture, and that He himself would explain to me what I should write on this subject; that same night also were opened to me, so that I became thoroughly convinced of their reality, the worlds of spirits, heaven, and hell, and I recognised there many acquaintances of every condition in life. From that day I gave up the study of all worldly science, and laboured in spiritual things, according as the Lord had commanded me to write. Afterwards the Lord opened, daily very often, my bodily (lekamlig) eyes, so that in the middle of the day I could see into the other world, and in a state of perfect wakefulness converse with angels and spirits."

CHAPTER VI.

WHAT BEFELL SWEDENBORG IN LONDON—HIS INTRODUCTION INTO THE SPIRITUAL WORLD—RESIGNS HIS ASSESSORSHIP—THE NATURE OF DELUSIONAL INSANITY—HIS THEOLOGICAL WORKS—CUNO'S ACCOUNT OF SWEDENBORG—FAMILIAR SPIRITS—ACCOUNTS BY ROBSAHM AND HARRISON—NATURE OF HIS ECSTASIES—HIS TRIALS AND TEMPTATIONS—PECULIARITY OF HIS RESPIRATION.

IT is to be understood that Swedenborg travelled alone and was a man of retiring habits. Beyond the Diary, we have no word of his proceedings at the Hague, but there is a curious account of what befell him in London. The Rev. Aron Mathesius, who went to London as minister to the Swedish Church, and chaplain to the Embassy in 1766, made some inquiries about Swedenborg, which led him to the house of Mr. Brockmer in Fetter Lane, with whom Swedenborg had lodged in 1744. Brockmer said that Swedenborg was brought to him by one of the Moravian Brethren with whom he had sailed from Holland. Mr. Swedenborg behaved very properly in his house, and went every Sunday to the church of the Moravian Brothers in Fetter Lane.

"One day," goes on Brockmer,* "he said to me he was glad the Gospel was preached to the poor, but complained of the learned and rich who, he thought, must go to hell. Under this idea he continued several months. He told me he was writing a small Latin book, which would be gratuitously distributed among the learned men in the Universities of England.

"After this he did not open the door of his chamber for two days, nor allow the maid-servant to make the bed and dust as usual.

"One evening, when I was in a coffee-house, the maid ran in to

---

* "Life and Writings of Swedenborg," by William White, vol. i. p. 221.

call me home, saying that something strange must have happened to Mr. Swedenborg. She had several times knocked at his door, without his answering or opening it.

"Upon this I went home, and knocked at his door, and called him by name. He then jumped out of bed, and I asked him if he would not allow the servant to enter and make his bed? He answered, 'No,' and desired to be left alone, for he had a great work on hand.

"This was about nine in the evening. Leaving his door and going upstairs, he rushed up after me, making a fearful appearance. His hair stood upright, and he foamed round the mouth.

"He tried to speak, but could not utter his thoughts, stammering long before he could get out a word.

"At last he said that he had something to confide to me privately, namely—that he was Messiah, that he was come to be crucified for the Jews, and that I (since he spoke with difficulty) should be his spokesman, and go with him to-morrow to the synagogue, there to preach his words.

"He continued, 'I know you are an honest man, for I am sure you love the Lord, but I fear you believe me not.'

"I now began to be afraid, and considered a long time ere I replied. At last I said: 'You are Mr. Swedenborg, a somewhat aged man, and, as you tell me, have never taken medicine, wherefore I think some of the right sort would do you good. Dr. Smith is near, he is your friend and mine, let us go to him, and he will give you something fitted for your state. Yet I shall make this bargain with you, if the Angel appears to me and delivers the message you mention, I shall obey the same. If not, you shall go with me to Dr. Smith in the morning.'

"He told me several times the Angel would appear to me, whereupon we took leave of each other and went to bed.

"In expectation of the Angel I could not sleep, but lay awake the whole night. My wife and children were at the same time very ill, which increased my anxiety. I rose about five o'clock in the morning.

"As soon as Mr. Swedenborg heard me move overhead he jumped out of bed, threw on a gown, and ran in the greatest haste up to me, with his nightcap half on his head, to receive the news about my call.

"I tried, by several remarks, to prepare his excited mind for my answer. He foamed, and cried again and again, 'But how—how—how?' Then I reminded him of our agreement to go to Dr. Smith. At this he asked me straight down, 'Came not the vision?' I answered, 'No; and now I suppose you will go with me to Dr. Smith?' He replied, 'I will not go to any doctor.'

"He then spoke a long while to himself. At last he said: 'I am now associating with two spirits, one on the right hand, the other on the left. One asks me to follow you, for you are a good fellow, the other says I ought to have nothing to do with you, because you are good for nothing.'

"Finally, he was put under the charge of Dr. Smith, who engaged apartments for him with Mr. Michael Caer, wig-maker, in Warner Street, Cold Bath Fields, three or four houses from his own.

"Whilst I was with Dr. Smith Mr. Swedenborg went to the Swedish Envoy, but was not admitted, it being post day. Departing thence, he pulled off his clothes and rolled himself in very deep mud in a gutter. Then he distributed money from his pockets among the crowd which had gathered.* In this state some of the footmen of the Swedish Envoy chanced to see him, and brought him to me, very foul with dirt. I told him that a good quarter had been taken for him near Mr. Smith, and asked him if he was willing to live there. He answered, ' Yes.' "

Mr. Brockmer then tells how he walked to the lodgings provided for him, how six men were left as guards over him, and how the Swedish envoy thanked him for his kindness to Mr. Swedenborg.

Mr. Brockmer continued to visit Swedenborg, who at last had only one keeper. One day he went out into the fields, and ran about so fast that his keeper could not follow him. Mr. Swedenborg sat down on a stile and laughed. When his man came near him, he rose and ran to another stile, and so on.

"When the dog days began he became worse and worse. Afterwards I associated very little with him. Now and then we met in the streets, and I always found he retained his former opinion."

Mathesius adjoins to his copy this testimony :—

"The above account was word by word delivered to me by Mr. Brockmer, an honest and trustworthy man, in the house and presence

---

* " He then went to a place called Gully Hole, undressed himself, rolled in very deep mud, and threw the money out of his pockets among the crowd."—*Arminian Magazine.*

of Mr. Burgman, Minister of the German Church, The Savoy, London, while Swedenborg lived.

"ARON MATHESIUS.

"STORA HALLFARA, 27*th August*, 1796."

"Plainly a straightforward and well authenticated story, possibly somewhat coloured by the influence of Mathesius, and by the inevitable treachery of a twenty-four years' memory; but fitting into the incoherences of the Diary with singular credibility, and full of touches characteristic of a timid, prudent, and credulous London lodging-house keeper."

Mathesius gave to the Rev. John Wesley a report of Mr. Brockmer's statement, which was published in the *Arminian Magazine* in January, 1781. In May, 1782, Wesley published thoughts about Swedenborg, in which he reproduced Mathesius' story, apparently from memory, in a garbled and unfair manner. At this time Swedenborg's writings had become known and had gained some believers. One of his most zealous disciples, Robert Hindmarsh, a printer, not liking the story, called upon Brockmer accompanied by three friends some time in or after 1783.* Hindmarsh read over the two accounts—that of Mathesius, and the garbled statement given by Wesley—and examined Brockmer thereupon. Brockmer is reported to have said :—

"To the best of my knowledge and recollection some things in that account are true, others are absolutely false, and the whole is exaggerated and unfairly stated. It is true that Swedenborg once called himself the Messiah, but not true that he always persisted in it whenever I met him afterwards. It was true that his hair stood upright, for, as he wore a wig, it was necessary to keep his hair cut short, in which case any person's hair will stand upright; but it is not true that he looked frightful or wild, for he was of a most placid and serene disposition. It is true that he had an impediment in his speech, and spoke with earnestness; but not true that he foamed at the mouth."

Hindmarsh, feeling how little he was taking by his motion, then addressed this wide question to Brockmer :—

---

* WHITE, p. 226. Hindmarsh's statement was originally published in a Swedenborgian periodical in 1791.

"Supposing it to be true that Swedenborg did actually see and converse with angels and spirits, did you ever observe anything in his behaviour that might not naturally be expected on such an extraordinary occasion?"

To which he represents Brockmer returning this accommodating answer:—

"If I believed that to be true, I should not wonder at anything he said or did; but would rather wonder that the surprise he must have felt on such an occasion did not betray him into more unguarded expressions than were ever known to escape him; for he did and said nothing but what I could easily account for in my own mind, if I really believed what he declares in his writings to be true."

To Wesley's version of the story Hindmarsh got a contradiction which threw discredit on it, but not upon the original account of Mathesius. It is not surprising that the Swedenborgian apologist should be anxious that Brockmer's denial should cover both versions.*

Mr. White upholds the substantial accuracy of Brockmer's statement as reported by Mathesius, and adds, "I freely

---

* Lest I should be accused of missing out anything material, Wesley's version and Brockmer's contradiction are given below.

"Many years ago the Baron came over to England and lodged at one Mr. Brockmer's, who informed me, and the same information was given me by Mr. Mathesius, a very serious Swedish clergyman, both of whom were alive when I left London, and, I suppose, are so still, that while he was in his house he had a violent fever, in the height of which, being totally delirious, he broke from Mr. Brockmer, ran into the street stark naked, proclaimed himself the Messiah, and rolled himself in the mire. I suppose he dates from this time his admission into the Society of Angels. From this time we are undoubtedly to date that peculiar species of insanity which attended him with scarce any intermission, to the day of his death.

"Hindmarsh says Brockmer told him 'that he had never opened his mouth on the subject of Swedenborg to Mr. Wesley,' adding Swedenborg was never afflicted with any illness, much less a violent fever, while at my house; nor did he ever break from me in a delirious state, and run into the street stark naked, and proclaim himself the Messiah. Perhaps Mr. Wesley may have heard the report from some other person; and it is well known that Mr. Wesley is a very credulous man, and easily imposed upon by any idle tale, from whatever quarter it may come.'"—WHITE, vol. i. p. 229.

admit, for it would be sheer perversity to do otherwise, that a production like the 'Book of Dreams' would be held as sufficient warrant for the consignment of any author to a lunatic asylum." Nevertheless, he does not think that through this admission we have made the slightest advance towards a comprehension of Swedenborg's case. Dr. Wilkinson shyly passes over the story, but Dr. Tafel sustains his part as an uncompromising apologist of Swedenborgianism.

Though there is no proof that Mathesius was a personal enemy of Swedenborg's, he was an opponent of his doctrines, and Swedenborg had shown his dislike to him by refusing to take the sacrament from him when dying. On the other hand, Hindmarsh was an out-and-out Swedenborgian devotee. Hence we may fairly suppose that both parties drew up their statements under the influence of preconceptions. But, allowing the full weight to Hindmarsh's statement, it is manifest that he failed to get Brockmer to contradict the story, though he was willing to gratify his visitors so far as to contradict some particulars incorrectly stated, such as that Swedenborg's hair stood erect, and that he foamed at the mouth, additions which an uncultivated person is apt to give to an exciting narrative. In fact Brockmer's statement as reported to Hindmarsh really contains an admission of the substantial accuracy of Mathesius' narrative. Dr. Tafel makes a solemn examination of the statement of Mathesius published in the *Arminian Magazine*, and a translation of a somewhat longer statement from a manuscript in Swedish in Mathesius' handwriting, and parades a few discrepancies* as proofs that the whole story is a dishonest invention of the Swedish clergyman. He prints in opposing columns portions of the one narrative containing 393 words against another containing 604 words, and observes that quite a number of particulars which had escaped Mathesius' memory in 1781 emerged from it as fresh as ever in 1796; but he affords no proof that Mathesius had trusted his memory with these particulars. The impression one would

---

* The only one of any magnitude is that in 1781 statement Brockmer left Swedenborg with two men, and in the 1796 statement there are six men.

form is that the document published in English was a shorter version of the other, and that both were reproduced from notes. The Swedish version is the most circumstantial, but it is a desperate expedient to try to confute them by comparing the one with the other.* Dr. Tafel, in the second volume of Swedenborg's work on "The Brain," claims that he has shown Mathesius' narrative to be a web of falsehoods, and says that Brockmer denied the truth of almost all the statements which Mathesius made on his authority. It seems to me that the learned Doctor is precipitate in congratulating himself on his success.

It is strange that, not ignorant of the life and writings of the Rev. Francis Okely, a Moravian preacher, Dr. Tafel discreetly omits all mention of his testimony. This gentleman, a man of irreproachable character, had made Swedenborg's acquaintance shortly before the seer's death, and had read some of his writings. In his "Reflections on Baron Swedenborg's Works,"† Mr. Okely wrote:—

"There is no denying, that in the year 1743 (1744), when Swedenborg was first (as he said) introduced into the spiritual world, he was for a while insane. He then lived with Mr. Brockmer, as Mr. J. Wesley has published in his *Arminian Magazine* for January, 1781. . . . As I rather suspect J. W.'s narratives, they being always warped to his own inclination, I inquired of Mr. Brockmer concerning it, and have found all the main lines of it truth."

From all this it is clear that Swedenborg's belief that he could converse with spirits gained possession of his mind during a period of nervous excitement and mental derangement which culminated in an attack of acute insanity. Mr. White observes, "It is only pert scientific ignorance which imagines that Swedenborg's life and writings for seven-and-twenty years

---

* The statement made by some Swedenborgians that the Rev. Aron Mathesius became himself insane in 1784, and remained so to the rest of his life, is denied by Mr. White, who seems to have communicated with his relatives. At any rate he was not insane when he made the statements in point. He left London in bad health in 1784 and went to Stockholm; five years after he married, and in 1805 was made pastor of a parish in Sweden, where he died in 1809, leaving two children.

† Quoted by WHITE, vol. i. p. 228.

subsequent to 1745 are in any way accounted for by asserting that he was out of his mind in 1744." If it be assumed that this attack of insanity entirely passed away, we can see that the thing can be made light of, but this is precisely the point in dispute. As we take it the mental excitement calmed down, self-control in a great measure returned, the extravagant behaviour ceased, but the nervous excitability remained, the hallucinations continued, and Swedenborg remained for the rest of his life under the invincible delusion that he was specially inspired, and could enter the society of spirits when he wished. A few more words and we complete the record of his doings in the work-day world.

In 1745, Swedenborg left London for Stockholm, where he arrived on the 7th of August, having been absent above two years. He returned to his duties as Assessor on the 22nd of August; but from the published record of attendance we see that he was frequently absent. In June, 1747, he sent a petition to the king declining the offered post of Councillor of Mines, and desiring leave to retire on half his salary, as he felt it incumbent to finish the work on which he was now engaged. The king graciously granted his request, and thanked him for his faithful services. The College asked the Assessor to continue his attendance until all cases commenced during his attendance were decided. To which the Assessor kindly agreed. On the 17th of July he bade goodbye to his colleagues, saying that he intended as soon as possible to commence his new journey abroad.

The Royal College thanked the Assessor for the minute care and fidelity with which he had attended to the duties of his office up to the present time; they wished him a prosperous journey and a happy return, after which he left. Dr. Tafel* argues from all this that Swedenborg would not have been treated with such regard had he shown symptoms of mental derangement.

It is, of course, impossible that he could have been afflicted with those obtrusive forms of insanity which cannot escape

---

* TAFEL, preface to the second volume of "The Brain," by Emanuel Swedenborg.

recognition even from the ignorant observer; but the form of derangement under which his mind laboured, what is called monomania or delusional insanity, is quite compatible with a man continuing to perform routine work which he has been accustomed to do for thirty years.

There is proof enough, that at first, Swedenborg was much more cautious in talking about his supernatural gifts than he afterwards was. In the second volume of the "Arcana Celestia," N. 1880, he says:—

"Some have, through me, seen the friends, which they had in the life of the body, as present as heretofore, whereat they were amazed; they have also seen their husbands and children, and have desired that I would tell them they were present, and that they saw them, and that I would acquaint them concerning their state in another life; but this I was forbidden to do, and for this reason, because they would have said that I was out of my senses, or would have thought that what I told them was the effect only of a wild imagination, inasmuch as I was well aware, that although with their lips they allowed of the existence of spirits, and the resurrection of the dead, yet in their hearts they did not believe any such thing."

Insanity may be difficult to detect even to a skilled observer. I have had frequent conversations with men and women without being able to detect any signs of mental aberration, and yet I knew from trustworthy persons that they laboured under insane delusions. In every large asylum there are two or three patients who to many people do not appear to be insane at all. The reason of their being committed to the asylum is not so much the absurdity of their delusion as its character. Their delusion leads them in some way to meddle with, injure, or annoy, other people. A man, for example, imagines that somebody owes him money, or has cheated him out of money, or an elderly lady that some one wishes to marry her but is prevented by a vile plot from declaring himself. If, on the other hand, the delusion be so far removed from the sphere of human action that it injures or infringes on the feelings or safety of no one, the subject of the delusion may go through life without anybody taking the trouble to challenge his sanity, and indeed without any one, save a few private friends, suspecting that the person was insane. Though this is a mere truism to any one accustomed to deal with lunatics, it may save misgivings with some readers to quote a few authorities who certainly did not write with an eye to support any views of mine.

"There are plenty of people," writes Dr. Clouston,* "doing their work in the world well, and yet they labour under monomania of pride or suspicion in a mild form. The now famous case of Mr. Wyld, who held an important Government office, and did his work well all his life, and yet had laboured under the delusion of grandeur, that he was a son of George the Fourth, and left all his money to the town of Brighton, because that monarch had been fond of that place, is one in point. He was held to be sane in everything he did but his will-making. I am constantly consulted by their friends about the insane delusions of persons who do not show them to anybody but their near relations, and continue to do their work and occupy responsible positions. I now know in Scotland, lawyers, doctors, clergymen, business men, and workmen, who labour under undoubted delusional insanity, and yet do their work about as well as if they had been quite sane, though they are not such pleasant people as they would have been if sane, especially to their relatives."

In the "Manual of Psychological Medicine," by Bucknill and Tuke, we read :—

"It is of the utmost importance to ascertain the *character* of the hallucinations, for on this will often depend the danger which attaches to it, and the necessity for the deprivation of the patient's liberty. It is obvious that 'Delusional Insanity,' of a destructive character, must demand early recognition and care; that a man who hears a voice commanding him to commit an act of violence towards others, or to destroy himself, requires strict watching or confinement; whilst a man who only hears a voice proclaiming his rank and wealth may be harmless, and require no restraint whatever."

In a discussion held by the Medico-Legal Society of New York on the question, "Is Spiritualism an evidence of Insanity?" the president, Mr. Clark Bell, made the following observation † :—

---

* "Clinical Lectures on Mental Diseases," London, 1887, p. 264.
† *The Medico-Legal Journal*, September, 1888, p. 221.

"Take the case of Mr. Luther R. Marsh, whom I have known for a great many years, with whom I have conversed upon this subject for the past two years quite fully. Mr. Marsh believes, as much as he believes in his existence, that he actually sees the dead in material forms, that they communicate with him, and advise him on many occasions. Upon that subject he has no manner of doubt. The question, '*Is Mr. Marsh therefore insane?*' would be a fair proposition to propound under the theory of this paper. I am satisfied that if the members of the Medico-Legal Society conversed with Mr. Marsh they would decide unanimously that he was perfectly sane. He may be entirely in error in regard to his belief. It is a deeply religious feeling with Mr. Marsh. I have no belief in spiritual manifestation myself, but cannot think all who have are insane. Mr. Marsh regards his belief akin to those miracles and manifestations related in the Bible, of which the 'Witch of Endor' and other phenomena are examples."

Mr. Clark Bell probably holds that Mr. Marsh's erroneous beliefs do not warrant people depriving him of his civil rights, or shutting him up in an asylum. As for Swedenborg, we know so much of his mental condition that, as already said, the choice lies between receiving his supernatural pretensions or declaring him subject to insane delusions.

Had Swedenborg fought with his delusions, or had he been led by his friends to turn his thoughts from them, his mind might have recovered its former clearness and power,* but he did the very contrary. He nourished his delusions, he gave up all his scientific studies, and passed his whole time in

---

* The following passages from the "Spiritual Diary" may be cited in support of this view:—

"5 *Dec.* 1747.—When I have been walking about in the heavens, and allowed my thoughts to lapse into worldly anxiety, heaven instantly disappeared."

"4 *March*, 1748.—I have now been nearly three years, or thirty-three months, with my mind withdrawn from corporeal things, and in society with spiritual and celestial spirits as a man with men, at which the spirits wonder. When, however, I am intensely absorbed in worldly things—as when concerned about necessary expenses—I to-day wrote a letter, the spirits could not speak with me; they were as if absent from me. This has happened before. Hence I know that spirits cannot converse with a man who is much devoted to worldly and corporeal cares. Such cares draw the mind down, and immerse it in nature.'

reading the Bible and a few religious books. He learned Hebrew, and discovered mystical meanings in the plainest passages of Scripture. His old speculations indeed reappeared, but the form was altered. They were given as what he learned from the spirits, instead of being presented as the result of his own cogitations. In his voluminous writings the process of self-deception can be clearly traced, though, in order to do so, it is needful to go a little into detail.

The remaining twenty-five years of Swedenborg's long life were principally spent either in Stockholm, Amsterdam, or London. To these foreign cities he went to get printed his many theological treatises. His claims to converse with the spiritual world were first made in the "Arcana Celestia," the earliest volume of which appeared in 1749, and then a volume every year, till the work was completed in eight quartos. This book consisted of a commentary upon the hidden meaning of Genesis and Exodus, interspersed with revelations from the spirit-world explaining his new theology.

His books were written in Latin, but have all been translated into English, French, and German, and some of them into other tongues. Swedenborg had unfortunately consulted the spirits about the first issue of the "Arcana Celestia," and they advised him to throw off a large edition, which nevertheless fell flat on the market.* After this, he seems to have had a wholesome distrust of the spirits' advice in business matters. He must have spent a great deal of money in bringing out religious books. Though the price asked was small, there was never much sale, and copies were freely gifted away to bishops, senators, and other place dignitaries, the least likely of all men to become converts to the new doctrine. For twenty years Swedenborg's books were issued without any name, and it only oozed out very slowly who the

---

* "I have received letters informing me that not more than four copies have been sold in the space of two months. I communicated this to the angels. They were surprised, &c. I have been taught by manifold experience that angels and spirits will sanction counsels as wise and advantageous which are quite the reverse. They only regard the good intention, and can be induced to affirm anything which promises to advance it."—"Spiritual Diary," No. 1164, 4th March, 1748.

strange author was that claimed to converse with the unseen world. In England, Swedenborg's works excited little attention, and no opposition. In Sweden, his book on "Conjugial Love" was seized, and an inquiry was ordered; and there was even a plot by his nephew, Bishop Filenius, to get him shut up in an asylum. In a letter to the King of Sweden he boldly avowed his intercourse with spirits, but denied doing anything contrary to the Christian religion. The king, who had already conversed with Swedenborg about his visions, was obviously disposed to let him alone, and the inquiry into his heretical tenets was allowed to drop harmlessly. It was a time of religious scepticism and indifference, and, as the retired Assessor seemed able to look after his private affairs, and led a quiet and decorous life, he was probably regarded as a harmless dreamer by the Gallios of the time. Certain it is that neither Swedenborg nor his few followers ever underwent any serious persecution. As his fame as a seer increased, owing to the circulation of his books and the rumours about them, his company was more sought after, and he became more communicative. He did not introduce the subject; but, when asked in a serious and respectful manner, would speak in an open and matter-of-fact way of what he had seen in the spirit-world.

Here we may give a few details. Emanuel Swedenborg was of the middle height, fair like a Swede, with blue eyes. In the portrait taken when he was forty-six, he appears a handsome man, with a noble and benign expression. He wore the ordinary attire of a gentleman of the time—wig and coat, knee-breeches, stockings, shoes, and gold buckles, with sword by his side. He was neat in his dress, though sometimes so absent of mind that in Stockholm his servants had to keep watch over him to revise his attire when he went out. Living alone, his habits were simply intended to suit himself. He sometimes worked all night, and went to bed during the day. "When I am sleepy," he said, "I go to bed." Both in Amsterdam and London he is described as giving very little trouble. At Stockholm, where he lived in a small house which he had got built, he lighted his own fire, and heated his coffee at the stove. He lived principally on bread and milk, rarely took wine, and scarcely ever tasted flesh. He possessed a good constitution, and, even in his old age, was alert and vigorous. He was of a serene and kindly disposition, and was fond of children. Though not averse to female society, he would never see women alone. He had an impediment in his speech, which sometimes caused him to stutter. He seems to have been able to converse in French and German, but never learned to speak English fluently. He always travelled alone, without any servant, saying that his guardian spirit would take care of him. What filled up this simple and unostentatious life was the converse of a seer with the unseen world. He lived amongst the spirits; sometimes he was surrounded by thousands of them. They were always speaking to him, or he was speaking to them, suggesting thoughts to him, tempting him, teasing him, threatening him, plotting against him. Even his bodily ailments are attributed to the spirits. Hypocritical spirits gave him the toothache. A wicked adulterer was with him some days, and induced pains in the toes of his left foot and in his loins and breast. Some spirits tried to suffocate him, but internal respiration was sustained by the intervention of the Lord. Other spirits penetrated to his heart, but were not allowed to do him harm. Some bad spirits were suffered to enter the right hemisphere of his brain and the left side of his chest, but not his left brain, which would have been fatal. Those who on earth had been in favour of justification by faith alone, showed great animus against him. Swedenborg records that when a preacher in a chapel in London enlarged on this doctrine, the spirits made such a hubbub contradicting him that the preacher's words were inaudible to the seer.

How ready Swedenborg was to assign any disease to the influence of spirits may be judged from the following passage[*]:—

"It has also been granted me to know the origin of the anxiety, grief of mind, and interior sadness, called melancholy, with which man is afflicted. There are certain spirits who are not yet in conjunction with hell, being as yet in their first state. They love undigested and malignant substances, such as those of food when it lies corrupting in

---

[*] "Heaven and Hell." London, 1851, N. 299.

the stomach. They consequently are present where such substances are to be found in man, because these are delightful to them; and they there converse with one another from their own evil affection. The affection contained in their discourse thence enters the man by influx; and if it is opposed to the man's affection, he experiences melancholy, sadness, and anxiety; whereas, if it agrees with his affection, he becomes gay and cheerful. Those spirits appear near the stomach, some to the left, some to the right, some below, and some above, with different degrees of proximity and remoteness; thus they take various stations, according to the affections which form their character. That such is the origin of anxiety of mind has been granted me to know and be assured of by much experience; I have seen those spirits, I have heard them, I have felt the anxieties arising from them, and I have conversed with them, they were driven away, and my anxiety ceased; they returned and it returned; and I was sensible of its increase and decrease according to their approximation and removal. Hence was made manifest to me the origin of the persuasion entertained by some, who do not know what conscience is by reason that they have none, when they attribute its pangs to a disordered state of the stomach."

Strange writing this for an accomplished chemist and anatomist, the possessor of all the science of his day. Luther, it may be recalled,* attributed his headaches to the agency of the devil, and called physicians ignorant blockheads for holding that the infirmities of idiots, the lame, the blind, and the dumb, proceeded from natural causes; but between Luther and Swedenborg there were more than 200 years of wonderful progress in physical science.

When asked to communicate with some of the dead whom he did not know, Swedenborg naively replied † :—

"I cannot converse with all, but with such as I have known in this world; with all royal and princely persons, renowned heroes, and great and learned men, whom I have either known personally, or from their actions or writings; consequently, with all of whom *I can form an idea;* for it may be supposed that a person whom I never knew, nor of whom I could form any idea, I neither could nor would wish to speak with."

The rational explanation of this seems to be that these

---

* See "The Blot on the Brain," p. 48.
† WHITE, vol. ii. p. 67.

visionary interviews with the illustrious dead, or with his old friends who had gone before, were constructed from materials furnished by his memory to his imagination.

One would have thought that Swedenborg might have suspected the objective reality of his visions when the spirits of people still living appeared to him. He was satisfied with the following explanation:—

"Every man as to his spirit is associated with his like in the spiritual world. I have been frequently permitted to see the spirits of persons now living upon earth in the heavenly and infernal societies to which they respectively belonged, and have conversed with them for days together. I have often wondered that a man while in the body should be totally unacquainted with the state and place of his spirit."

"Every body," he wrote in another place,* "is connected with two spirits from hell and two angels from heaven; and without such connection no one could live for a single moment. The infernals rule in him who is wicked, but are subdued and forced to serve in him who is good."

J. C. Cuno, a merchant in Amsterdam, and a well-known writer in his day, who cultivated the friendship of Swedenborg, tells us in a letter †:—

"Last Thursday I paid him a visit, and as usual found him writing. He told me that the same morning he had been in conversation with the late King of Sweden for three hours in the spiritual world. He had met him there already on Wednesday, but as he had seen that he was deeply engaged in conversation with the Queen, who is still living, I would not disturb him then. I let him talk on, but at last asked him how it was possible to meet in the spiritual world with a person who is still in the land of the living? He answered me, 'It was not the Queen herself, but her familiar spirit' (*spiritus familiaris*). 'What sort of a thing is that?' I continued, for of this new kind of appearances I had never heard from him before, nor had I read about them. He then informed me that every man had his good or bad spirit, who is not only constantly near him, but sometimes also withdraws from him, and appears in the spiritual world. But of this the man still living knows nothing, the spirit, however, knows every-

---

* "Arcana Celestia," N. 50, 968-986.
† Dated, March, 1771. TAFEL, vol. ii. p. 484.

thing. Such a familiar spirit has everything perfectly in common with his human companion; he has in the spiritual world visibly the same figure, the same countenance, the same tone of voice, wears also the same garments as the man on earth; in short, Swedenborg said, the familiar spirit of the Queen appeared exactly as he had so often seen the Queen herself in Stockholm, and had heard her speak.

"In order to lessen my astonishment, he added, that Dr. Ernesti of Leipzig had appeared to him in a similar manner in the spiritual world, and that he had had a regular disputation with him.

"It is inconceivable to me how I myself can refrain from laughing when I hear such extraordinary things of him. And what is more, I have often heard him relate similar things in large parties consisting of ladies and gentlemen, among whom I knew very well were persons given to mockery; but to my great astonishment no one thought of laughing. As long as he speaks, it is as if every person who hears him was charmed, and compelled to believe him. He is reserved to no one. Whoever invites him, is sure to have him."

Lest any one should doubt the truth of this narrative, we may observe that it is fully confirmed by a passage in the "True Christian Religion,"* in which Swedenborg describes a discussion held by a council in heaven on justification by faith.

"Amongst the spirits of the apostolic fathers and Protestant divines there appeared one spirit who made himself very busy. On being asked who he was, he replied in a deep tone of voice, 'Yes; I am consociated with a famous man, a leader of the troops that compose the army of church worthies.' And because he spoke in so deep a tone of voice, I said, 'Pardon me, if I ask you further, whether you know where that famous leader lives?' He said, 'I do know. He lives not far from Luther's Tomb.' This, it appears, was Dr. John A. Ernesti of Leipzig, who published some virulent attacks on Swedenborg. This was not the only familiar spirit present, for Swedenborg gravely tells us, 'When the debate was thus concluded, the president was desirous to close the council with prayer; but suddenly a man started up from the party on the left, having on his head a tiara, and over that a cap, and he touched his cap with his finger, and said, "I also am joined by spiritual consociation with a man in your world, who is honourable for his eminent station; I know this, because I speak from him as from himself." I then inquired where that honourable person lived.† He replied, "At Gottenburg; and I

---

* N. 137. † This was Dr. Ekebon, Dean of Gottenburg.

was once of opinion, from the ideas in him, that this new doctrine of yours has a tincture of Mahomedanism." At these words, I perceived that all those on the right, where the apostolic fathers stood, seemed astonished and changed colour; and I could hear these exclamations often repeated—"Oh! what a scandal! What an age is this?" In order, however, to appease their just indignation, I waved my hand, requesting to be heard, and said, "I know indeed that a person of that distinction did bring some such charge against me in an epistle, which he afterwards published; but had he known at that time what a blasphemous charge it was, he would have torn the letter to pieces, and committed it to the fire, rather than to the press. It was such contumely which the Lord condemned in the Jews, when they ascribed His miracles to some other power than that which is Divine (Matt. xii. 22-32), and to this He adds in the same place, 'Whosoever is not with me is against me; and he that gathereth not with me scattereth abroad' (ver. 30)." At these words the associate spirit hung down his head, but presently raising it again, he said, "This is the severest speech I have yet heard from you;" but I resumed my discourse, and said, "The fault is in the two accusations brought against me—of naturalism and Mahomedanism—which are both wicked lies and deadly stigmas, invented in subtlety, with a design to prejudice the hearer, and deter him from the holy worship of the Lord." Then, addressing myself to the former associate spirit, I said, "Desire your friend at Gottenburg, if it be possible, to read what the Lord says in the Revelation (iii. 18; and also ii. 16)." As I concluded, the council began to grow noisy.'"

Now, will any man read this and seriously maintain that such a discussion ever took place in heaven? It is clearly a fiction of Swedenborg's imagination. These memorable relations, as he calls them, resemble the visions, or dreams, or fables common in the literary essays of the time. They were regarded as a mere pleasant way of putting the author's meaning, but the fact that Swedenborg gravely maintained such relations to be literally true suggests irresistible doubts of his sanity. Though habitually basking in a benign self-confidence, Swedenborg now and then shows his sense of the world's neglect in an amusing way, for he had no sense of the ludicrous. In the "Apocalypse Revealed,"* Swedenborg tells us that he fell in with George II. in the spiritual world. The

---

* English translation; London, 1876, N. 716.

quondam monarch was much astonished to learn that Swedenborg's works on the New Jerusalem, though published in London and presented to the English bishops, were so shamefully neglected as not even to be thought worthy of a place in their catalogues. The king inquired by what means the clergy were kept so universally in subjection to the bishops, and he was informed "that it proceeded from the power which every bishop has in his diocese of nominating for the king's approbation a single candidate for the churches, and not three as in other kingdoms."

It strikes me that this is not quite the way in which vacancies in the ranks of the Episcopal clergy were filled up, but it is difficult to get correct information about such matters in Scotland, and perhaps even more so in Heaven.

Other incongruous hallucinations he explained to himself to be correspondences or emblems of truths in the spiritual world, or to be delusions framed by the bad spirits which tormented him. He said that his state was so ordered by the Lord that he could be possessed by spirits without injury. "Others so possessed," he observes, "become *non compos*, while I remain altogether in my right mind." The spirits were not allowed to instruct him in anything about the Word or any doctrine from the Word. "All I have received," he writes, "has been from the Lord alone. He appears before my eyes as the sun, in which He is, even as he appears to the angels."

In the days of the primitive Church men could hold converse with the spirits, but through their sinful and sensuous lives the power was lost, nevertheless it has been allowed to men to speak with spirits and angels for ages back. In such cases the spirits speak with man in his mother tongue, and only a few words. Even in his own day he said that men might attain the gift of conversing with spirits if they did not lead unnatural and sensual lives. From this we may assume that Swedenborg had a high estimate of the holiness of his own life. In the course of his writings he now and then allows us to see that he appreciated the unique position which he held as the only living being who could have converse both with men and spirits.

REVILINGS OF EVIL SPIRITS.

The following passages are taken from Robsahm's "Memoirs of Swedenborg"*:—

"Respecting his temptations I collected information from his modest servants the old gardener and his wife, who told me with sympathising and compassionate words that Swedenborg often spoke aloud in his room, and was indignant when evil spirits were with him; this they could hear the more distinctly because their room was near his. When he was asked why he had been so restless during the night, he answered that permission had been given to evil spirits to revile him, and that he spoke to and was indignant with them. It often happened that he wept bitterly, and called out with a loud voice, and prayed to the Lord, that He would not leave him in the temptation which had come upon him. The words which he cried out were these:—'O Lord, help me! O Lord my God, do not forsake me!' When it was all over, and his people asked him about the cause of this lamentation he said: 'God be praised! it is over now. You must not trouble yourselves about me; for whatever happens to me is permitted by the Lord, and He does not allow me to be tempted more than He sees that I can bear.'

"Once it was very remarkable, that after such a lamentation he lay down, and did not rise from his bed for several days and nights. This caused his people much uneasiness; they talked with one another, and supposed that he had died from some great fright. They thought of having the door forced open, or of calling in his intimate friends. At last the man went to the window, and, to his great joy saw that his master was still alive, for he turned himself in bed. The next day he rang the bell, and then the housekeeper went in, and told him of her own and her husband's uneasiness at his condition; whereupon he said with a cheerful countenance that he was doing well, and that he did not need anything."

Had some relative or friend of Swedenborg lived in the same house with him, they would have had something noteworthy to tell. We are indebted to Robsahm for the following information:—

"I am acquainted with two Englishmen, who are sea-captains and Swedish naturalised citizens; the name of the one is Harrison, on board whose ship Swedenborg was once a passenger. During almost the whole voyage he lay in bed, and nearly the whole time he spoke

---

* TAFEL, vol. i. p. 39.

as if he were in company. The cabin-boy and the mate said to the captain that Swedenborg must be mad; he answered, 'He may be what he pleases, but as long as he remains quiet, I have no authority over him; he is always prudent and discreet in speaking to me and in answering me; you see yourselves that we have the most favourable wind; and if this weather continues as it is, I shall make the quickest passage I have ever made."

Swedenborg himself wrote* :—

"I was once suddenly seized with a disease that seemed to threaten my life; my whole head was oppressed by pain, a pestilential smoke was let in upon me from the Jerusalem which is called Sodom and Egypt, Rev. xi. 8. I was half dead with intolerable agonies, and I expected every moment to be my last. Thus I lay in my bed three days and a-half. My spirit was reduced to this state, and in consequence of it my body. I then heard about me the voices of persons saying, 'Lo! he that preached repentance for the remission of sins, and exhorted us to look to the man Christ only, lies dead in the streets of our city.' On their asking several of the clergy whether he was worthy of burial, they answered, 'No; let him lie to be looked at;' and they passed to and fro and mocked. All this befell me of a truth while I was writing the explanation of the eleventh chapter of the Revelation."

This must have been about the year 1758. The relation seems to refer to a real illness; but from what follows it seems that Swedenborg saw a similarity in his condition to that of the two witnesses described in the Apocalypse.

Though Swedenborg treats it as a rule that spirits cannot see men, nor men spirits, he often talks of spirits tempting men, approaching them we suppose on the spiritual side. In one of what he calls his memorable relations,† he tells us that in the spiritual world an angel who excelled in wisdom on seeing him said :—

"'I was surprised as I saw you in the way coming towards us, to

---

* "The True Christian Religion," N. 567; "The Apocalypse Revealed," N. 531.

† The passage quoted is taken from "The True Christian Religion," N. 260. It may be also found in Swedenborg's book on "Conjugial Love," N. 326.

observe that sometimes you were in sight, and sometimes out of sight, or at one moment visible, and the next invisible; surely you are not in the same state of life with us.' To this I replied, with a smile, 'I am neither a stage-player nor a Vertumnus, but I am alternately dwelling sometimes in your light, and sometimes in your shade, thus I am a stranger here, and at the same time an inhabitant.' On this the wise personage looked at me attentively, and said, 'You speak strange wonderful things, tell me who you are?' I said, 'I am in the world in which you have been, and from which you are departed, which is called the Natural World, and I am also in the world in which you now are, which is called the Spiritual World; hence I am in a natural state, and at the same time in a spiritual state, in a natural state with men on earth, and in a spiritual state with you. When I am in a natural state, I am invisible to you, but when I am in a spiritual state I become visible, and this peculiarity in my nature is of the Lord's appointment.

"'It must be well known to a man so enlightened as you are, that an inhabitant of the natural world is invisible to an inhabitant of the spiritual world, and contrariwise, so when I let my spirit into the body, I was no longer visible to you, but when I let it out from the body, I became visible.'"

Some spirits were allowed to view the world through Swedenborg's organs. "They were able," he says, "to lead me to see through my eyes and to hear through my ears. They might also have talked and written to others through me, but it was not permitted, neither to touch others through my hands."

The following is recorded in his "Spiritual Diary":—

"19*th March*, 1748.

"When I had been writing certain things, a spirit, who was near me on the left, thanked me when I had finished for having assisted him. I was aware he thought himself to be myself, as is usually the case. He departed and told others what he had written, but said he was not sure whether he ought to consider that he had copied it by means of his own hand. . . . Such are the co-operations of spirits with man."

The spirits of fraudulent tradespeople tempted him to steal things of small value in shops, and actually moved his hand. He said that spirits had often guided his hand, "as though it were quite their own, so that they thought it was not I but themselves who were writing."*

The evil spirits tried to induce him to throw himself under the wheels of carriages in the streets of London. The spirit of a woman called Sara, who had once wanted Swedenborg to marry her, incited him to commit suicide. Here is another of his deranged sensations recorded in his "Spiritual Diary":—

"*27th November*, 1748.

"On shaking hands with a certain person, I had a feeling that it was not I but somebody else who grasped the hand. A spirit said that he distinctly felt that it was he who took the hand instead of me. So it seems that a spirit really had possession of my hand with its sense of touch."

Swedenborg had a peculiarity in his breathing which he thus described :—

"My respiration has been so formed by the Lord as to enable me to breathe inwardly for a long time without the aid of the external air, my respiration being directed within, and my outward senses, as well as actions, still continuing in their vigour. . . . I have also been instructed that my breathing was so directed, without my being aware of it, in order to enable me to be with spirits and to speak with them. . . . It was granted me to gather the same thing from much experience before I spoke with spirits, and to see that breathing corresponds with thought—as, for example, during my childhood, when I tried purposely to hold my breath, also at morning and evening prayers, and when I attempted to make the rhythm of my breath correspond with my heart's pulsation, in which case my understanding began almost to be obliterated. Furthermore, afterwards, when I was writing and using my imagination, at which time I could observe that I held my breath, which became in a manner tacit."†

The reader can easily note how intense thought slows the respiration, and the respiratory act seems to interrupt a prolonged effort of thought. Lunatics have sometimes a power of making their respiration difficult to hear and even inaudible. The inspiration is noiseless and the expiration retarded. This peculiarity seems most common in melancholia. I am not

---

* WHITE, vol. i. p. 300.
† WHITE, vol. i. p. 263.

aware that it has ever been observed to have any connection with special delusions. It seems that in Swedenborg's trances respiration was slowed, and this he called internal respiration.

Dr. Mickle * had a porter in his employment who was subject to severe attacks of breathlessness. In this state he became morose and suspicious to the verge of insanity. A few days before his death he confessed to Dr. Mickle that when in his "bad turns" he for years had had visual hallucinations or illusions, and that, as in dyspnœal lividity he spoke to me, he could see a man and dog at the foot of his bed (hallucination). Had this porter possessed the power of suspending his breathing which Swedenborg claimed, he might apparently have produced hallucinations at will. At any rate, Swedenborg's visions in some way corresponded with a change in the rate of his respirations, probably by inducing a change in the circulation of the brain. Writing in the "Spiritual Diary" † he says :—

"When heaven had been opened to me, so that I could speak with spirits, I was so fully introduced into this respiration, that for the space of almost an hour I did not draw any breath, there was only so much air inhaled that I was able to think. In this manner I was introduced by the Lord into internal respiration. Perhaps also in my dreams, for I noticed again and again that after falling asleep (external) respiration was almost entirely withdrawn from me, so that on awaking I gasped for breath. This kind of respiration, however, ceases when I do not observe, write, or think on any (*i.e.*, spiritual) subject, and reflect only upon this, that I believe these facts, and that they take place in innumerable ways. Formerly I was not able to see these varieties, because I could not reflect upon them ; but now I am able to do so, because each state, each sphere, and also each society (of heaven), especially the interior ones, have in me a suitable respiration, into which I come without reflecting upon it. By this means it is also granted me to be present with spirits and angels."

---

* "On Insanity in Relation to Cardiac and Aortic Disease ;" London, 1888, p. 24.

† No. 3464, quoted by Tafel, vol. ii. p. 144.

CHAPTER VII.

Summary of his Theology — The Spiritual World — Faith and Charity — The Formation of Character — He sees the Spirits of Luther, Melancthon, Calvin, St. Paul, David, and Mohammed — The State of the Soul after Death — The Interior Memory — All Good Actions are from God — Swedenborg's Descriptions of the World of Spirits, Heaven, and Hell.

In Swedenborg's mind everything became systematized; he spun a system as naturally as a silk worm spins a cocoon. While he accepted his hallucinations as real, he interpreted them agreeably to the cast of his mind, and his preconceived theories of God and the universe. In his scrutiny of Nature and of Scripture he grasped at everything which confirmed these views, and benignly explained away everything which appeared to tell against them. The result was a new form of religion under the old name of Christianity. While recognising the plenary inspiration of the Old and New Testaments, he often gave entirely new meanings to the plainest passages, in order to strain them into accordance with his own doctrines. Swedenborg's theological views are scattered over numerous books and pamphlets. Between the first sketches of the spirit world in the "Arcana Celestia," and the finished summary of his doctrines, published eighteen years after, in the "Vera Christiana Religio,"* there are certain differences;

---

* This work, published at Amsterdam in 1771, contains a complete summary of Swedenborg's doctrines. I have used the English translation, "The True Christian Religion containing the Universal Theology of the New Church," by Emanuel Swedenborg, published by the Swedenborg Society, 36 Bloomsbury Street, London, 1874. Swedenborg's books are full of repetitions; the same views in almost the same words may be found in many of his numerous treatises.

some notions are dropped, others altered, but the general outline is preserved. Swedenborg's main ideas may be found in all his larger works.

Swedenborg asserts for the doctrines he presented to the world the claim of a direct revelation from God.

"I have discoursed," he tells us,* "with spirits and with angels now for several years; nor durst any spirit, neither would any angel, say anything to me, much less instruct me, about anything in the Word, or any doctrinal derived from the Word; but the Lord alone, who was revealed to me, and afterwards continually did and does appear before my eyes as the sun in which He is, even as He appears to the angels, taught me and illuminated me."

Swedenborg makes a distinction between the doctrines thus solemnly revealed to him, and the observations he made in the world of spirits, and the conversations which he held with the angels.

His theology may be thus briefly summed up. God is the source of all power, energy, and action, in this world and all other worlds, this Divine efflux fills and sustains all things. There are two worlds; a spiritual world, inhabited by spirits and angels, and a natural world, inhabited by men.

"This," he says,† "is a fact hitherto unknown in the Christian world, lest, therefore, men should have doubts about the reality of heaven and hell, resulting from such ignorance, and should become naturalists and atheists, it has pleased the Lord to open my spiritual sight, and as to my spirit, to elevate me into heaven, and to lower me into hell, and to exhibit to my view the nature of both."

The spiritual world first existed and continually subsists from its own sun; "in appearance, it is a globe of fire, like our sun, is of much the same magnitude, and at the same distance from the angels as our sun is from men; but it does not rise or set, but stands immovable in a middle altitude between the zenith and the horizon, whence the angels enjoy perpetual light, and perpetual spring."

---

* "Angelic Wisdom Concerning the Divine Providence" (originally published at Amsterdam, Anno 1764); London, 1833, N. 135.

† "The Nature of the Intercourse between the Soul and the Body," from the Latin of Emanuel Swedenborg, originally printed in 1769; London, 1826, pp. 7, 9.

The sun of the spiritual world is pure love, because love is the principle of light. "They who deduce the origin of worlds from any other source than the Divine love operating by the Divine wisdom, fall into hallucinations like those of persons disordered in the brain who see spectres as men, phantoms as luminous objects, and imaginary entities as real figures; for the created universe is a coherent work, originating from love operating by wisdom, as you will see, if you are able to examine the chain of things in their order, from those which are first to those which are last."

God became man on earth in the form of Christ, but there is no difference between God the Father and God the Son. Thus while he rejects the doctrine of the Trinity, he abhors Socinianism. Unless God be approached in thought as a man, all idea of God is lost. There are in man two receptacles, one which is the receptacle of good, called the will, and the other, which is the receptacle of truth, called the understanding. That good belongs to love is evident from this consideration, "that when a man loves, this he wills, and when he brings it into act he calls it good, and that truth belongs to wisdom appears hence, that all wisdom is composed of truths," even the good which a wise man thinks, is truth, which becomes good when he wills it and does it.

Swedenborg defines faith to consist in a belief that the Lord will save all who live a good life and believe aright. He rejects imputed merit or faith by justification alone. His attacks on this doctrine come up with endless repetition in his different writings.

"Is it not," he asks, "contrary to the Divine essence that God should change the order established from eternity that every one should be judged according to his life? Justice and judgment cannot allow that one person should take upon himself the wickedness of another, and so make the wicked innocent, and wash away his guilt. Surely this is contrary to all righteousness, both Divine and human. Faith answers to light, and charity to heat, so, faith without charity, is like the sun in winter, which allows living things to perish with cold. As light and heat should go together, so ought faith and charity. Faith without charity is not faith; and charity without faith is not charity; and neither faith nor charity has any life in it but from the Lord. A man may attain faith by trying to do good works and purify his life, then the Lord enters into his soul and causes his natural faith to become spiritual faith, and his natural charity to become spiritual charity, and thus makes both alive. A man's nature and quality depend upon the nature and quality of his will, and not of his understanding, for the will easily draws over the understanding to its party and makes a slave of it. God might have made the whole world receive the Word at once, but it was the order of Creation that man should approach truth through his own free will, and that his blessedness or misery should depend upon his free determination in spiritual things."

Swedenborg regards man as born prone to evil, inclined to indulgence in all lusts, coveting the property of others, and hating those who oppose him; but his will is restrained by his understanding, which shows him the necessity of restraining his desires in order to retain the good will of others. Swedenborg would have disdained to call Utilitarianism morality at all; in fact, his description of a hypocrite would suit a Utilitarian exactly. It is through the understanding that man receives a knowledge of truth from good. This makes him willing to receive the influence of Divine love. Thus man by his free will, and God by His sanctifying influx co-operating in the work of regeneration by which man becomes a new creature, gets a new will and a new understanding to desire and discern what is holy. On the other hand, it is the full triumph of wickedness when the natural will rules over the understanding; men then become like devils who can understand spiritual truths, but cannot retain them.

Every man who leads a good life, and who avoids evil actions as sins, whatever his form of religion, goes to heaven, though of course a true form of faith is most conducive to a good life; goodness consists in the purity of the motive, not in the actions themselves.

Thus a man who leads a decorous life, from the fear of offending his fellow-men, or from the hope of gaining advancement or wealth while his secret inclinations are towards selfish gratification, is not worthy of heaven, and indeed could not enjoy it, for in the spiritual world all hindrances to the gratification of one's ruling desires are removed. Hence hypocrites could not live in heaven, as there every man is seen as he is —his real character is beyond disguise. On the other hand, no man is punished in the next world for his past misdeeds.[*] These he leaves behind him at death with his body, but he takes with him the character which he has formed on earth. If he be wholly selfish, and have acquired a taste for wickedness and sensual pleasures, these tastes determine his pursuits and companions in the next world. A large number of men, being neither decidedly good nor evil, remain in an intermediate state till either the good or the evil in them preponderates, when they pass away to hell or heaven. There is no fallen angel called Satan. All angels or devils were once men. He says that he knew men in the body who are now devils.

Though the resurrection of the body has no place in Swedenborg's faith, the next world resembles the present one: though they have left their body of skin and bones and muscles, they have a substantial body which has the same appearance and the same organs, as opposed to a natural body. People who die old, or changed from disease, at first assume this appearance, but gradually go back to the form they held in their flower, and as they advance in goodness become more

---

[*] In the "Arcana" Swedenborg had not arrived at this matured view. He gives (N. 817) a graphic account of a villain who was punished for a crime committed on earth. The spirit of this man in the lower earth began to dig a hole in the ground as is usual when a corpse is to be buried. "Immediately there appeared a bier covered with black cloth, and presently one rising from the bier came to me, and in an affecting tone informed me that he was dead, and that he was of opinion he had been poisoned by that person, and that this opinion possessed him just at the hour of death, but that still he was ignorant whether or no his suspicion was well grounded. The wicked spirit on hearing this confessed that he was guilty of the murder. 'After confession followed punishment,' he was twice rolled in the dirt which he had dug up, and made as black as an Egyptian mummy, both as to his face and body, and thus he was carried up aloft, and presented to the view of spirits and angels, whilst this cry was uttered, 'Behold, what a devil!' he became also cold, and in this state he was remitted amongst the cold infernals and cast into hell."

In N. 966 Swedenborg tells us, "It is to be observed that no one suffers any punishment and torment in another life on account of hereditary evils, but for the actual evils which he himself has committed."

and more beautiful. The senses in the spiritual world are much keener than they ever were. The spirits live in houses, eat and drink,* wear clothes, and walk, stand, sit, lie down to sleep, and do everything as it is done on earth. Men and women marry in heaven, but have no children. He describes at length one of these celestial weddings, which is full of symbolical ceremonies.

In the spiritual world Luther† kept on lecturing on theology in a house like what he had at Eisleben, till privileged to converse with Swedenborg, who convinced him of the fallacy of the doctrine of justification by faith alone. On the other hand, the Elector Frederick of Saxony was among the blessed. This Prince told Swedenborg that he had often blamed Luther when on earth for separating charity from faith, when Paul even gives charity the preference, saying there are these three, faith, hope, and charity—but the greatest of these is charity.

Swedenborg also conversed with Melancthon, whose condition in the spiritual world he describes in some detail. Melancthon had a house provided for him similar to what he inhabited in this world—the same kind of chamber, table, writing-desk with drawers, and also a similar library. As soon then as he came into his new habitation, like one awaking out of sleep, he seated himself at his table, and proceeded to write as usual on justification by faith alone, and so continued for several days without writing a word about charity. The angels hovering near him not being satisfied with this erroneous doctrine withdrew from him.

After this he was banished to a kind of work-house where similar spirits were confined. But as he had been one of the Reformers of the Church he was released by the Lord's command, and sent back into his former chamber, where he found only his table, paper, and ink; still, however, in con-

---

* In the "Arcana Celestia," N. 1880, he says that spirits have all the senses save that of taste, but in his later writings this restriction seems forgotten, and he even talks of the excellent dishes served in the spiritual world at the tables of the rich.

† "The True Christian Religion," N. 796.

sequence of the ideas which were rooted and confirmed in his mind, he continued blotting over sheet after sheet with his former erroneous notions, so that it was impossible to keep him from sinking down at times among his imprisoned companions, from whence he was again alternately released. When he was released he appeared clad in a rough, hairy skin, because faith without charity is cold.

As for Calvin he fares worse, and in the end falls into very strange company for so austere a personage. Swedenborg meets him in the spiritual world, and severely rebukes him for his doctrines of election and eternal damnation. The last thing we hear of Calvin is that he betook himself to a cave inhabited by those who had confirmed themselves in the execrable doctrine of predestination. As Dante saw those he hated in the Inferno and Michael Angelo painted the figures of his enemies in hell, Swedenborg saw those who separated Faith from Charity suffering for this doctrine in the spiritual world.

Possibly it was from hearing St. Paul so often cited in favour of justification by faith alone that Swedenborg was led to form an unfavourable opinion of him, which was reflected in his visions. In his "Spiritual Diary," there are some startling entries about the apostle of the Gentiles. "That Paul wrote epistles does not prove him good, for even the impious can preach well and write epistles." He accuses Paul of setting up a train of adulterous thoughts in his mind. The apostle brought some hypocrites to tease the Assessor, which he knew from the aching of his teeth. Swedenborg knew Paul's nefarious character and experience, for he had spoken with him more than with others. "He underwent many dangers and punishments on earth that he might be the greatest, and, in the other world, the rest of the apostles rejected him from their society."

There are also some strange entries about King David. Here is one of them, "David is wicked, and a slave of deceitful spirits, who say they treat him like a dog. His mind is full of cruelty and adultery, and, without conscience he meditates and contrives mischief."

The Catholics have a separate heaven from the Protestants,

where the simpler and better sort soon learn the truth, but the popes, and cardinals, and saints do not fare so well. A hundred saints were sent up from "the region below," in order that Swedenborg might inspect them. He conversed with Francis Xavier who talked like an idiot. Xavier explained that he becomes so whenever he thinks that he is a saint. St. Geneviève appeared to the Parisians in the other world in shining raiment, but when some of them began to worship her, she became like an ordinary woman and chided them for their folly.

The Mahomedans have two heavens of their own. Owing to their views on polygamy, they cannot get on with the Christian spirits. In one of their heavens they live virtuously with several wives.

"As the idea of Mohammed is always connected with religion in the minds of Musselmans, therefore some Mohammed or other is always placed in their view. It is not Mohammed himself who wrote the Koran, but some other who fills his place. In order that he may be distinguished, there is a fire near him like a small torch, but it is visible only to Mahomedans."

"The real Mohammed, who wrote the Koran, is not at this day to be seen among them.* I have been informed that at first he was appointed to preside over them; but being desirous to rule over all the concerns of their religion as a god, he was removed from his station, which was beneath the Roman Catholics, and was sent down to one on the right side, near the south. A certain society of Mahomedans was once instigated by some evil spirits to acknowledge Mohammed as a god, and in order to appease the sedition, Mohammed was raised up from the earth or region beneath and produced to their view, and on this occasion I also saw him. He appeared like corporeal spirits, who have no interior perception. His face was of a hue approaching to black, and I heard him utter these words, 'I am your Mohammed,' and presently he seemed to sink down again."

The Pagans, especially the Africans, have a heaven of their own, where they receive religious instruction from angels. They excel all other Gentiles in clearness of interior judgment.

---

* "The True Christian Religion," N. 830.

The Jews fare badly in the spiritual world, "most of them still firmly believe that they will go to the land of Canaan, and insist that the deceased Jews will rise again and leave their sepulchres to enter that land. When they are told that the land of Canaan is not large enough, they answer that it will be enlarged." It might be supposed that the inhabitants of the spiritual world would recognise the falsehoods of the religious notions they have held on earth. In many cases, this does not happen.

Swedenborg describes spirits who still maintained the erroneous notions they had held on earth. There were materialists who insisted that they had never died, and atheists who still agreed that there was no God. There were misers who still tried to hoard useless money.

Since, with Swedenborg, we have entered the spiritual world, the reader may be interested at hearing some of the details which he so freely gives, especially in his book upon heaven and its wonders, the world of spirits and hell, described by one who had heard and seen what he relates.*

Swedenborg minutely describes the feelings of a man passing by death into another world.† In order that he might do so more accurately, he himself was brought into a state of insensibility like that of dying persons, the faculty of thought and memory remaining unimpaired. The conjunction of the soul and body ceases with the action of the heart, because the heart corresponds to the affection which belongs to the love, which is the very life of man, for it is from love that every one derives the vital heat. The respiration of the body was almost taken away, but the interior respiration, which is that of the soul, remained. Two angels from the celestial kingdom sat at his head. They did not speak, but communicated their thoughts by looking at him. When they see that the man perceives their faces, they know that he is dead. They examine the man's thoughts, and if these are pious and holy they try to keep them up. The celestial angels do not leave

---

* I have used the translation of the Rev. Samuel Noble, London, 1851.

† "Arcana Celestia," vol. i. N. 168-189. "Heaven and Hell," N. 450.

the resuscitated person unless he is of such a character that he desires to depart from them. When he does so, the angels of the spiritual kingdom come to him, who open his eyes to the new world, for up to this time the man has but a faint and obscure perception of the new life.

"Those angels seemed to unroll, as it were, the coat of the left eye towards the nose, that the eye might be opened and the faculty of sight imparted. It appears to the spirit as if such an operation were actually performed, but it is only an appearance. After the coat of the eye has seemed to be thus drawn off, a lucid but indistinct appearance is observed, like that which, on first awaking from sleep, a man sees through his eyelids before he opens them. This indistinct, lucid appearance, as seen by me, was of a sky-blue colour; but I was afterwards informed that there are varieties in the colour as seen by different persons. After this there is a sensation as if something was gently drawn off the face, and when this operation is completed, the resuscitated person is introduced into a state of spiritual thought. That drawing off of something from the face is likewise, however, only an appearance, and by it is represented the passing from the state of natural thought into the state of spiritual thought. The angels use the utmost caution lest any idea should proceed from the resuscitated person, but such as partakes of love. All this being done, they tell him that he is now a spirit. After the spiritual angels have imparted to the new-born spirit the use of light, they render him all the kind offices which in that state he can possibly desire, and instruct him respecting the things that exist in the other life, as far as he is capable of comprehending them."

He is then left in the company of good spirits; but if the character which he had formed in the world has led him to a taste for base things, he soon desires to be away from them. In the end he becomes associated with such bad spirits.

Robsahm once asked Swedenborg how a man felt when he suffered the punishment of death. He answered:—

"When he first awakes in the spiritual world and finds that he is living, he is seized with the fear of his expected death, and tries to escape. Soon good spirits come to him and tell him where he is, and he is then left to follow his own inclinations, which lead him to the place where he abides for ever."

The following passage occurs in the "Spiritual Diary" in reference to the execution of Count Brahe on the 23rd July, 1756:—

"Brahe was beheaded at ten o'clock in the morning, and spoke with me at ten at night—that is to say, twelve hours after his execution. He was with me almost without interruption for several days. After two days he began to return to his former life, which consisted in loving worldly things, and after three days he relapsed into the evils which he had made his own before he died."

Another entry refers to his old friend Polhem, the engineer:—

"Polhem died on Monday and spoke with me on Thursday. I was invited to the funeral. Polhem saw the hearse, the attendants, and the whole procession. He also saw them let down the coffin into the grave, and conversed with me while the interment was going on, asking why they buried him when he was alive. When the priest pronounced that he would rise again at the day of judgment, he asked why this was, since he had risen already. He wondered that such a belief should prevail, considering that he was even now alive; he also wondered at the belief in the resurrection of the body, for he said he felt himself then in the body, with other remarks."

Polhem during life had been a materialist, and after death he went on trying to mould animals—such as birds, cats, and mice—out of a certain composition. "He sits in a dark chamber amongst men's bones, for he has no knowledge of the living, but of the dead."

Some spirits who are deeply depraved are led at once by their lusts to hell; others pass quickly to heaven, but the greater number remain generally for a few days, and seldom longer than a year, in the world of spirits till their ruling love declares itself. In this state their occupations correspond to those they most affected when on earth. A man skilled in the science of correspondences may foresee his own state after death, provided he knows his own love, which however is difficult, as men favour what is their own, and call their evils good.

Swedenborg further tells us:—

"When a man's actions are brought before him after death, the angels to whom the duty of making the inquiry is assigned look into his face, and then the examination proceeds through his whole body, beginning from the fingers of both hands. As I wondered what this could be for, it was discovered to me. All particulars of a man's thought and will are inscribed on his brain, for there they exist in their first principles. Thence also they are inscribed on his whole body, because all things belonging to his thought and will proceed thither from their first principles, and are there terminated, as being there in their ultimates. This is the reason that whatever things proceeding from a man's will, and thence from his thought, are inscribed on his memory, are not only inscribed on the brain, but also on the whole man, and there exist in order according to the order of the parts of the body. It was hence made evident to me that man is such in the whole as he is in his will and in his thought thence derived, so that a bad man is his own evil, and a good man is his own good."

Swedenborg tells us* that everything which enters into a man's will and thoughts remains in his memory for ever, so that the minutest events of his life can be recalled in the world of spirits. In the interior memory, whose existence is not known to men, are stored his acquired habits and the tone of his thoughts, and what pertains to the rational and spiritual side of his nature. It is the book of his life. In the exterior memory are recorded the man's perception of the material world, and what he has committed to heart. In the spiritual world the outer memory remains quiescent, or he is not permitted to use it. Some of the natural things in the outer memory are changed into corresponding spiritual things.

Some persons regarded on earth as men of learning on account of their knowledge of the ancient languages, such as Hebrew, Greek, and Latin, but who had not cultivated their rational faculty by the information contained in the books written in these tongues, were found to be as simple as those who knew no language save their own, and yet a conceited persuasion remains with them that they were wiser than others. But those who had been opposed to the truths of the Church, and had occupied their thoughts with mere matters of science,

---

* "Arcana Celestia," N. 2475, 5212, 9386. "Heaven and Hell," N. 464.

by means of which they had confirmed themselves in falsities, had not cultivated their rational faculty, but only the faculty of reasoning. This, in the world, is supposed to be rationality; but it is a faculty with which rationality has no connection, being a mere talent for confirming as true whatever a man pleases, and, from preconceived principles and from fallacies, seeing falsities as truths, but not truths themselves.

To reconcile the providence of God with the free-will of man is one of the old difficulties of the framers of systems of theology. Swedenborg taught that, as God is the sole subsisting and self-subsisting Principle, everything is really sustained by Him, hence the sense of liberty and rationality in man, which appears to him as his own, in reality comes from God. Man's good actions are thus not his own; and it is an error, and in some cases a heinous sin, to believe that man works out his own salvation. The more distinctly regenerated man appears to himself at his own disposal, the more evidently he perceives that he is the Lord's. "It has been granted to me," he writes,* "also to be in a similar perception and appearance now for many years; from which I am fully convinced that I neither will nor think anything from myself, but that it appears as from myself; and it is also given me to desire and love this."

This is very like Pantheism. One feels curious to know what Swedenborg would have said about Spinoza. It does not appear that the Swedish theologian ever read the works of the Jewish philosopher of Amsterdam.

The world of spirits lies between heaven on one side and hell on the other. Between heaven and hell there is a perpetual equilibrium. The societies in hell are perpetually striving against those in heaven. It is this sustained equilibrium which allows the freedom of the will to those who are in the world of spirits. Heaven is in the form of a grand man—*i.e.*, it is a vast region with the outlines of a human figure. As the natural world exists in leasts, so does the spiritual world; it contains innumerable societies also in the form of a man. These societies occupy different parts and

---

* "Angelic Wisdom concerning the Divine Providence," N. 44 and 158.

organs, corresponding to the qualities in which they excel. The best situations are in the head and breast, who pre-eminently enjoy love, peace, wisdom, charity, and faith. "They who are in the arms and hands are, in the power of truth, derived from good. They who are in the eyes are those eminent for understanding. They who are in the ears are in attention and obedience. They in the nostrils are those distinguished for perception. They in the mouth and tongue are such as excel in discoursing from understanding and perception. They in the kidneys are such as are grounded in truth of a searching, distinguishing, and castigatory character. They in the liver, pancreas, and spleen are grounded in the purification of good and truth by various methods. So with those in the other members and organs."

In heaven there are plains, and hills, and rivers, everything as on earth. The angels have the perfect human form. The angels have splendid palaces and beautiful gardens. The Dutch style of gardening is evidently preferred, trim walks, and trees neatly clipped, the flowers and plants changed every day. The angels seem very fond of disputing about theology. This may, however, be owing to Swedenborg's affecting such society, and neglecting the less disputatious ones. Aristotle's definition of happiness as virtuous energy seems to hold good for heaven. The angels are always busy about something. After hundreds of years they retain the ruling taste which they had upon earth, and follow similar pursuits. The children who die young are brought up in heaven by angels who were women that loved children. They are allowed to adopt children in proportion to the amount of their maternal love. Little girls brought up in heaven have a liberal allowance of pretty clothes. When they see spots on their frocks, they know that they have committed some faults.

Swedenborg takes a cheerful and practical view of human merit. Every one who leads a good life, avoiding evils as sins, in the end gets into heaven; hereditary evil tendencies, and occasional sins which do not enter deeply into a man's character, are left behind at death. It is by no means needful that a man should give away his possessions; the rich get to heaven as easily as the poor. He goes over the different texts in the

New Testament which say that it is difficult for a rich man to enter into heaven and that the poor are blessed, and assures us the words "poor" and "rich" have different meanings. Rich men are those puffed up with worldly knowledge; poor men, those who hunger after spiritual knowledge. Those who practise great austerities form a morose disposition, which renders them unfit for the joys of heaven. He observes that it is believed that the bad may be saved as well as the good, provided they only, at the hour of death, speak with confidence of the Lord's intercession, and of mercy as procured by that intercession. The angels declared that they had never yet seen any one, who had lived wickedly, received into heaven by an act of immediate mercy, how much soever when in the world he might have spoken from such trust or confidence, as in a more eminent sense is meant by faith.

Swedenborg repeats in many forms his conviction that no one's life can possibly be changed after death, and that to transmute an evil life into a good one, or the life of an infernal into that of an angel, is utterly impracticable; since every spirit is, from head to foot, such in quality as his love is, consequently, such as his life is; and to metamorphose this into an opposite one were to destroy the spirit altogether. Those confirmed in wickedness and falsehood can enter heaven if they choose, but instead of joy they feel torment. He tells us of a certain devil who appeared like a leopard, but who had the art to transform himself into an angel of light, and passed the chasm between heaven and hell. As soon as some angels approached he was seized with convulsions and fell down, with all his joints contracted; and then he appeared like a great serpent, folding and writhing himself, till at length he made his escape through the ground, and, being received by his associates, he was conveyed down into a cavern, where he presently revived by the stinking odour of his own delight. "I once also saw," he tells us, "a certain Satan[*] punished by his associates, and on inquiring into the reason was informed that he had stopped his nostrils and approached the heavenly

---

[*] In Swedenborg's terminology a Satan is a man who has passed from falsehood to evil, a devil one who has passed from evil to falsehood.

odours, and on his return had brought some taint of them along with him in his clothes."

Swedenborg's descriptions of hell are dismal and disgusting, rather than striking and terrible. As heaven is in the form of a grand man, the entire hell is in the form of a grand devil, like that of a man, though hardly so handsome. Each society in heaven has its opposite in hell—the hypocrites, the spiteful, the covetous and avaricious, the violent, the adulterous are all drawn together by their ruling taste to one particular resort, where they tempt, cheat, and maltreat one another. He saw the murderous dealing blows on other spirits, but the knife is taken from them ere it enters their victims. There are whole cities in hell, squalid, filthy, smelling of all foulness which, in their vitiated taste, the inhabitants prefer to the perfumes of heaven. Each society has at its gates some emblem denoting its character. This to the angels appear very hideous, but to the inhabitants it has a different aspect. Hell is under the supervision of the angels, who sometimes have to repress dreadful riots. The inhabitants are compelled to work so many hours a day. Each male spirit is allowed to select a female, and is punished if he cohabits with any other. These women are artful and fond of dominion. They tempt their partners to murder them, knowing they cannot die. The female spirits were seen to tear one another's hair.

In Swedenborg's day devils were shut up in hell, and no longer suffered to possess men's bodies as of old. The faces of the dwellers in hell are horrible, like those of wild beasts; sometimes nothing is seen save grinning teeth, but they appear like human beings to one another. There are evil spirits in hell who have totally forgotten what they were on earth, the souls of kings and men of mark mingled with those of mean men, drawn together by a community of wicked tastes. "Infernal torments," he observes, "are not, as some suppose, stings of conscience, for they who are in hell have no conscience, and consequently cannot be so tormented. Such as have had any conscience are amongst the blessed."

Those who deny the divinity of the Lord, like the Socinians, are amongst the lost; though, as we have seen, the Mahomedans are admitted to Paradise, Swedenborg finds the Quakers in the lowest hell, and accuses them of secret profligacy while on earth. This may be cited as a proof of his own credulity. In hell he meets with Gustavus Vasa, who rescued Sweden from a foreign yoke and introduced the Reformed religion. The king had become a mere idiot as a punishment for his love of dominion. Swedenborg also saw the heroic figure of the great Gustavus seated on his war-horse. He was still suffering for his adulteries on earth. As for the Assessor's old patron, Charles XII., he was a most horrid devil, who had married a wife more obstinate than himself. Swedenborg tells us he was let down to the lowest hells; a column of angelic spirits like a wall of brass encompassed him and protected him from the murderous assaults of the evil spirits. He heard piteous lamentations and cries to God for mercy. "They were," he writes, "in a state of despair, saying that they believed their torments would be eternal; but it was granted me to comfort them."* He does not say how. In the "Arcana" there are passages which seem to signify that punishment is so given as to lead to amendment; but in his later writings, such as "Heaven and Hell," a more vindictive spirit exists. Bad spirits become so besotted in evil that all taste for good, or contact with good, is even more painful than the continued indulgence of evil. In truth, Swedenborg does not seem to have much advantage over Calvin. There is a difficulty in denying the prescience of God; it is not predestination which is so dreadful, it is the thing predestinated. Swedenborg says it is the wicked that choose their own fate, God does not choose it for them; but he looks passively on, and hell is as full as heaven. We have some fanciful nonsense about the necessity of an equilibrium between the two. Surely God is above all—above free-will as above fate. If He will not change the evil nature of the wicked, He can in mercy return them into the nothing from which He called them.

---

* "Arcana Celestia," N. 699.

CHAPTER VIII.

The Language of Spirits—Their Ideas of Space—The Doctrine of Correspondence in Nature—The Inner Sense of the Bible—He offers to Interpret the Hieroglyphics.

SCATTERED over Swedenborg's theological writings there are speculations or revelations about the language of spirits which show both the penetrating power of his intellect and his proclivity to whimsical theories. Every spirit or angel, when conversing with a man, appears to speak in his proper language—French, with a Frenchman; English, with an Englishman; Arabic, with an Arabian. The reason of this Swedenborg tells us is* :—

"Because when angels converse with man, they turn towards him, and conjoin themselves with him; the effect of which is, to bring both parties into a similar memory, and his speech flows from it, both parties possess and use the same language. Besides, when an angel or spirit approaches a man, and by turning towards comes into conjunction with him, he enters into all the man's memory, so completely, that he is scarcely aware that he does not know, of himself, all that the man knows, including the languages with which the man is acquainted. I have conversed with the angels on this phenomenon, and have remarked to them, that they might possibly suppose that they were speaking with me in my native tongue, because it so appeared to them, whereas it was not they who thus spoke, but myself, and that this might be demonstrated from the fact, that angels cannot utter one word of any human language, and because also, the language of men is natural, whereas they are spiritual, and spiritual beings cannot utter anything in a natural manner."

This means, that in conversing with a man through

---

* "Heaven and Hell," N. 246.

ordinary speech, one uses words, letters, or other symbols, which excite the thoughts with which the words have become associated, whereas spirits, by arousing thoughts on the mental side of a man, excite the corresponding words in his memory. Thus, in the one case, the passage is from words to ideas; in the other, from ideas to words. Swedenborg tells us that the spirits infuse ideas into men's minds through the cerebellum, but he does not otherwise explain the process, which, perhaps, is too much to expect. At anyrate, many ideas, which men believe to be their own, are really infused into their minds by good or bad spirits. In Swedenborg's own case, he frequently was able to detect the spirit or syren who tried to infuse vicious or voluptuous ideas into his mind. These syrens were chiefly women, who, during life, had made themselves adepts in all alluring arts. After passing to the spirit world, they would persist, in spite of severe punishments, in infusing themselves into men's thoughts and affections. Swedenborg complains that these syrens discoursed with other spirits during the night, suggesting obscene thoughts, and imitating his voice and style so artfully, that they could not be distinguished. On one occasion, he tells us, after he awoke from a quiet sleep, "Certain good spirits began to chide me for having infested them so cruelly, as they said that they supposed themselves to be in hell; to whom I replied that I knew nothing about the matter, &c." Of course it was the syrens who had been practising on the good spirits. One night Swedenborg wakened out of sleep and heard spirits about him, who were desirous to ensnare him. Falling asleep again he had a dismal dream, and, on waking, there suddenly presented themselves some chastising spirits, who inflicted summary punishments upon the syrens by clothing them, as it were, with bodies which were visible, and giving them corporeal senses, and then thrashing, or dashing them about in a violent manner. The punishment, he tells us, lasted for a long time, and all who had endeavoured to ensnare me were discovered. As they were syrens, they studied, by every art, to elude punishment; sometimes they wished to slip away and hide themselves; sometimes to pretend that they were not the persons who had offended; sometimes to transfer the punishment to others by translation of ideas. Sometimes they feigned themselves to be infants; sometimes to be good spirits, with a variety of other artifices; but all to no purpose. I wondered that they were so severely punished, but it was perceived that their crime was of an enormous kind, arising from the necessity that man should sleep in safety.

Swedenborg tells us that he heard the voices of the spirits who addressed him quite clearly, and noticed that their voices did not seem any fainter when they were at a distance. To use his own words* :—

"As I heard the sound of man's voice in discourse, so I heard also the voice of spirits, insomuch that the spirits sometimes wondered that their discourse with me was not heard by others; for, in respect to hearing, there was no difference at all between the voices of men and spirits; but whereas the influx into the internal organs of hearing is distinct from the influx of man's voice into the external organs, therefore the discourse of spirits was heard by none but myself, whose internal organs by the Divine mercy of the Lord were opened."

Some spirits told him that they not merely spoke from man, but that they actually spoke in man, and that his memory was really theirs. In other cases, the man mistook the memory of the spirits for his own, on which account some of the ancients conceived the idea that they had existed in another state before being born on earth. Hence arose the error of the transmigration of souls. In the spiritual world they have a spiritual language, which is not like any natural language. Every man cometh, without effort, into the use of this spiritual language after his decease. In the "Arcana" he speaks of this as consisting not of a language of words, but a language of ideas of thought, which is the universal language of all languages. In some passages he talks of the thoughts of the angels being indicated by vibrations of flames, or by their thoughts being displayed by modifications of the light of heaven, and their affections by modifications of its heat. In "Heaven and Hell," written four years later, he says the

---

* "Arcana Celestia," N. 1634.

spiritual language is spoken through the mouth by means of a spiritual atmosphere which enters the lungs. The angels even use written characters, and have writings which they carefully preserve. The angelic speech is highly musical; vowels are much in use. It is more abstract than any human language. The angels can express in a minute what would take a man an hour to say. The language of the angels deals with ideas of ideas, and thoughts of thoughts, and affections of affections, therefore, the conceptions of the spiritual world are ineffable, and so we need not say any more about them. It is to be observed, however, that, though Swedenborg talks in high terms of the angels, in his own memorable relations he seems to be subtler than they are, and to suggest new ideas to them about the subjects which he loves to discuss.

In the ancient Church, men had a language which was conducted through internal respiration and was heard through the Eustachian tube. They also expressed their ideas by numberless changes of the face, and especially of the lips, in which there are many series of muscular fibres at this day not unfolded, and which in those primeval times were read off by the sight. This method of conversing is unfortunately lost, though perhaps the German method of teaching the deaf to speak, and to follow speech by watching the lips, may be considered an imperfect approach to it. Swedenborg tells us that when internal respiration ceased, external respiration such as is now the custom succeeded, and with this came the language of words to express the ideas of thought.

The relation of ideas to space is an old difficulty of the metaphysicians. The schoolmen used to dispute whether two spirits could occupy the same space at the same time. Jacob Behmen writes:—

"The soul, when it departs from the body, needs not to go far, for at that place where the body dies, there is heaven and hell; and the man Christ dwells everywhere. God and the devil is there, yet each in his own kingdom. The paradise is also there, and the soul needs only to enter through the deep door in the centre. Is the soul holy? Then it stands in the gate of heaven and the earthly body has but kept it out of heaven; and now when the body comes to be broken, then the soul is already in heaven; it needs no going out or in, Christ has it in His arms."

Nevertheless one would not have anticipated that Swedenborg, who thought lightly of the metaphysicians, would have perplexed himself with such a question. He held that the spiritual body had the same shape as the natural body and that there were in heaven plains and houses and gardens and other things which must be extended in space. It must, however, be remembered, that Swedenborg's mind worked under the belief that he had communicated with the spiritual world. He was thus induced to uphold the reality of his visions and phantasms, and his reason laboured to reconcile doubts and difficulties. But as the morbid condition of his nervous system worked independently of his will, his hallucinations were not always as he wished, nor always as he expected. His visions had not the congruity of a poet like Dante whose imagination was under the control of his will and regulated by his tastes. One of the difficulties Swedenborg had to reconcile was that he was introduced into heaven and hell without changing the place he held in the world, and that spectres appeared together who could not be expected to be seen at once in the same places. He explained this by saying that there was no space in the spiritual world, but only the appearance of space.

One angel or spirit may in an instant be made present with another, provided they meet in similar affections of love, and thence of thought; for a difference with regard to these two circumstances is what causes the appearance of space. Distances in another life are nothing else but varieties in state. The angels approached quicker to one another in proportion to the ardour of their desires to meet.

"That such is the nature of presence in the spiritual world," writes Swedenborg,* "was made plain to me from this consideration that there I could see Africans and Indians very near together, although they are so many miles distant here on earth; yea, that I could be made present with the inhabit-

---

* "The True Christian Religion," N. 64.

ants of other planets that are in other worlds, which revolve about other suns."

In one passage, he tells us, that the spirits who conversed with him took positions towards one another, corresponding to the parts of the shape of the grand man where they resided in heaven. We suppose the spirits of the left heel would be in a corner of the room, while those belonging to the right eye would be on the other side near the ceiling. The following passage shows the whimsical perplexities which the unaccountable behaviour of the spirits sometimes aroused in the still inquiring mind of the old Assessor. He observed that when he removed to an adjoining room the spirits did not follow him, and even when he changed his clothes that the spirits were estranged, not knowing where they were. "Spirits desire to have their ideas connected with place, and thus rendered determinate. . . . The reason is, that an idea is not fixed and finited without space, or, which is the same thing, without structure. Spirits draw back the foot when thinking of places, which is a kind of sign that places and material things serve as fulcra for their thoughts."[*]

The doctrine of correspondence has a large place in Swedenborg's writings. The whole natural world which lies below the sun corresponds to the spiritual or heavenly world,[†] "and not only the natural world collectively, but also in its individual parts, wherefore, every object in the natural world exists from something in the spiritual world, just as the effect exists from its efficient cause." Hence by an intelligent scrutiny of the natural world it was possible that one could infer what occurred in the spiritual world. In the Golden Age, men thought from correspondences, and the natural objects of the world which they had before their eyes served them as mediums for contemplation and converse with the angels. In the silver age this natural gift was lost, but the science of correspondences remained so that the wise could learn it with effort as men learn a dead language. In the course of time even this was lost, though scattered perceptions of correspondences existed in ancient learning, mythology and

---

[*] White, vol. i. p. 302.   [†] "Heaven and Hell," N. 89.

poetry. That correspondences exist in the universe the student of nature will be ready to believe. In the movements of the planets we discern geometrical laws. In the arrangement of the different parts of plants such as the leaf and the flower, we observe invariable arithmetical relations. These and many other things in nature awake in us the thought that the human intellect, however weak, is akin to the Divine mind which made and sustains the universe. The principle of beauty which exists throughout nature, in the flower of the field as in the shell at the bottom of the sea, is it not also a Divine idea? Does music not consist of correspondences? Tones of a certain character arranged in a certain pitch and succession arouse in us emotional states, joy, sadness, love, pity, and raise our minds to the perception of the ideal, and the contemplation of the infinite. There is therefore some correspondence between the vibrations of sound and the passions of the soul. We trace correspondences in the ancient mythologies; poetry delights in similes and allegories; heraldry has its emblems and devices often based on correspondences more or less fitting. Language tends to lead us away from these correspondences and substitute arbitrary symbols to answer to thoughts, yet language is built up of correspondences. Philologists teach us that all complex ideas are derived from simple figures. The words used for the soul or spirit are derived from those used for the breath or heart, the just or right from what is straight, the wrong from what is crooked, the polite from what is smooth, the rude from what is rough, and so on. Some complex correspondences run through all educated thought, the microcosm or the world, the microcosm or the human frame, the body politic and the individual body. Men delight in finding out and recognising correspondences. A bull's head borne in a dish portended murder, a pair of spurs under a cover signified that it was time to go on a foray for provisions. The taste for fables and riddles will never die out.

Some of Swedenborg's correspondences satisfy the mind; others are difficult to seize. Light corresponds to intelligence; heat to love; pure water to truth; rain to Divine truth from heaven; clouds are Divine truths reduced to their simplest parts, or the word in its literal sense. A fish corresponds to general truths, a fisherman therefore is a searcher for truth. In some of Swedenborg's correspondences a trace of poetical similitude remains, but in others the morbid divergence of his intellect leads him into mere guess work and extravagance. Many of his correspondences are the result of knowledge acquired in his visits to the spiritual world. Animals correspond to the affections of angels or spirits, tame, peaceful, and useful beasts to good affections, and the fierce and useless kinds to evil lusts and affections. The moral world is the cause of the existence of the animal world; all animal life proceeds from moral affections in the spiritual world. Trees, according to their species, correspond to perceptions of good and truth, hence the ancients had their oracles in groves. There are animals in heaven quite the same as those on earth. He mentions sheep, goats, doves, and birds of paradise. Most of the domestic animals, as well as some beasts of prey, occur in the world of spirits. In the spiritual world Swedenborg heard two Presidents of the Royal Society, Sir Hans Sloane and Martin Folkes, disputing whether seeds and ova were generated by the sun's heat or through the influx of God in nature.

"In order to determine the dispute, a beautiful bird was exhibited to Sir Hans Sloane, and he was told to examine whether in the least thing it differed from a similar bird on earth.[*] He held it in his hand, examined it, and said there was no difference. At the same time he knew that the bird was nothing else than the external representative of an affection of a certain angel, and that it would vanish or cease with the angel's affection, as indeed it did."

In the hells there are dogs, foxes, wolves, swine, mice, serpents, owls, and bats. He informs us that the beasts and wild creatures in the natural world, whose souls are evil affections, such as mice, poisonous serpents, crocodiles, basilisks, and vipers, together with various kinds of noxious insects, were not created from the beginning, but took their rise with hell

---

[*] WHITE, vol. ii. p. 225.

in lakes, fens, stinking and filthy waters,* and wherever there were effluvia arising from rottenness. In fact, since animals arose from affections in the spiritual world, it follows that man must have preceded animals, since all angels and spirits and devils were once men. All men called into being live for ever; but beasts, though they have souls or living principles, intuition and affections, have neither will nor thoughts from the understanding, and have no existence after death.

Swedenborg regarded the human body as the conjunction of the spiritual and natural world; and in its structure he delighted to carry out his science of correspondences. The countenance answered to the changes in the soul, not by any system of pre-established harmony as Leibnitz taught, but as cause and effect. The heat corresponded to the will and the affections; the lungs to thought; the human body in all its parts corresponded to heaven. These analogies in Swedenborg's mind were not mere similes or forms of speech. It was his besetting tendency to put together theories as a bird takes straws and twigs to put together a nest, to treat these theories as real entities, and to dwell in them. His dreams and incongruous hallucinations were interpreted under this easy and elastic science of correspondences, and made to work in the art of deception. Swedenborg states his belief that dreams were sent to him from heaven like those of Joseph and Pharaoh. The angels explain to him how dreams were infused into his mind.†

Take the following‡ as an example of the fantastic visions that presented themselves to his mind, and the way in which he interpreted them.

"There appeared some spirits in black, and in a cloud so dark as to excite horror; afterwards there appeared others not so horrible, and it was signified to me that I should see something. Instantly there was seen at first some children who were combed by their mothers so cruelly that the blood flowed out, by which was represented that such is the education of infants at this day. Afterwards there appeared a tree, and it was perceived as if it was the tree of knowledge, into

---

* "The White Horse," p. 77.   † "Arcana Celestia," N. 1977.
‡ *Ibid.*, N. 2125.

which a large viper was seen to raise itself, of such a size as to beget horror, it appeared to be of the length of the trunk. The tree with the viper vanishing, there appeared a dog, and instantly a door was opened into a chamber, enlightened with a yellowish light as of lighted coal, and therein were two women; it was perceived that the chamber was a kitchen, but I am not at liberty to relate the things which were there seen. It was told me that the tree, into which the viper climbed, represented the state of the men of the Church, as they are at this day, in that they entertain mortal hatred towards each other instead of love and charity, covering such hatreds also under deceit and pretences of uprightness; and likewise that they cherish impious thoughts concerning the things appertaining to faith, but the things seen in the kitchen represented those hatreds and impious thoughts, according to their real quality."

In one place he relates a vision of children and women in raiment of different colours, and observes, "It was not discovered to me what these things signified."

Here is portrayed the fate of the sceptic in the world of spirits:—

"There appeared to me a certain spirit in a dark habit sitting at a mill, and, as it were, grinding corn, and beside him there appeared small mirrors. I wondered who he was, but he came to me and said that he was the person who sat at the mill, and that he had an idea that all and everything was merely the creature of phantasy, and that nothing real existed."

Brought up in a strict reverence for the Bible, Swedenborg might have found in its pages insuperable objections to his new beliefs; but his complacent and elastic intellect showed him how to escape. A double meaning was known to exist in some parts of Scripture. The parables in the gospels are the clearest and best instances of correspondences. There runs through them both a natural and a spiritual sense. The parable always remains true to nature, whereas the fable violates it, as when beasts are made to speak. The theology of these days delighted to find types of the Christian dispensation throughout the Old Testament, often strangely incongruous, but which it was then thought heretical to contest. Swedenborg gets over all difficulty of reconciling his doctrines with

Scripture by the assumption that the Scriptures have an external and internal sense; and here he takes rank among the Mystics. He differs from them, as not only he professes to find hidden or unsuspected meanings in the Bible, but he also pretends to have a special revelation through which he was enabled to find meanings in the Scriptures which no one would have suspected, and which indeed do not look at all credible after they are pointed out. All the Old Testament save those books generally assigned to Solomon were susceptible of these explanations; but in the New Testament only the gospels and the Apocalypse had the internal sense. The "Arcana Celestia" form a commentary upon the meaning of Genesis and Exodus; according to Swedenborg there is no historical or literal truth in Genesis up to the twelfth chapter when the history of Abraham begins. After this there is both a historical and a representative sense in the narrative.

In the view that the opening chapters of Genesis have an allegorical meaning Swedenborg is at one with several of the early Fathers of the Church. Such explanations may avoid some of the difficulties in the account of the creation, but what Swedenborg calls the true meaning or the internal sense has rarely any semblance of probability or congruity. The six days in which the world was created are the six states of the regeneration of man's soul. The first is infancy, the second the commencement of action of the Spirit of God, the third repentance, the fourth love illustrated by faith. In the fifth stage man confirms himself in truth and goodness; and in the sixth stage, he speaketh what is true and doeth what is good. By the beasts created are signified things appertaining to the will; by the fowls things pertaining to the understanding. The river Hiddekel is reason; Euphrates science; Assyria the rational mind. To eat of every tree in the garden is to know by perception what is good and true. To eat of the tree of good and evil is to search into the mysteries of faith by means of the sensual and scientific. The serpent that tempted Eve is the sensual principle in man. Abel is charity; Cain faith without charity; the flood of waters an inundation of evil. In this way Swedenborg pored through the Old Testament in search of correspondences. He wrote a large volume on the mysteries contained in the Apocalypse. It was then customary with Protestant divines to find a condemnation of Papacy in this book. Swedenborg found a condemnation both of Catholicism and of those doctrines of Protestantism which he disliked. Babylon and the harlot seated on the seven hills was indeed the Catholic religion; but the great red dragon signified those in the Reformed Church, who made God three and the Lord two, and who said men were saved by faith alone. The beast coming out of the earth signified the clergy who are in faith separate from charity. The beast coming out of the sea signified the laity who were in the same condition. It is now held both by scholars like Renan and by divines like Farrar, that the Apocalypse has reference to some of the past and current events of the time in which it was written, and that the beast was Nero. But Swedenborg's mind had no grasp of historical events. In fact, though his comments on the moral precepts of Scripture are often searching and noble, he did scarcely anything to make the meaning of the Bible clearer, while he used it to confirm and illustrate his new views, with very little regard for its obvious meaning. No text however clear stood in his way. One would have thought that Christ's answer to the Sadducees, that after the resurrection men neither marry nor are given in marriage, but are as the angels which are in heaven,* was a direct contradiction to his doctrine that marriage was a universal and lasting institution in heaven. Swedenborg explained this by saying that Christ referred to spiritual nuptials, that is, the soul's conjunction with the Lord Himself which is effected on earth. It is also worthy of remark that Swedenborg, like the Sadducees, said that there was no resurrection. He maintains that when the apostles saw Christ after the crucifixion it was because their spiritual eyes were opened, so that His spiritual form could be seen by them.† In this way Swedenborg gets rid of the very central fact of Christianity.

---

* Mark xii. 25; Swedenborg on "Conjugial Love," N. 41.

† See "The True Christian Religion," N. 793.—"The reason why the disciples saw Him was because their spiritual eyes were at that time

There is still preserved a letter of Swedenborg's to the Academy of Sciences of Stockholm, in which he offers to explain the hieroglyphics inscribed on the columns and walls of the temples in Egypt. These, he wrote, were nothing else than the correspondences of natural and spiritual things. Had Champollion appeared in his day to show that the hieroglyphics really contained alphabetical characters, Swedenborg would either have calmly rejected his views, or would have complacently told him that his deciphered texts contained both an external and internal sense.

---

opened; and when this is the case, the objects of the spiritual world appear as distinctly as those of the natural world."

"Heaven and Hell," N. 76.—"This also is done in an instant, when it is the pleasure of the Lord, that the things of the spiritual world should be seen by man; nor is he at all aware, at the time, that he does not behold them with the eyes of his body. It was thus that angels were seen by Abraham, Lot, Manoah, and the prophets; it was thus that the Lord was seen by the disciples after His resurrection; and it was thus, also, that angels had been seen by me."

CHAPTER IX.

SWEDENBORG COLLECTS INFORMATION ABOUT THE PLANETS AND THEIR INHABITANTS—HIS CLAIRVOYANCE—STORY OF THE FIRE AT STOCKHOLM—THE QUEEN OF SWEDEN—THE DE MARTEVILLE RECEIPT.

HEAVEN and hell were recruited by drafts from innumerable worlds, so Swedenborg, in the course of his spiritual converse, got acquainted with spirits from the planets, from whom he derived the only personal information which we have of other earths.*

The planet Mercury is peopled by philosophers. They are very fond of knowledge; but as they are little given to applying it, are deficient in judgment. On it being pointed out to them that knowledge is only valuable for its uses, they replied, "To us knowledge is use." They are averse to discourse consisting of vocal expressions, and Swedenborg conversed with them "by a species of active thought." They are allowed to wander about the other worlds in search of knowledge. The Mercurials are like human beings on earth, but of a more slender make; their cattle are also more slender in build, resembling deer.

In Venus there are savage giants who are given to rapine. They are much occupied in looking after their cattle. In the world of spirits they have to go through a good deal of tribulation before they can get into heaven. On some occasions when this was accomplished, Swedenborg informs us that he felt such joy that it drew tears from his eyes. On the other

---

* See "The Earths in the Universe, and their Inhabitants; also their Spirits and Angels, from what has been Seen and Heard by Emanuel Swedenborg," being a translation of his work, "De Telluribus in Mundo Nostro Solari," Londini, 1758; London, 1875.

side of Venus the inhabitants are mild and gentle. They have seen the Lord Jesus Christ, and worship Him as God.

Swedenborg thought highly of the people in Mars. They converse by internal respiration, helped by the action of the muscles of the face. The men have no beards, but a blackness where we have it, extending backwards under the ears. They live on fruit and pulse and a kind of round vegetable which buds forth from the ground, probably resembling a pumpkin. Their clothes are made from the fibres of the bark of trees. They have fluid fire, to light up the moonless nights.

The planet Jupiter is very thickly peopled, for though they only live to about thirty years, they marry early. They dwell in low houses of wood, the ceilings of which are painted blue, variegated with stars. They have also tents in which they take their meals. Large horses run wild in Jupiter, and the Jovians are much afraid of them, though they never suffer any hurt from them. They added that the fear of horses is innate or natural to them. "This led me," goes on our informant, "to consider the cause of that fear, and it seemed to be grounded in the spiritual signification of horses; for a horse, in a spiritual sense, signifies the intellect formed of scientifics, and inasmuch as the inhabitants of Jupiter are afraid of cultivating the intellect by worldly sciences, hence comes an influence of the fear of horses."

Some spirits of Jesuits from our earth got into this planet and did a good deal of mischief by spreading false reports. Though the Jovians sometimes use the voice in speaking, they principally converse by the changes seen in the countenance. When death is near, the Jovians are warned by the apparition of a bald head. Those who are destined for heaven are carried away like Elijah in chariots with bright horses.

In Saturn the inhabitants, knowing that their real life commences after death, take very little interest in Saturnian affairs. They do not even bury the bodies of the dead, but cover them with branches of forest trees. When questioned about the great belt seen through our telescopes, the Saturnian spirits said it appeared to them only as something whitish, like snow in the heaven in various directions.

The Moon is inhabited by sturdy dwarfs with long faces. As there is no atmosphere, they speak from air which is collected in the abdomen, and make a loud noise. The moons of Jupiter and Saturn are also peopled. Besides this, Swedenborg describes five other worlds beyond our solar system, all inhabited by beings like men.

The souls of the people of these different planets and stars have each their abode in allotted parts of the figure of the grand man, of which heaven is composed. The people of our earth hold the skin, those of Mars the pons Varolii, and so on.

In these strange narratives, presented to us as the result of supernatural revelations, Swedenborg shows himself possessed of all the astronomical knowledge of the day, but of no more. It does not look an unfair test to expect that he might have communicated facts which could have been afterwards verified by later astronomers, such as the existence of Uranus and Neptune.

The old discoverers who landed in America or Australia found animals, and plants, and states, and cities, such as men had never imagined though coherent with nature's plan; but Swedenborg, visiting the planets and wandering beyond the solar system, brought back nothing save information which had a suspicious likeness to what he took away with him. One would have thought that Emanuel Swedenborg had been not only the explorer but the creator of the worlds he describes. Naturally when it was rumoured about that the old Assessor possessed such wonderful powers, he was charged with messages and inquiries from interested friends about persons in the world of souls; but these commissions he was very chary of undertaking. It was perhaps too much to expect that Swedenborg should find out Lavater's friend, Felix Hess, in the spiritual world, or tell what had become of the lost prince of Saxe-Coburg Saalfeldt, for, as he sententiously observed, it is very difficult to find out one particular spirit amongst the countless number of deceased persons, and we hear nothing of a spiritual post-office or directory for departed souls. Nevertheless, it is somewhat surprising that the angels and spiritual guides with whom the seer consulted did not save him from such blunders as that there was existing a people in Central

Africa who were in the possession of the true faith, or that the Book of Jasher, and that of the Wars of Jehovah, were preserved in Great Tartary.

Naturally the followers of the New Church make the most of some stories which, if true, would seem to justify for Swedenborg the claim of clairvoyance or second sight. We are told that, once being at Gottenburg at a friend's house, he went out about six o'clock and returned looking pale and alarmed. He told the rest of the company that a dangerous fire had just broken out in Stockholm, and that it was spreading fast. He also said that the house of one of his friends was already destroyed, and that his own was in danger. After eight o'clock he exclaimed, "Thank God, the fire is extinguished three doors from my house." This occurred on Saturday evening, and on Monday evening a messenger, despatched while the fire was raging, arrived from Stockholm with an account of the fire agreeing exactly with Swedenborg's description. The distance between the two places is about three hundred miles. Kant, the celebrated metaphysician of Königsberg, investigated this affair by correspondence, and declared that he had reason to believe that it took place as related.

As Swedenborg's pretensions were known at court, the Queen of Sweden, Louisa Ulrica, asked him lightly whether he had seen her brother, August Wilhelm, the *late Crown Prince of Prussia*, in the other world, and on Swedenborg's replying "No," she desired him to greet her brother from her. A few days after Swedenborg appeared at an early hour, while the Queen was in her own room surrounded by her ladies of honour. He boldly approached the Queen, and told her that her brother sent greeting and apologies for not having answered her last letter, but that he had now sent a reply through Swedenborg, which was repeated to her privately. The Queen was greatly moved, and said, "No one but God and my brother knows this secret."

One account* is that the communication related to the Queen's last interview with her brother at Charlottenburg;

---

* No less than twenty-one versions of this story are given in TAFEL's "Documents," vol. ii. part i.

but the Queen's narrative of the occurrence, which was published ten years after her death, states that it referred to a correspondence with the Prince of Prussia, which she carried on during the war between Sweden and Prussia, and which she did not wish to be known at the time. This affair made sufficient noise to be reported by the different ambassadors to their courts. M. Thiebault, a professor in the Royal Academy of Berlin, relates a conversation he had with the Queen about Swedenborg: " A thousand events," said she, "appear inexplicable and supernatural to us who know only the immediate consequences of them, and men of quick parts, who are never so well pleased as when they exhibit something wonderful, take an advantage of this to gain an extraordinary reputation. Swedenborg was a man of learning, and very able in his profession; he has always had the reputation of being an honest man—and I cannot comprehend by what means he obtained the knowledge of what no one could know. However, I have no faith in his having had a conference with my late brother."

It would appear that the Queen had some correspondence with her brother which she believed had been kept quite secret; but there are reasons for supposing that she might have been watched, and that more persons might have known about it. What the precise information was, and how it came to Swedenborg's knowledge, is not known to us. At any rate, there are possibilities which would need to be exhausted before we are driven to conclude that the secret came from the world beyond the grave.

There are eleven accounts of the story of the lost receipt from different sources. Two of these are from Swedenborg himself to different persons, and one from Mr. Letocard, secretary of the Dutch Embassy in Stockholm, who lived at the house of M. de Marteville, and who was a witness of the whole affair. Some time after the death of M. de Marteville, Dutch Ambassador in Stockholm, his widow received a demand for payment of a bill for silver plate which her husband had got. She had reason to believe that it had been already paid, and after searching in vain for the receipt she mentioned the matter to Swedenborg, desiring his assistance. Some days after Swedenborg came to her house, and told her that he had conversed with the spirit of her deceased husband, who told him the receipt was in the secret drawer of a writing-table—where it was really found. Another account supplied by Madame de Marteville's second husband differs in some important particulars. He says that the spirit of De Marteville appeared to Madame de Marteville in a dream and told her where she would find the lost receipt, and that next morning Swedenborg came to her house and told her that her husband's spirit had appeared to him during the night, but said he had not time to converse with Swedenborg as he had to go to his wife in order to tell her something of importance.

Mr. White observes that there are not perhaps in literature three better attested narratives of the supernatural than the preceding. It would take a good deal of reading to verify this observation. When one opens the door to such stories they rush in like a flood. There are many narratives of second sight, clairvoyance, and ghost-seeing, which are attested by apparently honest witnesses.

Unhappily when one agrees to believe in these stories the mind is not at rest. On making a collection of them from different times and countries, and comparing them with one another, we find that these supernatural communications go to support different religions and incompatible doctrines. In general they reproduce the prejudices and errors of the ghost seer. Consider the two large volumes which the Psychical Research Society have published, full of attested stories of communications to relatives and friends at great distances, often announcing a death or some serious accident. Are we to believe that there are more powers in the human mind than are habitually exercised, but which are exerted rarely and under unknown conditions? Some stories of clairvoyance have much impressed me; but if clairvoyance could be put under scientific examination it would be very soon proved. This, however, seems certain, that under some abnormal conditions of the nervous system, the ordinary powers of the senses are very much increased, so that things are felt and apprehended which in ordinary circumstances could not possibly be perceived. This has been observed mainly in hysteria, somnambulism, hypnotism, and other kindred conditions; but what are the limits of this power of heightened feeling and perception has not been defined, and is still a subject of question.

EMANUEL SWEDENBURG

CHAPTER X.

The Last Judgment—The New Church—Swedenborg's House in Stockholm—His Book on "Conjugial Love"—Letter to Hartley—The True Christian Religion—Letter to Wesley—His Last Illness—Dying Declaration—His Death—Remarks on the Nature of his Neurosis.

From the corruption of the times and the accumulation of hereditary evils through the wickedness of past generations, Swedenborg ventured to predict that the last judgment was near at hand. Some people will be relieved to learn that it is already past. The last judgment took place in 1757, the same year as Clive began the British rule in India by the victory of Plassy. The last judgment consisted in the clearing out of the settlements of souls in the world of spirits. Whole cities and communities were broken up, and multitudes of spirits shifted to heaven or hell. Though Swedenborg was present, he gives but a feeble description of the scene. He is particular in telling where people of different faiths were placed in the vast assembly. Justice was done to the spirits in accordance with his already published views.

An able expositor* of Swedenborg's religion and philosophy has observed that his claims to supernatural illumination, and to record events heard and seen by him in the spiritual world, may be considered, apart from the doctrines which he has delivered, as derived from and confirmed by the Divine Word, and illustrated by rational considerations. In truth, much of what Swedenborg has written shows a profound insight into human nature, and is calculated to exalt and support morality; but it may be safely said that Swedenborgianism, as a religious

---

* "Outlines of the Religion and Philosophy of Swedenborg," by Theophilus Parsons, LL.D. London: F. Pitman.

system, will only be received by those who believe in his converse with the world of spirits; or, to put it in another way, that those who receive his system will also receive his claims to supernatural illumination. With these people I need not have much controversy. My explanations they will reject for their own, which they will defend by what arguments they can gather together. There seem to be certain tendencies to spiritualism in the present time, perhaps a kind of rallying against the materialism of scientific men. Such tastes or aspirations ought to favour the spread of Swedenborgianism, and I should not be surprised if the New Church were yet to take considerable extension. Its very negations may help it at the present time.

Much of the influence of Swedenborg's writings has been below the surface. No doubt they have had a decided though mediate effect in modifying the religious views of our century, especially about a future life. The doctrine that heaven is a character, not a locality, has been taught by some of the greatest Protestant divines of the age, and the notion of hell as a mere torture-place is rapidly falling into utter disbelief. It was to be expected that men of an imaginative and enthusiastic turn of mind should find a fascination in the writings of the Swedish mystic, and, without going so far as entering the New Church or leaving their own, should have adopted some of his views, and taught them in the pulpit and elsewhere. It appears that we may count General Gordon as one who accepted Swedenborg's explanations of the inner sense of the Old Testament. Writing from Jerusalem to a friend, Gordon says that the Holy Land is only interesting because we have it in ourselves. "The kings who built walls or portions of walls were kings who succeeded wicked kings or who had repented, the building of walls meaning the bringing into control irregular portions or suburbs of city—*i.e.*, of self, after some outbreak or tumult." This is quite Swedenborgian. Gordon adds: "In reality, I think it was spiritually given me to see the line of the walls before I could see it in the ground." Thus men of Gordon's enthusiastic temperament mistake the exuberant outburst of their own conceptions for the voice of inspiration.

In Stockholm, Swedenborg lived in a small house which he got built in the southern suburb. It had a garden and summer-house, where he used to receive visitors. He had no opinion of his countrymen. The Swedes, he said, were the most wicked of nations. On the other hand, very few Swedes have done honour to their countryman by joining the New Church. He always retained his old liking for the Dutch. In the spiritual world he found that they were greatly favoured in having cities of their own. Owing to the stubbornness of their disposition, especial arrangements were made to get them insinuated into heavenly truths. Swedenborg praises the English for the sincerity and independence of their character. In the world of spirits they have a city like London. There is also one of inferior description for wicked Londoners, a species of spiritual Whitechapel. The indifference of the English to strangers is thus finely touched off: "They regard foreigners as one who from the roof of a palace surveys through a telescope those who dwell and wander about at a distance from the city." From the goodness of their internal discernment he thought that the English would be the readiest to receive the New Church, which perhaps has turned out correct. There are now seventy-seven Swedenborgian places of worship in Great Britain, though the number attached to each church is probably small. In 1768, Swedenborg went to Amsterdam, to get through the press his book on "The Delights of Wisdom concerning Conjugial Love." This was the first of his theological treatises to which his name was affixed. In this long and somewhat diffuse work Swedenborg shows an originality which bears him above conventional views, and a deep knowledge of the human heart. Along with a pervading sentiment of serious tenderness, he now and then exhibits an amount of shrewdness and common sense, contrasting strangely with some of the memorable relations with which he intersperses his moral reflections. To do the book justice, an analysis of considerable length would be necessary. The following brief notes may at least give some notion of its contents.

The distinction of sex is real and pervading and survives death; a man remains a man and a woman a woman to all eternity. Perfect chastity is the union of one man with one woman. Conjugal love is the attraction of woman's mind for man's mind. In woman the affections rule; in man the understanding. "Woman," as he puts it in his quaint way, "is the love of man's understanding; the will of the wife conjoins itself with the understanding of the man, and thence the understanding of the man with the will of the wife." Men love the sex in general; women love one man in particular. A man cannot truly love a woman in whom there is no trace of sympathy, and the first spark of love is insinuated from the woman, which she often does unknowingly. If husband and wife have a real affinity their marriage will last through eternity. If a couple has lived on good terms they generally keep awhile together in the world of spirits; if they find one another deficient in sympathy they separate, and in time find other partners. Swedenborg remarks that sometimes when a married pair meet for the first time after death there is a violent quarrel. Those who have died in infancy and have been brought up in heaven soon find their affinities and get happily married. Those who really love one another and are fitted for one another have a perpetual desire to be one. In a highly poetical and beautiful relation Swedenborg describes an interview he had with one of the most ancient of men and his wife. "I looked steadfastly at the husband and the wife by turns, and I noticed as it were the unity of their souls in their faces; and I said, 'You two are one!' And the man answered, 'We are one; her life is in me, and mine in her; we are two bodies and one soul. There is a union between us like that between the two teats of the breast, the heart and the lungs. She is my heart and I am her lungs.'" In the end all the spirits fall into Swedenborg's own style. He told the children of his old love, Emerentia Polhena, that he frequently saw their mother in the world of spirits, but the bride destined for Swedenborg in heaven was the Countess of Gyllenborg, a lady of a poetical and religious turn of mind, who wrote a book entitled "Mary's Better Part."

In the second portion of his work Swedenborg discourses on the cause of coldness and unfaithfulness in marriage, and on scortatory love and the perversion of sexual feeling. His acquaintance with these subjects is remarkable; it is such as a physician might have gained in a lifelong experience. Swedenborg allows a young man to keep a mistress, if, from various reasons, marriage is impossible. He also suffers a married man to keep a concubine under certain conditions which are defined at length. They are principally bodily disease, or insanity on the part of the wife, and in general such reasons as would entitle the husband to a judicial separation. If the man under such conditions have a concubine he cannot live at the same time with his wife.

As Swedenborg himself observed there was in his nature a strong erotic tendency. Even after his assumption of the rôle of religious reformer the tendency of his thoughts is shown by frequent allusions to matters which it is customary to avoid. Nevertheless he led a pure life, and was very guarded in his intercourse with women.

In a letter to the Rev. Thomas Hartley, rector of Winwick, Northamptonshire, who became a convert, Swedenborg gives a short account of his life. The letter is dated London, 1769. After mentioning that he had been Assessor in the Metallic College, but had quitted the office, Swedenborg writes:—

"The sole reason of my withdrawing from the business of that employment was, that I might be more at liberty to apply myself to that new function to which the Lord had called me. A higher degree of rank was then offered me, which I declined to accept, lest pride on account of it should enter my mind. In 1719, I was ennobled by Queen Ulrica Eleanora, and named *Swedenborg;* from which time I have taken my seat with the Nobles of the Equestrian Order, in the triennial assemblies of the States. I am a Fellow, by invitation, of the Royal Academy of Sciences at Stockholm, but have never sought admission into any other literary society, as I belong to an Angelical Society, in which things relating to heaven and the soul are the only subjects of discourse and entertainment; whereas in our literary societies, the attention is wholly taken up with things relating to the world and the body."

After some details about the bishops and other personages with whom he was connected by marriage, Swedenborg goes on:—

"I converse freely, and am in friendship, with all the Bishops of my country, who are ten in number; and also with the sixteen

Senators, and the rest of the Grandees, who love and honour me, as knowing that I am in fellowship with Angels. The King and Queen themselves, as also the three Princes, their sons, show me all kind countenance; and I was once invited to eat with the King and Queen at their table (an honour granted only to the peers of the realm), and likewise since with the hereditary Prince. All in my own country wish for my return home—so far am I from having the least fear of being persecuted there, as you seem to apprehend, and are also kindly solicitous to provide against; and should any thing of that kind befall me elsewhere, it will give me no concern.

"Whatever of worldly honour and advantage may appear to be in the things before mentioned, I hold them as matters of respectively little moment, because, what is far better, I have been called to a holy office, by the Lord Himself, who most graciously manifested Himself in person, to me His servant, in the year 1743, and then opened my sight into the spiritual world and endowed me with the gift of conversing with spirits and angels, which has been continued to me to this day. From that time, I began to print and publish various arcana, that have been either seen by me, or revealed to me; as concerning heaven and hell, the state of men after death, the true worship of God, the spiritual sense of the Word, and many other most important matters, tending to salvation and true wisdom; and the only motive which has induced me at different times to leave my home, and visit foreign countries, was the desire of being useful, and of communicating the arcana intrusted to me. As to this world's wealth, I have sufficient, and more I neither desire nor wish for."

Some of the anecdotes told about Swedenborg and his converse with the spirits are mere legends. I quite agree with Dr. Tafel that the graphic story reported by Atterbom of the seer's receiving the ghost of Virgil and holding a long conversation with him in his house at Stockholm is, if not a pure invention, at least too much embellished to be used for truthful purposes. Klopstock, the author of the "Messiah," tried to interview Swedenborg at Copenhagen in 1768; but the German poet cut short the colloquy in impatience at what he called the drawling way in which the seer brought in the names of royal personages. Though Klopstock does not appear to advantage even in his own story, for a man of his high pretensions, Swedenborg showed a strange hankering after kings and great dignitaries, even after they had sunk their rank in the world of spirits. Now and then he could do defunct royalty a good turn. In 1770, Swedenborg, sailing to London, was entertained by General Tuxen at Elsinore. He showed much pleasure in listening to the singing and playing of Mrs. Tuxen and her daughters. The General tells us :—

"I took the liberty of saying to him, that since in his writings he always declared that at all times good and evil spirits of the other world were present with every man, I would make bold to ask whether now, while my wife and daughter were singing, there were any from the other world present with us? To this he answered, 'Yes, certainly.' And on my inquiring who they were, and whether I had known them, he said that it was the Danish Royal Family, and he mentioned Christian VI., Sophia Magdalene, and Frederic V., who through his eyes and ears had seen and heard it."

Beyond getting published and distributing his Latin books, Swedenborg made scarcely any efforts to propagate his opinions. He always said that men would only receive his doctrines if they found them consonant to what was in their own minds. None of his larger works seem to have been translated into any spoken language in his life time. Had he been an eloquent preacher like Mohammed or Luther, or had he gained some disciples with a gift of oratory fit to move the multitude like Farel or Whitfield, Swedenborg might have seen many proselytes. As it was, he had an impediment in his speech, and his style of writing was not of a popular character. Towards the end of his life he made a few converts especially in England and Germany. He himself said that they amounted to about fifty.

Swedenborg left Stockholm for Amsterdam in the summer of 1770 to get printed "The True Christian Religion," his whole body of divinity. He left Amsterdam for London in August, 1771. On Christmas eve he had an apoplectic shock, by which he was somewhat paralysed on one side, and his speech affected. During three weeks he lay in a lethargic condition, taking very little sustenance. He was much distressed, saying that his spiritual sight was withdrawn; but in answer to his prayers it was again restored to him. Swedenborg's attention had been aroused by the great religious revival of Wesley and Whitfield. He sent to Wesley a copy of his "True Christian Religion." While preparing for his great circuit, the Rev. John Wesley received a letter written in Latin in the following terms,* which he read aloud to those present:—

"GREAT BATH STREET, COLDBATH FIELDS,
February, 1772.

"SIR,—I have been informed in the world of spirits that you have a strong desire to converse with me. I shall be happy to see you if you will favour me with a visit.—I am, Sir, your humble servant,

"EMAN. SWEDENBORG."

Wesley acknowledged that he had felt a desire to converse with Swedenborg, and that he had never mentioned it to any one. He wrote in reply that he was then closely occupied in preparing for a six months' journey, but would wait upon Mr. Swedenborg after his return to London.

"Mr. Smith further informed me," goes on Mr. Hawkins, " that he afterwards learned that Swedenborg wrote in reply, that the visit proposed by Mr. Wesley would be too late, as he, Swedenborg, should go into the world of spirits on the 29th day of the next month, never more to return." This correspondence led Mr. Smith to examine the writings of Swedenborg, and in the end he became convinced of their truth, and laboured to disseminate them.

Swedenborg refused to see the Rev. Aron Mathesius, of whom mention has been made; but they brought to his bedside the Rev. Arvid Ferelius, another Swedish clergyman in London, to whom Swedenborg said that his end was near. The minister then said to him, "' that as many persons thought that he had endeavoured only to make himself a name by his new theological system, which object he had indeed attained, he would do well now to publish the truth to the world, and to recant either the whole or a part of what he had advanced since he had now nothing more to expect from the world which

---

* See TAFEL's "Documents," vol. ii. p. 564. These statements are taken from a report given by a friend of what he heard from Mr. Samuel Smith, an early Wesleyan minister.

he was soon about to leave for ever.' Upon hearing these words, Swedenborg raised himself half upright in bed, and, placing his sound hand upon his breast, said with great zeal and emphasis, 'As true as you see me before you, so true is everything that I have written. I could have said more had I been permitted. When you come into eternity you will see all things as I have stated and described them, and we shall have much to discourse about them with each other.' Ferelius then asked whether he would take the Lord's Holy Supper? He replied with thankfulness that the offer was well meant, but that being a member of the other world, he did not need it. He would, however, gladly take it, in order to show the connection and union between the Church in heaven and the Church on earth."

His faculties were clear to the last. On Sunday, the 29th day of March, 1772, hearing the clock strike, he asked his landlady and her maid, who were both sitting at his bedside, what it was o'clock, and upon being answered it was five o'clock, he said, "It is well; I thank you; God bless you." And then, in a little moment after, he gently gave up the ghost.

He was buried in a vault beneath the Swedish Church in Ratcliff Highway.* It was not till the year 1857 that a tablet was erected by his English followers to indicate where lie the remains of "the Swedish philosopher and theologian."

The reader of this work can hardly have come so far without some conclusions forming in his mind about the nature of Swedenborg's revelations. Nevertheless, it may be expected that I should here give a summary of my views about his condition. Those who believe that Swedenborg's claims to intercourse with the spirit world are founded on truth will not feel the need of any explanation, but those who cannot admit this will probably be willing to listen to suggestions as to how his delusions arose or may have arisen. My view then is that Swedenborg inherited a neurotic tendency from his father, who was himself a spirit-seer. Illusions or hallucinations seem to

---

* Wilkinson's "Life," pp. 231. 232.

have been manifested in his childhood, and even to have been encouraged by his parents.

Swedenborg himself wrote*:—" From my fourth to my tenth year I was constantly engaged in thought upon God, salvation, and the spiritual diseases (*passiones spirituales*) of men; and several times I revealed things at which my father and mother wondered, saying that angels must be speaking through me."

This tendency was outgrown in his youth; and the studies of his robust manhood were not favourable to fantastic ideas until passing through the sciences of anatomy and physiology he began to ponder deeply on the nature of the soul. Dissatisfied with the religious creed of his country, and recoiling from the scepticism of the age, his mind wandered about seeking for an explanation of the mysteries of our being, of the purpose of life, of the destiny of the soul after death, and its relation to God. On these subjects he thought deeply and searched earnestly. He worked out some conclusions, but recognised that they were deficient in proof. He felt the weakness of the human understanding, and the innumerable deceptions to which it is subject, and longed for some clue to lead him through the maze. Thus he was ready to welcome the indications in dreams and the correspondences of nature as affording special guidance from on high. In Swedenborg's mind predisposition was very powerful to give a definite and realistic form to his theories, and to seize upon all facts, or apparent facts, to confirm or illustrate them. Swedenborg's delusions seemed to be the result of the excessive growth of certain qualities which were always prominent in his character. It was probably under the strain of the severe labour of preparing his anatomical treatises that his brain and whole nervous system got into the excited state shown by the dreams and other nervous disturbances recorded in his Diary. This condition probably commenced as early as 1736, and became intensified by slow degrees. There were hyperæsthesia of the senses and excitement of the brain. There were flashes of light in his eyes, sounds in his ears, and strange feelings throughout his whole frame, partly the result of new impres-

---

* See Letter to Dr. Beyer, TAFEL, " Document," 243.

sions from the outer world to which he became open through the unwonted sensitiveness of his nervous system, and partly the result of subjective sensations from his deranged condition of health. These impressions were gradually elaborated under the powerful predisposition of his mind into Divine visions, heavenly voices, and the contact of spirits. Some of them might be called deranged sensations, others might be classed as illusions, if one looks at the subjective phenomena, which were real; or as hallucinations, they not being the result of impressions coming from the outer world. These illusions, or hallucinations, seem to have been more vivid at the time Swedenborg wrote the "Arcana" than during the later years of his life. He had hallucinations of sight, hearing, smell, taste, and touch. The spectres which affected his vision appeared to him as if outward; but not representing refractions of light from real objects they turned with the observer. In the "Arcana," N. 1274, writing of spirits and angels, Swedenborg tells us:—
"Situations and distances have their relations, and are estimated with a regulated respectivity to the human body, so that they who are to the right appear to the right, and they who are to the left appear to the left, in whatsoever direction the body be turned, and this holds true with regard to other quarters."

Swedenborg distinguished between the interior or spiritual sight and the exterior or natural sight. A living man could see natural objects only; a spirit could not see men in the body. Swedenborg himself could see both. Probably spectres appeared to him more hazy and less distinct than real objects.

In the following passage from the "Arcana," N. 1972, he lets us know that he had different degrees of perception:—

"As to what concerns visions, or rather sights, which appear before the eyes of the spirit and not before the eyes of the body, they are more and more interior; what I have seen in the world of spirits I have seen in a clear light, but more obscurely the things which exist in the heaven of angelic spirits, and still more obscurely the things which exist in the heaven of angels, for the sight of my spirit was seldom open to that degree, nevertheless it was given me to know by a certain perception, the nature of which cannot be described, what they discoursed about, and this frequently by intermediate spirits, sometimes the things there existing appeared to me in the shade of the light of this world, being an incomprehensibly mild and pure light equally enlightening the understanding and the sight."

There must have been great hyperæsthesia of smell in his case. He is continually haunted by the odours of spirits. Those of bad spirits were most unpleasant, one of the least disgusting being the smell of burnt bread, which was diffused by spirits who, when in the world, had been addicted to oratory of a deceitful character.

Swedenborg describes himself as being three or four times brought into a state intermediate between sleeping and waking. All the senses were as active as when the body was perfectly awake; not only the senses of sight and hearing, but that of touch, which was then more exquisite than usual. In this state, he tells, spirits and angels were seen in complete reality, and were heard to speak, and, what is more wonderful, even felt by touch. It is in this state between sleeping and waking that hallucinations are most common. The following passage* is note-worthy. It shows the elaboration of simple hallucinations, through whimsical reasonings under a strong mental predisposition, into very complex hallucinations.

"Awaking one morning out of sleep, I saw, as it were, several apparitions (*larvæ*) in various forms, floating before my eyes; and presently, as the morning advanced, I observed false lights (*luces fatuæ*) in different forms, some like sheets of paper written all over, which, being folded over and over, at last appeared like falling stars, which in their descent through the atmosphere vanished; and others again like open books, some of which shone like little moons, while some flamed like lighted candles. Among the latter were some books which were carried up aloft, and lost when they arrived at their highest altitude, and others which fell down to the ground, and were there reduced to dust. From these appearances I conjectured that, in the region below these meteors, there were some spirits disputing on matters of speculation, which they reckoned of great importance; for in the spiritual world such phenomena appear in the atmospheres, in consequence of the reasonings of those who are beneath. Presently my spiritual sight was opened, and I observed a number of spirits

---

* "The True Christian Religion," N. 335.

whose heads were encompassed with leaves of laurel, and who were clothed in flowered robes, which indicated that they were spirits who in the natural world had been distinguished for their great learning; and as I was in the spirit, I approached and joined their company. I then found that they were disputing sharply and warmly with each other about CONNATE IDEAS, whether men receive any at their birth as the beasts do. Those who maintained the negative side of the question turned away from those who maintained the affirmative, and at length they formed two separate parties, like the ranks of two armies going to engage sword in hand; but having no swords, they carried on the battle with sharp-pointed words and arguments."

Here a certain angelic spirit presented himself in the midst of the assembly, and delivered a discourse to prove "that neither men nor beasts have any connate ideas." The angel talked much in the same style, and reproduced the views of Emanuel Swedenborg. The result was gratifying. After this discourse he tells us: "I looked around and saw at a little distance from me, Leibnitz and Wolfius, who were both very attentive to the arguments produced by the angelic spirit. Leibnitz immediately approached and declared himself convinced; but Wolfius walked off, both denying and affirming, for he had not the same strength of interior judgment as Leibnitz." Swedenborg does not appear to have noticed Locke on this memorable occasion. It is to be hoped, nevertheless, that the shade of the English philosopher was present, or at least that Leibnitz's withdrawal of the views given to the world in the "Nouveaux Essais" was reported to him in some way.

Swedenborg was once or twice in another state, of which he gives the following instance[*] :—

"Walking through the streets of a city, and through fields, and being at the time in conversation with spirits, I was not aware but that I was awake, and in the use of my sight, as at other times. I thus walked on without mistaking the way, being, at the same time, in vision, beholding groves, rivers, palaces, houses, men, and other objects. But, after walking thus for hours, I suddenly returned into my bodily sight, and discovered that I was in a different place. Being exceedingly astonished at this, I perceived that I had been in the

---

[*] "Heaven and Hell," N. 441.

state experienced by those, of whom it is said, that they were *carried of the spirit* to another place."

This is not different from ordinary somnambulism, save that, on coming out of his sleep-walking condition, Swedenborg was able to recall what he had been doing. It occasionally happens, however, that the sleep-walker, or hypnotised person, on awaking remembers the hallucinations and delusions which have passed through his mind. Dr. Bernheim[*] has observed that many subjects who had been previously hypnotised manifest susceptibility to the same suggestive phenomena in the waking condition without being again hypnotised,—that is to say, the delusions and hallucinations to which they have been subjected in the hypnotic state could readily be renewed in the waking state. As hypnotism is but somnambulism artificially induced, one might expect that the suggestions to which Swedenborg yielded in the condition of somnambulism would be easily excited in the waking state. With Swedenborg it was a case of auto-suggestion coming from his powerful predisposition.

It is evident that in Swedenborg's case sensory disorders were much commoner than motor ones, but in the general excitement of his nervous system, motor symptoms could not be absent. We have already noted the tremors which he regarded as an indication that spirits had entered his body. He also mentioned that he felt incitements to stretch out his hand and take things, which did not appear to come from his own will. Then he had fits or swoons which sometimes threw him on the ground. He was several times seen by different persons to be in a state of intense reverie or ecstasy, which sometimes passed into continued trance. These swoons and trances seem to have had a relation to the slowing or temporary arrest of his respiration already mentioned. He was never observed to have a regular epileptic fit, and the benign serenity of his disposition forms a strong contrast to the irritability of temper which in the great majority of cases attends those subject to epilepsy. Though all his dreams and visions did not take the deep colour of his mind, Swedenborg

---

[*] See his book on "Suggestive Therapeutics," translated by C. A. Herter, M.D., New York and London, 1889, p. 78.

was sure, through his ingenious explanations and system of correspondences, to find in them the meaning which he favoured.

We have seen that, after a period of great nervous excitement at the Hague, Swedenborg had in London in 1744 an attack of acute insanity (*paranoia acuta hallucinatoria?*) This calmed down in a few months, and gradually the will and intellect resumed their power, though not to struggle against the delusions that had now taken hold of the mind, but to find a meaning in them, to systematise them, and to propagate them. In spite of this Swedenborg's intellect retained much of its power; his mind worked on false premises, like the blinded Samson in the Philistines' mill. He remained the rest of his life in a state of delusional insanity, or paranoia. Anders Fryxell, the Swedish historian,* has truly observed that " the foundations of Swedenborgianism are two essential, though altogether contradictory, constituents, which were developed simultaneously in him—viz., a rationalistic doctrine of religion on the one hand, and an irrational spirit-seeing on the other." The explanation of this no doubt is that the doctrines propounded were the result of the speculations of Swedenborg's powerful mind working while still unsubdued by morbid influences, and that the spirit-seeing and attendant puerilities were the results of hallucinations and delusions formed after his nervous centres had become diseased, for had the higher centres of his brain not also become affected, Swedenborg would not have yielded to the misleading impressions of the peripheral nerves and of the basal ganglia. Instead of being active to recognise the character of these impressions and to correct them, all the powers of his mind were engaged in the work of self-deception. None who have taken the trouble to examine those affected with delusional insanity can have failed to find how hallucinations pass into delusions, or delusions appear in the mind as remembered hallucinations. The memory helps in the work of deception. In recalling his visions we doubt not that Swedenborg altered their shape as a fanciful person changes and embellishes the event which he is relating. Though I am told that there are orthodox

---

* Quoted by TAFEL, vol. i. p. 1241.

Swedenborgians who accept all the revelations of the seer, I have great difficulty in believing that any man could receive as really true the "memorable relations" with which Swedenborg illustrates his theological treatises. One might as well believe in the actual occurrence of the events related in the "Vision of Mirza," "The Pilgrim's Progress," or the "Tale of a Tub," which are much more life-like and realistic.

Take for example the narrative in his pamphlet in the "Nature of the Intercourse between the Soul and Body," in which he gravely tells us that he prayed to the Lord that he might be allowed to converse with some disciples of Aristotle, some disciples of Descartes, and some of Leibnitz, to learn their opinions concerning the intercourse between the soul and body :—

"After my prayer was ended," Swedenborg writes, "there were present nine men, three Aristotelians, three Cartesians, and three Leibnitzians, and they arranged themselves round me, the admirers of Aristotle being on the left side, and the favourers of Leibnitz behind. At a considerable distance, and also at a distance from each other, were seen three persons crowned with laurel, whom I knew, by an influent perception, to be these three great leaders, or masters themselves. Behind Leibnitz stood a person holding the skirt of his garment who, I was told was Wolff."

Then follows an account of a heated disputation between the advocates of these three schools of metaphysics. The matter is at last decided by three mottos being written on three bits of paper, "Physical Influx," "Spiritual Influx," and "Pre-established Harmony." These bits of paper were put into the crown of a hat. Of course spiritual influx, the theory favoured by Swedenborg himself, comes out; and an angel suddenly appearing assured the disputatious assembly of spirits that this did not take place through chance.

The whole description is obviously the figment of a brain too fond of scholastic disquisitions, and which transferred to the Elysian fields the recollections and dreams of a student in the University of Upsala.

One of the earliest aberrations of Swedenborg's strange mind was his tendency to receive mere theories as realities. This is well illustrated in his book "On the Worship and

Love of God," which, though published in 1745, was apparently written before the year 1743. In this book he treats of the creation and first appearance of Adam, and then of Eve, he explains the method of their origin, their first impressions, and their feelings before meeting and after meeting one another. All this he relates as if he were entirely convinced of the truth of his narrative.

One versed in the types of insanity now in vogue would look in Swedenborg's case for the symptoms of the mania of grandeur, and of the mania of persecution. Here we must bear in mind how much he had transferred his thoughts and interests to a world of his own fancy, and how much he had withdrawn from them the ways of ordinary men. In his claims to direct intercourse with the Divine Being we find the loftiest delusions of grandeur, and in his complaints of being infested for whole days by wicked spirits we recognise the delusions of persecution. It is surprising that through such strange experiences Swedenborg should have preserved so much serenity of disposition, and displayed in many things so much sagacity of thought. This would imply that the higher centres of the brain were less affected than the lower, which is the rule in what is called delusional insanity.

It is sad to think that it should have been the lot of so earnest a searcher after truth to wander so many years in the mazes of delusion; but the records of mental derangement contain some of the saddest things in fate. Swedenborg's moral and theological writings contain much that is noble and true, though marred by whimsical notions and erroneous statements. Nevertheless many of the sayings committed to writing will find acceptance amongst thoughtful men, bearing their own evidence in their fitness to other things in the plan of the world.

WILLIAM BLAKE.

THOUGH mystics who have had visions and religious ecstasies have appeared from time to time in all ages, it is difficult to find one like Swedenborg. The man who resembled him most was William Blake. In many things there was a marked difference between the Swedish assessor of mines and the English engraver. Blake was poor, scantily educated, a small tradesman's son. Swedenborg was rich and learned, and occupied a high position. Blake was of an enthusiastic temperament, very warm-hearted, a revolutionary in politics. Swedenborg was of a calm and benign disposition, and, though liberal in politics, he never showed any keen sympathy with the poor or down-trodden, or sought to disturb the inequalities of rank. Blake was married; Swedenborg remained single all his life. Blake's tastes were artistic and poetical; those of Swedenborg, scientific and philosophical. But both had a sublime opinion of their own merits. Both were deeply religious; both were mystics who sought for new light in the inner sense of the Scripture, and believed that they conversed with the spirits of the departed.

When Blake was eight or ten years of age he saw a tree filled with angels. Returning home, he naively related what he had seen, and only by his mother's intercession escaped a thrashing from his father for telling a falsehood.[*] It appears that Blake's brother also saw visions.

---

[*] See the "Life of William Blake, 'Pictor Ignotus,' with Selections from his Poems and other Writings," by Alexander Gilchrist; London, 1863, p. 7.

There is a most able estimate of Blake's mental characteristics in a paper on "Mad Artists," by Dr. W. A. F. Browne, in the *Journal of Psychological Medicine and Mental Pathology*, vol. vi. part 1.

When twenty-five years old, Blake married a girl of humble origin. She proved a faithful and sensible wife, and helped to keep him from breaking away from the real world. The necessity of working for their daily bread, no doubt prevented Blake from giving himself up entirely to the ideal as Swedenborg did. As it was his conduct was eccentric and imprudent, sometimes extravagant to the verge of insanity, if not beyond it. Having derived all her education from Blake, his wife believed in his visions, and obeyed his fancies. She also learned to assist him in his engraving work.

Blake, like Swedenborg, held frequent converse with the illustrious dead. They sought him wherever he was; by the sea-shore, on the downs of Suffolk, or in his own dingy rooms in London. Amongst others, he talked with Moses and the Prophets, Homer, Dante, and Milton. "All," said Blake, when questioned on these appearances, "all majestic shadows, gray, but luminous, and superior to the common height of man." He talked quite familiarly about his supernatural visitors. The spectres that entered his rooms were used as models; he would look at them, then draw a little, then look up again. Sometimes he would stop at his work, saying that the spirits had walked off. Once he drew King Saul in armour, but said that he could not finish the helmet, because, from the way Saul was standing, he could not see the whole of it. Some months after, the spectre of Saul came back, when he stood in such a position that Blake could see the rest of the helmet and finish the sketch.

On one occasion he was asked to supply a likeness of Sir William Wallace.* In presence of his employer, Blake cried out: "Sir William Wallace, there! there I see him in all his glory!" and forthwith he commenced to draw, but suddenly paused, and when he was asked why he did not go on, he replied, "I cannot finish him, Edward I. has stepped in between him and me."

"For years he had sighed for an interview with Satan, whom he had considered to be a grand and spiritual existence, but at last, unannounced and unexpected, when Blake was going up the stairs of

---

* BROWNE, *op cit.*

his house, a light streamed around him, and he saw the fiend glaring upon him through the grating of a window, when, opportunely, his wife conceiving that he was visited by a poetic vision, supplied such materials as enabled him to execute a portrait of his infernal visitant."

We have sketches of different kings and great men, with the inscription below, "Drawn from their spectres by William Blake." His brother, Robert, who died young, appeared to him and communicated a new process, by which he engraved illustrations to his "Songs of Innocence." The spirit of Joseph of Nazareth advised him how to mix his colours. The following narrative reminds one of Swedenborg's memorable relations :—

"The other evening," said Blake, in his usual quiet way, "taking a walk, I came to a meadow, and at the farther corner of it I saw a fold of lambs. Coming nearer, the ground blushed with flowers, and the wattled cote and its woolly tenants were of an exquisite pastoral beauty. But I looked again, and it proved to be no living flock, but beautiful sculpture. The lady thinking this a capital holiday show for her children, eagerly interposed, 'I beg pardon, Mr. Blake, but *may* I ask *where* you saw this?' '*Here*, madam,' answered Blake, touching his forehead."

He made no attempt to explain his apparitions, and though he had peculiar religious views, he never tried to propagate them, nor did he claim to have received any particular revelation. He wrote a number of verses, not very smooth, but full of spirit, with startling flashes of imagination. He wrote, too, a great deal of mystical poetry, the meaning of which could not be rightly apprehended by one who had not the key.

Blake would only paint in water-colours; his original designs are now very rare. Ruskin says that the Book of Job engraved by Blake is of the highest rank in certain characters of imagination and expression, " and in expressing conditions of glaring and flickering light Blake is greater than Rembrandt." The British public, always slow to appreciate originality, would have allowed the artist to starve had he not returned to the graver when need pressed.

Blake was born in 1757, and died in 1827. He read

some of Swedenborg's books, but never became a proselyte, though his friend Flaxman the sculptor did. Amongst Blake's writings there are five memorable fancies, obviously in imitation of Swedenborg's "Memorable Relations." The first four seem to have some meaning. The last seems simply grotesque —intended to turn Swedenborg's manner into ridicule. It is too long to quote, but the following passages may be amusing :—

"An angel came to me, and said, 'O pitiable, foolish young man! O horrible—O dreadful state! Consider the hot burning dungeon thou art preparing for thyself to all eternity, to which thou art going in such career.' I said, 'Perhaps you will be willing to show me my eternal lot, and we will contemplate together upon it, and see whether your lot or mine is most desirable.'

"So he took me through a stable and through a church, and down into the church vault, at the end of which was a mill. Through the mill we went, and came to a cave, down the winding cavern we groped our tedious way till a void, boundless as a nether sky, appeared beneath us, and we held by the roots of trees, and hung over this immensity. But I said, 'If you please, we will commit ourselves to this void and see whether Providence is here also; if you will not, I will!' But he answered, 'Do not presume, O young man; but as we here remain, behold thy lot, which will soon appear when the darkness passes away.'

* * * * *

"My friend the angel climbed up from his station into the mill. I remained alone, and then this appearance was no more; but I found myself sitting on a pleasant bank beside a river by moonlight, hearing a harper who sung to the harp—and his theme was, 'The man who never alters his opinion is like standing water, and breeds reptiles of the mind.'

"But I arose, and sought for the mill, and there I found my angel, . . . but I by force suddenly caught him in my arms, and flew westerly through the night, till we were elevated above the earth's shadow. Then I flung myself with him directly into the body of the sun. Here I clothed myself in white, and, taking in my hand Swedenborg's volumes, sunk from the glorious clime, and passed all the planets till we came to Saturn. Here I stayed to rest, and then leaped into the void between Saturn and the fixed stars."

Towards the end of the memorable fancy there is the following passage :—

"I in my hand brought a skeleton of a body, which in the mill was Aristotle's 'Analytics.' So the angel said, 'Thy phantasy has imposed upon me, and thou oughtest to be ashamed!'

"I answered, 'We impose on one another, and it is but lost time to converse with you, whose works are only analytics.'

"Swedenborg boasts that what he writes is new; though it is only the contents or index of already published books."

For mystical reading Blake preferred Paracelsus and Jacob Behmen to Swedenborg. Of the last he said that his truths were not new, and his falsehoods were all old. Two such independent spirits so like one another were sure to disagree in some points, just as we see in a lunatic asylum the man who believes himself to be the Duke of Wellington laughing at the pretentions of the man who calls himself Napoleon Bonaparte, or a St. Paul who derides John the Baptist as a senseless impostor.

In a chapter near the end of his "Life of Blake" Mr. Gilchrist considers the question whether he was mad or not mad, supporting the last opinion by citing the observations of friends who knew him. On this question Dr. Browne remarks :—

"On an analysis of an estimate arrived at by these critics, it will be discovered that, while one defines him as an eccentric, another as a visionary, a third as an enthusiast, a fourth as a superstitious ghost-seer, all feel it expedient to mollify or to apologise for modes of action inconsistent with the habits of other healthy men; it may be safely affirmed that if he was not insane in conduct, Blake betrayed undoubted symptoms of his mental malady in painting."

LOUIS II OF BAVARIA

THE INSANITY OF KING LOUIS II. OF BAVARIA.

THE events surrounding the end of this prince will always make it a striking chapter in German history. Although some time will probably elapse before the chief witnesses of the tragedy will tell to the world all that they know, so much has already been published about it* that it is unlikely the outline of the events will ever be materially altered.

A study worthy of the attention of psychologists is afforded,

---

* Our original sketch was published in the *Journal of Mental Science* for October, 1886. A translation of it, made by Dr. Victor Parant, appeared in the *Annales Médico-Psychologiques*, tome v., Janvier, 1887. At that time my principal sources of information were the extra edition of the *Berliner Börsen Zeitung* of 15th June, 1886, and a collection of cuttings from English and American newspapers. Also three pamphlets—

"Die Letzten Tage König Ludwig's II. von Bayern," von R. Graser. Stuttgart, 1886.

"Zur Königs-Katastrophe in Baiern" (Separatabdruck aus Dr. Wittelhöfer's "Wiener Mediz. Wochenschrift," Nr. 25 und Nr. 26, 1886). Vienna, 1886. The author of this pamphlet is Baron Mundy.

"König Ludwig II. von Bayern. Sein Leben, Wirken und Tod geschildert von George Morin." Munich, 1806.

Since then there have appeared two authentic accounts of the last events of the King's life—

"Die Letzen Tage König's Ludwig II. von Bayern," von Dr. Franz Carl Müller, ehem. Assistenzarzt des Ober. Med. Rath von Gudden, &c., Dritte unveränderte Auflage, pp. 53. Berlin, 1888.

"Bernhard von Gudden, Nekrolog." Archiv. für Psychiatrie, xvii. Band, 3 Heft.

Some additional facts are given in a paper on "König Ludwig II. von Bayern," at the end of the German translation of the historical portion of "The Blot on the Brain," under the title of Herrschermacht und Geisteskrankheit. Stuttgart, Lutz, 1887.

apart from the interest derived from the rank of the unfortunate prince, and the pathetic character of the event which brought his life to a close. We see the evolution of a hereditary disposition to insanity helped instead of hindered by external circumstances. The family of Wittelsbach was one of the oldest amongst the ruling princes of Europe. The Duke of Bavaria, a prominent figure in the Thirty Years' War, became an electoral prince of the German Empire in 1623. When Gustavus of Sweden entered Munich in 1632, he much approved of the taste displayed in the apartments of the palace of the fugitive Elector, and asked, " Who was the architect?" "He is no other," answered the attendant, "than the Elector himself." "I should like to have him," said the King, "to send him to Stockholm." Thus a taste for decorative architecture seemed to have appeared at this early date in this princely family. Maximilian Joseph I. was made king by Napoleon after the battle of Austerlitz, at the same time receiving the Tyrol as the reward of his alliance. In this prince the family taste for art showed itself in many ways. He acquired the Æginetan Marbles, the Dürer and the Düsseldorf Gallery. His son, Louis I., spent millions of money in adorning Munich with splendid buildings in the Greek and Italian styles, and was the patron of Cornelius and the elder Kaulbach. The weaknesses of a *virtuoso*, and the scandals and imprudences into which he was led by his mistress, Lola Montes, brought about his deposition in the stormy year 1848. He was succeeded by his son, Maximilian II., whose rule was unpopular, owing to his reactionary tendencies. Maximilian's brother became King of Greece, till his subjects got rid of him without much ceremony or difficulty in 1862, when he returned to Bavaria.

Maximilian married Mary of Hohenzollern, daughter of Prince Frederick William, the youngest son of Frederick William II. of Prussia. This lady was supposed to have introduced insanity into the Bavarian family. She died on the 17th of May, 1889, aged 63. It was, however, stated in the *Frankfurter Zeitung* that the King's paternal aunt, the Princess Alexandra, had been treated, about 1850, in the asylum at Illenau. She was possessed with the idea that she had swallowed a glass sofa. The Queen had only two children, Louis, born on the 25th of August, 1845, and Prince Otho, born on the 27th of April, 1848. It was a part of their father's plan of education to subject them to strict discipline, and to allow them few luxuries. When Louis succeeded to the throne on the death of his father in 1864, no one dreamed of the fate that hung over these two brothers, who bore a great likeness and were much attached to one another. Louis II. was then nineteen years of age. Tall, beautiful in person, endowed with great strength, carefully educated, and possessed of many pleasing mental gifts, it was not suspected that the hereditary tastes for music and art, and the desire to surround himself with beautiful objects, would grow into a consuming passion going beyond the bounds of reason.

From the beginning of his reign the young king neglected the duties of his position to follow his romantic tastes. Unhappily he soon fell under the fascinating power of a man ready to tempt and encourage him to use his wealth to realise the dreams and longings of an artistic nature. Louis formed an enthusiastic friendship for Richard Wagner, whose lofty ideas and tumultuous music were highly fitted to strike his imagination. He contributed largely to build the huge theatre at Bayreuth, and got the operas of the great composer performed on the grandest scale. Louis delighted to personate the Wagnerian heroes. He used to put on the pilgrim robes of Tannhäuser, or the armour of the chivalrous Tristan ; but his favourite character was Lohengrin, the son of King Parzival, described in an old Bavarian poem. This legend was revived in the well-known opera of Wagner, and King Louis, in a boat on the Starnberg Lake, used to rehearse the part of the Knight of the Holy Grail. We are[*] told that, finding the ordinary lake too realistic for this exalted personation, the Bavarian monarch got a large reservoir constructed on the roof of the Schloss at Munich, upon which, dressed in glittering armour, he sailed in a boat with a stuffed swan floating in front. As he wished to have blue water, it was

---

[†] GRASER, p. 24.

coloured with sulphate of copper. This solution acted upon the metal of the roof and streamed through the royal palace, spoiling the splendid furnishings, after which an optician was employed to give a blue tint to the water by coloured light. He then complained that the water was too calm, so that workmen were employed to turn paddles, which made waves so effectually that the King was thrown into the water, on which he gave up further nautical rehearsals on the roof of the palace. On another occasion the King represented the Genius of the Mountain, and got six men to carry him in a litter or jaunpaun over the Bavarian Alps.

His intimacy with Wagner, more advantageous to the musician than the King, was dissolved in the end of 1865, whether through popular clamour, Court intrigue, or through Louis tiring of the imposing personality of the composer. He, however, still kept up a correspondence with Wagner, and occasionally visited him across the frontier. In June, 1882, when Wagner went to reside for some months at Palermo, Louis sent a telegram to the King of Italy asking him to have the great tone poet received as a prince of the blood. When the composer died in 1883, Louis is said to have shown much grief. The King conceived some other warm friendships for artists and actors, to whom he would write long letters, sometimes of a very tender character. These friendships soon passed away, sometimes coming to a very abrupt end, when he would remark that "*this* comes of associating with such common people." From boyhood, he was extremely haughty, and considered it a liberty that a physician should feel his pulse when he was ill.

During the political contest which divided the German States into two great parties, Louis was principally occupied with Wagner's operas and their representation at Munich. When the dispute came to the decision of arms in the war of 1866, Bavaria took the side of Austria against Prussia, a step which could hardly be thought imprudent at the time, since it was generally believed that Prussia would be overpowered. Well organised, alert, and ready, and armed with the new needle gun, the Prussians defeated their adversaries on every side. "After Sadowa," we are told,* "the Bavarian Premier, Baron v.d. Pfordten, had to go to Nikolsburg to ask for peace; but he was obliged to do so on his own responsibility, and to sign a bill of exchange for the war indemnity of thirty million thalers without full power from his sovereign, who had retired to a lonely island, and strictly forbidden approach to it. With the greatest difficulty at last ministers forced their way against the injunction and penetrated to the King, in order to obtain his signature." Thus, more fortunate than her allies in Northern Germany, Bavaria escaped from the struggle with a small cession of territory, and less diminution of independence than might have been feared.

The Bavarian people were much pleased when, in 1866, the young King became betrothed to the Duchess Sophia, daughter of Duke Max, and sister to the present Empress of Austria. The old King, Louis I., was much attached to his grandson. Being struck with his resemblance to Adonis in a fresco at Pompeii, especially in the passionate expression of the eyes (*in dem schwärmerischen Ausdruck der Augen*), he composed a sonnet on the occasion, which was published in the *Allgemeine Augsbury Zeitung*, dated 27th February, 1867. He promises a happy future for the young King and his betrothed. About the same time Dr. Morel, who was at Munich on the Chorinsky case, and saw the King of Bavaria, was also struck with the expression in his eye. "It is an eye," he said, "from which future madness speaks." Of the King's attachment to the Duchess Sophia romantic stories are told; but in his life everything was romantic. "She had the untamed air of a wood nymph, was passionately fond of sylvan sports, of dogs, horses, and the excitement of hunting. As she lived on the edge of a romantic sheet of water, on which she often shot out in a light skiff, he called her 'The Lady of the Lake.' It pleased him to come and woo her in secret, and if he had a fault to find with her, it was that she was too coy. When preparations were being carried on for the wedding, Ludwig, who was fond of coming unawares on those

---

* See article on "Contemporary Life and Thought in Germany" by Professor Geffcken, in the *Contemporary Review* for August, 1886.

he loved, to afford them agreeable surprises, came with a band of wandering musicians, and disguised as a minstrel, to serenade his betrothed. He approached through a wild wood her father's castle, a little in advance of his musical comrades. What did he see in a glade? His betrothed toying with the locks of the groom who had been attending her on an equestrian excursion. He was sitting on a rock, and she was standing beside him, with her waist encircled by one of his arms. The King rushed to kill them both, and, as he was tall and muscular, he might have done so had not the other minstrels come to save them. He denounced her to her father, a bluff German. She said that, being subject to hallucinations, he fancied he saw what never happened." The *Debats* says that it was her domestic chaplain, and not a stableman, of whom she was enamoured. The lady got married soon after to a French nobleman.

Whatever may be the truth in these stories, Louis about this time began to shun the society of women. He refused all proposals of marriage, and repelled other advances with indignation. It was reported in the *Boston Post* that he commanded a famous actress, a very beautiful woman, to read to him, which she did almost daily or nightly. At these times he always went to bed, and ordered her to sit beside him. One evening while reading to him from some tragedy, she rose, the better to render it, and, whether by chance or purposely, she sat down upon the edge of the foot of the bed. He instantly ordered her to leave the kingdom for insulting his dignity by touching the royal bed, and she had to go, though the most popular actress in Munich.

We are told that, on one occasion, the King said abruptly to his secretary, who was living with his family near one of the royal country seats, "I have seen the countenance of your wife." The secretary remained silent, not knowing what to reply, on which Louis said again in a severe tone—"I have seen the countenance of your wife." The secretary, recovering his presence of mind, then said that he should take care that this would never again happen.

The French Emperor, in provoking a war with Prussia in 1870, thought he might count upon the neutrality, if not the assistance of Southern Germany, but Bavaria at once took part against France. The Crown Prince Frederick of Prussia on his way to the command of the German army stopped at Munich in July, 1870. The following entry occurs in his Diary :—

"King Ludwig strangely altered; much less handsome, lost his front teeth, pale, nervous in his speech, does not wait for an answer after putting questions, but while the answer is yet being given puts other questions referring to widely different subjects. He seems to be in the national cause with all his heart; his quiet determination is generally approved."

Even before 1870 rumours went about Bavaria that the King was mad—some said only music mad.

The Bavarian army took from the outset an active part in the struggle, and did some of the hardest of the fighting. Louis, who had no military tastes, did not accompany his army, but his brother, Prince Otho, gained the Iron Cross for his bravery. That his mind was beginning to be unhinged, perhaps by the strain of the war, seems likely from another entry in the Crown Prince's Diary :—

"30*th October*.—Prince Otto of Bavaria, who has been summoned to Munich on important business, came to take leave of me, pale, and as wretched-looking as if he were in a fit of the shivers, he sat before me, while I set forth the necessity of our having unity in military and diplomatic matters, &c., but whether he understood or even heard me, I could not make out."

It is now known that it was the Crown Prince of Prussia and the Grand Duke of Baden who were the main agents in the private overtures designed to get King William made Kaiser. Nevertheless at the time the most prominent figure in the scene was the King of Bavaria. A circular letter signed by him was sent to the German princes and the free towns inviting them to ask the King of Prussia to receive the German empire. In reality this letter was drafted by Bismarck, and simply copied out by Louis. As the head of the largest of the German States, Louis was the spokesman on the occasion when William was made Emperor at the Palace at Versailles, while the siege of Paris was going on. It may seem doubtful whether he, Louis, thought more of the political consequences of this event than that he was taking part in a grand and gorgeous pageant such as the world could not equal.

The reception of the Bavarian troops returning from the war was the last public appearance of the King. He gained some prominence in supporting Dr. Döllinger and the German Catholic party against the Ultramontanes, but he gradually withdrew his attention from politics, and used his wealth and power to gratify his artistic dreamings.

It ought to be borne in mind that we have as yet no continuous narrative of the King's neurosis, little more, in fact, than a series of anecdotes and observations, many of which have no dates. We may, however, take it for certain that the King's malady commenced in his youth, that it was of slow growth, but continuous and progressive, a rising self-will which, guided solely by his tastes and dislikes, brooked neither delay nor denial in the gratification of his fancies, a gradual diminution of mental balance and self-restraint complicated in the end with hallucinations, stormy fits of passion, and violent assaults on his attendants, and orders for the assassination of those who had offended him beyond his palace walls.

In the report of medical evidence read to the Bavarian Landtag, symptoms of insanity were distinctly recognised since 1880. Baron Mundy tells us that the King had been insane for at least ten years before his death.

The Germans, as a people, have a singular respect for the mere claims of birth and superior rank, and are disposed to acquiesce in an ostentatious display of power on the part of those who rule over them to an extent Englishmen can hardly understand. The King's vagaries were humoured with marvellous patience.[*] The lofty and æsthetic nature of his tastes with his patronage of art inspired awe and admiration. For a long time he was temperate both in food and drink, and free from the grosser vices.

Vanity seems to be the besetting weakness of men of artistic

---

[*] Contrast with this the prompt treatment of George III., and his recovery under the Rev. Dr. Willis.

tastes; but the King seemed to regard as nothing the sympathy and admiration of other men, whom he only used as the means of helping him to gratify his dreams of beauty and art. He hated to be seen, and only enjoyed plays and operas when performed in a half-darkened theatre, he himself sitting alone. Once, at the Court Theatre, the entire audience, that is, the King, fell asleep during the play which followed after the public performance. Nobody dared to awake him, and he slept for hours. When his majesty opened his eyes the play went on from where he had lost it, and was finished some time the next day.

At Court-dinners it was arranged that the guests were hidden behind vases of flowers and piled-up dishes, so that he might not be plagued by seeing them. A musical band drowned the sound of conversation. During the last years, as the love of solitude grew upon him, his dining-table was hoisted up by means of machinery through the floor, with everything ready, so that he could take his meals without seeing a human being. When he wanted a thing he must have it at once. When an idea occurred to him it must be immediately put into execution. If he read of a piece of architecture he would order a special train to go to see it. He would order his equerries to be wakened in the middle of the night to play at billiards with him, and dismissed one of them from his service because he came with his neckcloth awry. He often slept all day and remained awake all night, sometimes reading, sometimes wandering about in the moonlight amongst the grand scenery surrounding his castles, and during the winter he used to be driven about in a sleigh amongst the hill roads. The peasants would now and then see the splendid vision glide by, the out-riders, the four plumed horses at full gallop, the carriage, a marvel of beautiful design, illumined by electric light, and the King sitting within alone. Numbers of labourers were employed in keeping the roads in good repair, for fear of an overturn.

His most expensive taste was building new palaces. He built the colossal castle Neuschwangau on a precipitous rock, opposite the old Schloss of Hohenschwangu, also a model of the summer palace of the Emperor of China, and several new castles in solitary places among the mountains. These were decorated with rare taste, and at a cost that knew no stint. Of the millions that he squandered, a great deal of money no doubt fell into the hands of those who undertook to execute his artistic schemes. Dr. Schleiss, the King's surgeon, who seems to have at first doubted his insanity, though for many years he had seen little of him, is reported to have said :— "The King has his peculiarities; he is extravagant and good-hearted to excess; his passion is a love of architecture and the fine arts. For his eccentricities those are to blame who have been around him for so many years. These mercenary, selfish, lying, servile souls have done nothing but strengthen him in his wishes and heightened the fervid activity of his passions. They pillaged him, and pushed him into enormous expenses." Dr. Schleiss afterwards explained that the theory assigned to him that the King was only eccentric had not been stated by him in the form presented by the newspapers; but the words here translated have about them the ring of truth. The calculations of self-interest, the enthusiastic praises of the architects and painters and sculptors who had interviews with the King, the fear of bringing on a great scandal, and the dislike of disturbing existing relations near and far, combined with the veil which the King's retiring mode of life threw over his actions, long prevented the real condition of his mind being known save to a few.

Louis was esteemed to be a prominent supporter of the new German empire, the hegemony of Prussia, and was opposed to the pretensions of the Vatican in the Kultur-Kampf; his successor, it was feared, might be a partisan of the old state of things, an Ultramontane, a friend to Austria and the dispossessed princes of Germany. Most of the reports about the strange doings and fancies of the Bavarian monarch that appeared from time to time came from journals in Vienna and Pesth of reactionary tendencies. They caused some irritation in Germany, and were now and then contradicted. The Berlin correspondent of the *Standard* of 20th January, 1886, who had been making particular inquiries at Munich regarding the recent revival of reports hostile to King Louis, was now in a position to state, on the highest authority, that they are without foundation, and that the Bavarian ministers, so far from urging the King to abdicate, have discussed the propriety of prosecuting for libel those German and Austrian journals which have been publishing the reports in question. The highest authority is sometimes readier to conceal the truth than to tell it. The madness of the mysterious King and his degraded habits, the insanity of the Cæsars (Cesaren Wahnsinn), had about two years before been announced with Suetonian plainness in a feuilleton of the *Social Demokrat* of Zürich (21st February, 1884). Copies of this paper, passed from hand to hand, were eagerly read at Munich. The derangement of the poor King was ever becoming worse. It was no secret that his brother Otho had now been insane for years, under restraint, watched by keepers.

The King's dislike to being looked at went on increasing. At last the only woman whom he could tolerate was the Princess Gisela, daughter of the Emperor of Austria, married to Prince Louis, the second son of his uncle Luitpold, who had caught his fancy. He used to send presents to her by his equerry at any hour of the day or night. The messenger was ordered to deliver the gift to the Princess herself, and she had sometimes to get up during the night to receive a nosegay or other mark of the royal esteem. Louis had long been in the habit of drinking a good many glasses of champagne before he could fortify himself to grant public audiences to ambassadors. His ministers found more and more difficulty in getting interviews with him. Sometimes he would interrupt their conversation by repeating pieces of poetry. For several years during councils he sat behind a screen. The last Secretary of the Cabinet, Schneider, had never seen the King face to face. But the ministers said that his questions and remarks showed knowledge and shrewdness. Latterly his intercourse was almost entirely with servants of a lower grade. He took sudden likings for troopers of his guard, got them to attend upon him, and then chased them away in a few days. For years his chamberlain, Meyer, had to appear before him in a black mask, as his royal master did not like his face. A servant whom the King thought stupid had to come with a black seal on his forehead, to indicate that there was some fault in his

L

brain. The King generally rose at three o'clock in the afternoon, when he rang for his valet, who entered bending low. With a tablet on his knees he received the royal orders. Louis would ask him sometimes as many as twenty questions. When these were written down the King would give the order, "Now answer." When the business was over the servant had to go out walking backwards and bending low. A story is told that Louis, not thinking his lacquey had bowed low enough, cried out angrily, "Bend lower!" The man bowed and bent till his face nearly touched the ground, on which the Bavarian monarch gave him a kick on the chin. It appeared from the report laid before the Bavarian Landtag that thirty-two of his attendants testified to being beaten, kicked, knocked against the wall, or otherwise maltreated. Some of them had received large sums as a compensation. Many orders were given to his servants through the closed doors; by tapping they intimated that he was understood. His habits became more and more degraded. He ate immoderately, and drank a great deal, principally Rhenish white wine, mixed with champagne and flavoured with violets. They had to remove weapons from his reach. He several times ordered offending servants to be put in chains and confined on bread and water, others to be put to death, and their bodies thrown into the lake. Luckily he did not insist on seeing these orders carried out. He, however, ordered a Secretary of State, von Ziegler, to be confined, and fictitious reports were sent him daily about this man's condition, He sent a trooper to an officer of high rank at Munich with a letter as follows: "The bearer dined with me yesterday at noon, and is to be instantly shot." When the Finance Minister announced that there was a deficit, and that they could give him no more money for his building of palaces, he sent a message to the States Commission to flog the dog and put his eyes out. Three orders for the execution of offending ministers were shown signed by the royal hand. Louis had a great hatred of the Crown Prince of Germany, who came every year to inspect the Bavarian army. He repeatedly told his chamberlain, Hesselschwerdt, for several years, to get a band of men and seize upon the Prince, and throw him into a dungeon, where he was to suffer from hunger and thirst. Similar orders were issued against some of the Bavarian princes and ministers.

His servants testified that for years he had suffered from pains at the back of the head, to which he had ice applied. He was troubled with sleeplessness, for which he took chloral. He had frequent fits of motor excitement, when he would leap, dance, or hop about; sometimes he would tear his hair and beard. At other times he would stand still in one place.

He had many delusions and hallucinations of the senses. He often heard steps and voices. During frost and snow he thought that he was beside the sea. He used to bow to particular trees and bushes, took off his hat to busts, and made his attendants kneel to a statue believed to be that of Marie Antoinette. He would tell a lacquey to lift up things from the ground which were not there, and when the man looked at a loss would threaten to choke him. He fancied that he saw knives before his eyes.

One must remember that such symptoms and actions, concentrated as it were in a few sentences, did not represent the whole life of the unfortunate Prince. They were spread over years, and diluted with more sensible actions. What relation of frequency they bore to the rest of his doings, thinkings, and sayings, we have not the means of deciding. That Louis was suffered so long to drain the cup of power which has ere this intoxicated stronger heads, seems amongst the strangest things of history. We are in no way surprised to learn that the King's "privy purse and civil lists were very carelessly administered," and that after the final catastrophe the leader of the opposition made a violent attack upon the Bavarian ministers, to which Dr. von Lutz replied in an excited manner. A king who is incapable of governing is likely to light upon someone willing to perform this task for him, and had it not been for the importunity of his creditors, for his extravagant demands upon the treasury, and his threats to hang the Finance Minister if money were not forthcoming, the name of Louis II. might still be in the "Almanach de Gotha" as King of Bavaria, Count Palatine of the Rhine, Colonel of Infantry, Lancers, and Hussars, in the armies of Austria, Prussia, and Russia, &c. The King had been seized with a consuming admiration for that grand parade monarch, Louis XIV., and read everything he could collect about him and his Court, including the disasters which his own ancestor, the Elector of Bavaria, suffered for his alliance with France. It is said that he used to wander about at night, dressed like the Grand Monarque, whose portrait was used to represent the sun in one of his most splendid rooms. It is even said that he was heard to address the French King as if he really saw his figure and that he ordered courses to be laid for him and other imaginary guests at his table. His admiration went down to Louis XVI. and Marie Antoinette. Hearing of an opera performed at Vienna which dealt with Madame Pompadour, he immediately sent to one of his envoys to procure a copy, which neither the composer nor manager would give. It was only obtained by engaging some shorthand writers to take a copy during the performance of the play. He built on an island the palace of Herren Chiemsee, in which Versailles was reproduced, room by room. He had gone incognito many times back and forward to Versailles to compare the work, and his plans for decorating the interior struck the ministry with despair. The King sent agents to foreign princes to borrow money, to Brazil, Stockholm, Constantinople, and Teheran. The story of his promising the neutrality of Bavaria in the event of a war between France and Germany, as an inducement towards a loan from the Count of Paris, seems to have been true. He instructed his servant to organise a band to rob the banks of Vienna, Berlin, and Stuttgart.

Baron Mundy assures us that in the month of March of 1886, Dr. von Gudden, the Superintendent of the Asylum at Munich for Upper Bavaria, was consulted, who declared that it was mental disease, not eccentricity, that was the matter with the King. In spite of this, Louis still continued in the possession of his legal rights as King for more than three months, during which time he gave his formal assent to the Bills which had passed through the Bavarian Parliament.

Dr. Müller, assistant physician in the asylum, was in the

habit of visiting Prince Otho, about whose mental condition reports were regularly sent to the King his brother. In May, 1866, Müller spoke to Gudden about the report which he was then preparing, and at the same time he took the occasion to allude to what had appeared in the Vienna papers about the mental health of the King. Gudden was not a man who could be drawn to talk on a subject which he would rather have avoided; but, "on this occasion," writes Dr. Müller, "he took up the word and told us at length that the King was insane, as insane as his brother. There was no help for it, and a change in the government of Bavaria was only a question of time." Dr. Grashey came from Würtzburg to Munich on the 7th June, and found him busy collecting and arranging materials for a report on the King's mental condition. It was necessary that such a document should be of a weighty and solid character. Should the experts called in not be satisfied with the character of the evidence, should any one of them have disagreed with the rest, or have insisted that a personal examination of the King was necessary, the proceedings would probably have been suspended. Everything, therefore, depended on the medical report, and all subsequent action was founded on its absolute correctness. In preparing this report Dr. Grashey tells us that Gudden only slept two nights out of five—from the 7th to the 12th of June. On the 8th of June, Dr. Gudden came to Müller and said shortly, "In a few days a regency will be appointed. We go to-morrow to Hohenschwangau and announce this to the King; then we go with the King to Linderhof, where he will be treated. You go with me to undertake the treatment in Linderhof. Make the necessary preparations for a fortnight's journey."

Dr. Grashey was to go to Linderhof to prepare the chateau for the King's reception.

Thus it was not till the beginning of June, strange to say, that the Bavarian ministers were ready to take advantage of the article in the Constitution which provided for proclaiming a Regent in the case of the serious illness of the King. On the 10th of June, Prince Luitpold, the King's uncle, the third son of Louis I., was declared Regent; on the day before the

King's insanity had been certified on oath by four physicians. Here is a translation of their certificate :—

"1. His Majesty is in a far-advanced state of insanity, suffering from that form of mental disease which is well known to alienist physicians of experience as paranoia.*

"2. From the gradual and continuous advance of this disease, which has now lasted many years, His Majesty is incurable, and only a further diminution of mental power is to be looked for.

"3. Through this disease the free exercise of the will is completely excluded, so that the King is hindered in the exercise of the Government. This will last not only longer than a year, but during his whole life.

"Signed,   "GUDDEN,
"HAGEN,
"GRASHEY,
"HUBRICH."

On the 9th, a Commission reached Hohenschwangau to communicate the new arrangements to the King. Louis, who was in the adjoining Castle of Neuschwanstein, was first told by his coachman of what was preparing for him. He received the news with calmness, and at once prepared means of resistance. He collected all the gendarmerie about, issued a proclamation calling on his army to defend him, and sent for a regiment of Jägers at Kempten, but their commanding officer, knowing

---

* In a learned and critical essay on paranoia translated by Dr. W. Noyes, in the *Journal of Nervous and Mental Diseases*, New York, 1888, Nos. 3, 4, 5, and 6, Dr. J. Séglas observes that "paranoia is perhaps the one word in psychiatry that has the most extensive but most ill-defined acceptance." It is mainly used by German and Italian writers on insanity. The paranoia of Snell is not the same as the paranoia of Westphal, or of Meynert, or of Krafft-Ebing. Lest the reader should still desire a definition, I have tried the following :—

"Paranoia is a mental affection of hereditary origin, generally of a slowly advancing character, with illusions and hallucinations, and delusions, often of persecution or of grandeur. Sometimes the two varieties of delusion are combined. The emotional faculties are seldom deeply affected, and the logical power is the last to suffer, the patient reasoning acutely from false premises. The mental enfeeblement thus does not appear to be great. In the chronic form the disease is regarded as incurable. Some writers will not admit of an acute form of paranoia."

the Regent's proclamation, did not come. When the members of the deputation reached Neuschwanstein early next morning, they found a guard of gendarmes at the gate, who politely but peremptorily refused entry to the castle. Expostulation was of no avail. Our King has ordered, they said, and we obey. The Commission returned to the old castle, and in a short time a sergeant of gendarmerie appeared with a written order from the King to arrest them all. As the Commission had no armed escort, and as the sergeant was accompanied by a sufficient force, they judged it best to yield; and three of the Commissioners — Freiherr von Crailsheim and the Counts Holnstein and Törring — were at once marched off to Neuschwanstein. Precautions were at the same time taken that the others should not leave the old castle; and about an hour and a-half after, the remaining members of the deputation, including Dr. Gudden and Dr. Müller, were also arrested and marched off to Neuschwanstein. At a public-house on the road between the two castles they saw a number of people assembled — gamekeepers, woodmen, and peasants — who had all hastened to the help of the King. Had it not been for the district magistrate, these people would have given proofs of their anger upon the captives. When they came to Neuschwanstein they were introduced into the same chamber as their colleagues, but were soon lodged in separate rooms.

Dr. Müller gives the text of the order which the King wrote with his own hand what was to be done with the prisoners: "The skin should be torn from the traitors, and they should be starved." Dr. Grashey, who was not amongst the captives, speaks of the sentence in terms of refined meekness: "Some of his Highness's orders concerning the further fate of those arrested, and which cannot be mentioned on account of their incredible nature, remained unexecuted;" that is to say, none of the Commissioners were flayed alive. After being kept in confinement for about two hours, they were released from their dangerous position in the power of a lunatic ruler, through the exertions of the district magistrate, who explained to the gendarmerie the proclamation of the regency. They returned to Hohenschwangau, from which they drove away without looking after their baggage, making the distance to Munich in a remarkably short time.

Ere the day was over, the palace was surrounded by gendarmes, and all the King's servants, save two, were withdrawn from the vast building. Next day a council was held at Munich, and it was determined that, owing to the excited state of the people, the King should not be sent to Linderhof, a secluded place amongst the mountains, but to the Chateau of Berg, by the Starnberg Lake, which was nearer to Munich, being about twenty miles to the south. Dr. Gudden and his party were sent back to Hohenschwangau on the evening of Friday, the 11th, prepared to enter the palace and take the King away by force if necessary. They arrived about midnight.

The carriages for the whole party were to be ready at four o'clock, but at one o'clock in the morning the King's chamberlain, Meier, came, saying that the King had drunk a good deal of rum, that he was much excited, and had several times asked for the key of the tower, saying that he intended to throw himself over. They had told him that the key could not be found, but that they were seeking for it. There seemed danger that if an attempt were made to enter the King's room by force he would throw himself out of the window, and, as the palace was situated on a precipitous rock, he could thus make an end of himself at any moment. Gudden saw that no time was to be lost. He went with his party along the panelled corridors to a winding stair which led up to the ominous tower. About the middle of this staircase there was a corridor leading directly to the King's room. Gudden placed some of his keepers on the steps above leading to the tower, and himself stayed with the rest below, so that no one could be seen from the corridor. He then sent the chamberlain with the key of the tower to the King.

"Suddenly," writes Müller, "we heard quick footsteps, and a man of imposing height appeared from the door of the corridor, and spoke in short, broken sentences with a servant who stood near, bowing low. The attendants above and below went towards the doors, cutting off his retreat, and quickly seized the King by the arms. Gudden then stepped forward and said, 'Your Majesty, this is the saddest commission of my life which I have undertaken. Your Majesty has been certified by four alienist physicians, and on their certificate Prince Luitpold has undertaken the regency. I have been ordered to accompany your Majesty to Schloss Berg this very night. If your Majesty orders it, the carriage will be ready precisely at four.'"

The King uttered a short, painful "Ah!" and said, "What do you want? What is this?"

The King was then led back into the room which he had quitted, and Gudden began to talk to him about his brother, the Prince Otho, when the King abruptly asked, "How could you certify me to be insane when you had not before seen and examined me?"

Gudden replied, "Your Majesty, that was not needed. The evidence collected was very copious and decisive."

Ludwig then asked how long the cure would last? when Gudden said that to justify a regency it was necessary for the King's illness to last a year. To which Ludwig answered, "It will be shorter than that. They could do as they did with the Sultan. It is so easy to put a man out of the world."

Dr. Müller describes the King as a big, stately man of a powerful frame. He gazed at those around him with his great eyes, but from his glance the self-sufficiency had disappeared, and there was a marked hesitancy; his face was pale, his speech abrupt, but full of repetitions, and his movements uncertain. They had expected him to burst into a towering rage, and were evidently surprised at the self-command he showed. Before setting out he had a conversation with his chamberlain, whom he asked for poison. The party left in three carriages, the King being alone in the middle one, the doors of which were secured.

The journey lasted eight hours. They reached Berg about noon on Saturday, the 12th. Professor Grashey had gone on before to the chateau, in order to make arrangements, and everything was ready, save that the windows, from which it was feared the King might throw himself, were not barred. In his conversation with Dr. Müller, Ludwig repeatedly introduced the subject of poisoning. "It is easy," he said, "to put something in a man's soup, that he never awakes." As no answer was given to this suggestion the King asked, "What means are used to cause sleep?" "There are many—opium, morphia, hydrate of chloral, bathing, washing, and gymnastic exercises."

Ludwig then abruptly changed the conversation. "You wear spectacles. Are you short-sighted?" "In the one eye I am short-sighted; in the other, astigmatic."

Naturally the King wanted an explanation of astigmatism, and, after a few more questions, he led back to the subject that the medical attendant who was to relieve Müller would find some means to send him out of the world; to which Dr. Müller replied: "Your Majesty, I can answer for my colleagues as for myself. The duty of a physician is to heal, not to destroy."

It may be here noticed that the King repeatedly put these suggestions as if he were afraid of being secretly poisoned or murdered.

Professor Grashey describes the walk in the morning of the King and Gudden with the two keepers behind, and apparently this consideration, with the King's friendly deportment, tended to remove Gudden's fears of suicide or violence. Dr. Grashey tells us of a conversation which he had with Gudden the morning of the 13th. Gudden observed that the King was anxious about his life, that he was afraid of weapons, and only thought of suicide when in an excited state. When excited he was dangerous, especially as he used to drink a great deal of rum, which, of course, would not now be allowed him. Grashey saw the King and Gudden take their walk in the morning along a footpath which skirted the lake, which was about fifteen yards distant from the shore of the lake. In the intervening shrubbery he had placed a gendarme. The King and Gudden walked along, quietly talking, and about thirty paces behind there followed the two keepers. Gudden turned round and waved the keepers to keep a greater distance, which they understood. It did not occur to Grashey that under these circumstances there was any great danger of the King drowning himself in the lake, which was known to deepen so slowly that one would need to go about thirty yards before he was out of his depth. After they had returned, Grashey bade Gudden farewell, leaving for Munich about half-past four. During dinner Gudden said that they would not want the gendarme by the shore of the lake as he had come upon them suddenly during their walk, which had annoyed the King.

We are told about the precautions used to prevent the deposed King having any opportunity of committing suicide. The shutters of his bedroom were kept closed till the windows could be barred, he was constantly watched through holes made in the doors, the knives at table were blunted, and so on.

We now approach the fatal moment when the King and Gudden stepped out alone for an evening walk on the shore of the lake. Grashey says that he does not believe that Gudden really told the keepers not to follow. He bases his belief upon what he heard Gudden say about the case and his general character for prudence. Nevertheless, wise men occasionally do foolish things, and a cautious man may do something which costs him his life. Müller quotes the statement of the keeper, Mauder, that Gudden told the attendants to turn back: "*Es darf kein Pfleger mitgehen.*" At this time Gudden was at the door of the chateau, four or five steps behind the King. The keeper immediately went and reported to Müller that the keepers had been turned back by Gudden. Grashey insists that Müller should not have minded the statement of the keepers, but should have instructed the men to follow, so as to keep the King and the physician in view. To this Müller's observation may be considered a reply. "Gudden's words were a clear and decisive order. Had I disregarded the order and sent some one after them, and had the insane King provoked a scene, the blame would have been thrown upon me, and I should have taken upon myself the heavy responsibility arising from the disregarding of an order."

Müller quotes the testimony of Baron Washington, who warned Gudden of the danger of going out alone with the King. He affirms that Gudden was quite taken in by the apparent friendliness of the King, and that he laughed at their fears, which he thought overstrained.

They went out at 6.25, and at 7.30 Müller seems to have got alarmed, especially as it had been raining hard. What took place can only be inferred from circumstantial evidence. Grashey's theory is that Ludwig tried to persuade Gudden to allow him to escape, and that not being able to gain him over, the King got excited and ran into the water; that Gudden overtook him and seized him by the coat, on which the King pulled the coat from him so forcibly as to tear his finger nail; that the King then threw off his coat, and, as Gudden still clung to him, he seized him by the throat with the right hand and struck him with his left fist on the face, and then held him under the water until he was drowned. There is no doubt that Gudden was drowned first; his footsteps could be traced on the sand of the lake up to sixteen metres from the shore, where his footsteps were mingled with those of the King, after which the King's footsteps could be seen twenty-five metres farther. Beyond this there was the trail of the body, which had been washed by the current twenty-nine metres northwards, the head being upwards and the feet dragging on the ground. The only question I would ask is, How did Gudden succeed in overtaking the King, and why did Ludwig throw off his overcoat and coat? Ludwig was forty-one years of age, and very strong, and Gudden, though a vigorous man, was twenty-one years older; moreover, Ludwig, being the taller of the two, had an additional advantage in walking in shallow water. Both were said to be good swimmers. On the supposition that the King wished to escape by swimming, the difficulty is explained. He would naturally stop to throw off his coats, which would allow time for Gudden to make up to him. Of course, a man would not think of taking off his coat to sink more easily. That yielding to a new impulse he should then have destroyed himself is not contrary to experience. Müller says that the coats were found by the shore wetted through; Grashey says that they were found in the water, the arms within one another. They found the bodies at eleven o'clock. The King's watch had stopped at 6.54, the water having got between the glass and the dial. When found the rigor mortis had come on in both bodies. It would thus appear that the tragedy had taken place shortly after they had left the chateau.

This is the sum of what these two writers have to tell us about this terrible event.

Gudden died at his post like a brave and devoted physician. It is not surprising that in writing the obituary of his father-in-law, Dr. Grashey should try to defend his memory from the reproach of having made a wrong estimate of the King's disposition; but when his defence consists in a denial of Gudden's having forbidden the attendants to follow the King, it is clear the learned professor of Psychiatry believes that such an order, if given, would have been an error. In justice to Dr. Müller, I must say that I accept his statement about the keepers being really sent back. Those who knew the King best trusted him least. They said that he had a strange power of misleading people about his intentions and then suddenly carrying them out. To this fascinating power Gudden fell a victim. He was anxious to treat his royal patient with indulgence, and he carried this desire beyond the bounds of safety. It would appear that in gratifying the wish of his royal patient that the keepers should not follow them on their walk, the danger of suicide could not have been present to Dr. Gudden's mind, although it is said that the King had several times talked of making away with himself, had asked to be taken to the top of a tower, and had been even denied the use of a sharp knife since coming to Berg. It does seem strange that the experienced physician of an asylum should not have dreaded a violent assault from a lunatic whom he had been so recently instrumental in depriving of so much liberty, and who had actually ordered his eyes to be put out three days before. Moreover, even granting that there was a sufficient cordon of guards round the grounds of the chateau to prevent the King getting into the open country, an attempt at escape, even without any violence, would have been, at least, an awkward and distressing affair.

But all men make mistakes now and then, and there is already a goodly list of physicians, in charge of the insane, who have perished at the hands of those whom they sought to benefit. Bernhard von Gudden must be judged not by one incident, but by the tenour of his whole useful and honourable life. He was a skilful physician, an able superintendent, and a good man. As a neurologist, he occupied the first rank in learned Germany. His studies on the growth of the skull and of the brain, on the optic tract, and his experiments on the function of the brain, were a real gain to science.

Even the terrible close of the King's life did not silence those who doubted whether he had been insane, and the examination of his body by experienced pathologists was regarded as affording valuable evidence to put the question at rest.

They found considerable alterations of a degenerative character in the skull, brain, and membranes. These were regarded as due partly to original abnormal development, partly to chronic inflammatory processes.

Amongst the details which have got into print we note that the length of the whole body was 191 centimètres (6 ft. 3 in.); the girth round the chest 103c. As compared with the size of the body the skull was somewhat small. It was asymmetrical. The diameter from the left frontal to the occipital plate was 17·2; from the right frontal to right occipital, 17·9. The calvarium was unusually thin. On the inner plate of the skull there were degenerations of the bony tissue, especially at the frontal bone. There was an osseous growth springing from the clivus of two millimètres in length, and the bony tissue around was porous and brittle. There was a bulging of the left petrous bone of about one centimètre into the temporo-sphenoidal lobe. The pia mater was thickened, especially in the frontal region, where it was rougher and contained more blood. The arachnoid was thickened, with milky discoloration. At the upper part of the anterior central gyrus a portion of the pia mater and arachnoid about the size of a shilling had become thickened and hardened, and had impinged upon the table of the skull, causing absorption.

The brain, which weighed 1349 grammes, was full of blood and somewhat soft.

The stomach showed indications of chronic catarrh. While the want of symmetry and the defective development of the base of the skull were proofs of abnormal structural growth, the alterations in the soft parts might be said to indicate recent morbid action; otherwise the results of the examination, so far as published, contained nothing specific.

In the course of this sketch we have been more anxious to detail facts than to make reflections; but it is difficult to resist wondering at so strange a story. Bavaria for so many years to be ruled over by an insane King, and then to be treated as an hereditary possession in his family! For immediately after being freed from Louis II., we read that all the generals of the army and other functionaries had to swear allegiance to his brother Otho, who is, and has been for years, more insane than Louis ever was. Surely it is tampering too much both with Divine right and the sanctity of an oath to make a man King known to be clearly incapable of reigning, and to compel people to swear obedience to one whom they knew they would never be called upon to obey.

It must be deeply abhorrent to the traditions of Divine right that the relentless facts of pathology should intrude themselves into the palaces of Kings, but unless the princes of Germany shake off some of their prejudices, and show more wisdom and less exclusiveness in their marriages, they may find that a people so enlightened as the Germans will read their lesson for them, and, in the words of Schiller, will make it easier for their Princes to be men, and more difficult to be Kings.

CHARLES J. GUITEAU.

CHAPTER I.

THE ASSASSINATION OF PRESIDENT GARFIELD—THE GUITEAU FAMILY—CHARLES GUITEAU AS A CHILD—HIS UPBRINGING—JOINS THE ONEIDA COMMUNITY—LEAVES THE COMMUNITY—HIS QUARRELS WITH THE PERFECTIONISTS—BECOMES AN ATTORNEY—GETS MARRIED AND DIVORCED—TAKES TO RELIGIOUS LECTURING—TAKES TO POLITICS—REASONS ASSIGNED BY HIM FOR THE MURDER.

ON the 2nd of July, 1881, a telegraphic message ran through the world that James Garfield, the President of the United States, had been dangerously wounded by an assassin. Entering a railway station at Washington with that absence of ceremony which distinguishes the highest officials of the great republic, the President was walking along with Mr. Blaine, the Secretary of State, when a man issuing from a waiting-room with a loaded pistol approached from behind within a few feet of him, and fired two shots one of which entered his back. The President sank to the ground and swooned away. He was borne into a waiting-room, on reviving a little he was conveyed to the White House.

The President had only been in office for four months. He had risen from a humble position, without resorting to any doubtful arts, by the sheer force of wisdom, courage, and energy. He was a man who believed in the eternally right, and was prepared to carry it into politics. He had resolved that his election should not be signalised by a wholesale ejectment of the Government officials who had not shared in the political creeds of his party. Men had fondly hoped that a day of good feeling was now dawning when the North and South would live at peace together as citizens of one great country, and were all these bright hopes to be dashed away by the shot of a vile assassin? It was at first supposed that the bullet had perforated the liver, and was lodged somewhere in the cavity of the abdomen. Death was thought to be near at hand; but as the President lived on, day after day, people began to hope, and then to gather faith that his life would be saved. Daily bulletins describing the fluctuations of strength, and weakness, and suffering, and relief, signed by eminent physicians and surgeons, were eagerly read in all parts of the civilised world, and words of condolence came back, and well-meant suggestions for the relief of the illustrious sufferer, with messages of sympathy for his wife and aged mother. Never had such wide-spread interest centred round a sick bed before; and never since, save during the course of the malady of the Emperor Frederick of Germany which is still fresh in the public memory.

A gasp of relief ran through the world when it was announced that with many ingenious devices to prevent friction and shaking, the President had been wheeled away from the White House to a cottage at New Jersey, on the shore of the Atlantic.

"This is life," he said, when he felt the cool sea-breeze enter his chest. But the bullet travelled with him. It was still in the sufferer's back, lodged amongst the broken and crushed fragments of the bones of the spinal column, and could neither be found nor extracted. All the resources of the healing art, and the solicitude and prayers of millions were in vain. The President at last died, eighty days after the wound, a period of cruel suffering manfully borne. Men then began to turn their thoughts to the murderer. He had made no attempt to escape, his main anxiety seemed to be that he should be safely lodged in jail, and protected against the fury of the mob, who might have torn him to pieces on the spot. He was a little, thin, sallow man, about forty years of age, with dark hair. Mr. Blaine recognised him at once

M

as a dissatisfied seeker for office. His name was Charles Julius Guiteau. He was not brought to his trial till the issue of the illness of his victim could be determined. He was arraigned on the 14th of October, 1881, for the murder of James A. Garfield, President of the United States. Such was the bitter hatred pervading all classes of the community that at first no advocate could be got to defend the prisoner. The only man forthcoming was George Scoville, a legal practitioner at Chicago, who had married Guiteau's only sister Frances. Mr. Scoville was little versed in criminal law; he had never practised in the Courts of Columbia, and his knowledge of insanity seemed merely to have been got up for the occasion. The fact of the assassination was notorious, nor was it denied by Guiteau himself; and when the plea of insanity was put in, it was clear that this was the only defence which could give the prisoner the chance of escaping with his life, though, in the angry and excited state of the public mind, very few people could think with patience of any plea whatever being listened to. Furious messages were sent to the murderer through the post, with caricatures, and halters. Small-pox virus was sent in packets in the hopes of infecting him and Mr. Scoville. The prisoner was shot at on two several occasions, once by one of his guards, another time when in the van driving from the court-house. The jail had to be guarded by a body of troops to prevent an attempt being made to break into the building and lynch the murderer. Mr. Scoville was allowed by the Court a month's delay to prepare for the defence, and collect witnesses. In spite of the feeling of loathing and indignation against the accused which pervaded all classes, there were a few physicians who maintained from the outset that he was insane.

The most prominent amongst these was Dr. W. W. Godding, the superintendent of the Government Asylum at Washington, who was the first to examine the prisoner.[*] On the side of

---

[*] In preparing this paper great use has been made of "Two Hard Cases, Sketches from a Physician's Portfolio," by W. W. Godding, M.D. Boston, 1882. There is a long account of the Guiteau trial in the *American Journal of Insanity*, Vol. xxxviii., by Dr. John P. Gray, of the New York State Lunatic Asylum at Utica. These two works support opposite sides

the prosecution a number of distinguished physicians was summoned. It became clear that there would be a contest of authority on the vexed subject of the responsibility of the insane, and the lines to be drawn between wickedness and madness. Inquiries were made into the previous history of the criminal, and owing to the universal interest felt in the matter, most of the details of his life were soon known. Charles Guiteau was of Huguenot extraction. His family had been in the United States for three generations. Mentally, they were said to have been a strong race. His great-grandfather and grandfather had been leading country physicians. His grandfather, Francis Guiteau, had married Hannah Wilson, a woman of Scottish origin, who had borne eleven children, one of whom died in infancy. Of the ten who grew up, five are said to have died of consumption. One of them died of this disease in the Bloomingdale Asylum for the Insane. His derangement was said to be owing to distress of mind from having been led into a mock duel in the course of a love affair.

There was a conflict of evidence on some statements that two of Luther Guiteau's sisters had shown signs of mental derangement. At anyrate the aberration could not have been well marked nor lasted long. There was, however, no question that one of these sisters, Mrs. Maynard, had a daughter who was of weak intellect, and at that time was in a lunatic asylum. It was said she became insane when ten years old under the influence of a professional mesmeriser. The other sister, Mrs. Parker, had a son in an asylum in Illinois. Luther W. Guiteau, the father of the prisoner, was the youngest child of the eleven. For the last ten years of his life he had been cashier of a bank in Freeport, Illinois. He had always been correct in his business relations, had borne a good character, and had been elected to several public offices in the county. In recognition of the interest he took in education, his name

---

of the argument, Dr. Godding maintaining that Guiteau was insane, Dr. Gray that he was sane. I have also used the Report of the Proceedings in the case of the United States v. Charles J. Guiteau, in three parts. H. H. Alexander and Edward D. Easton, official stenographers, Washington. Government Printing Office, 1882.

was inscribed on one of the school-houses, which was called the Guiteau building. A number of respectable witnesses were brought forward to prove that Luther Guiteau never showed the slightest trace of insanity.

The argument that a man is or should be thought insane because his ancestors were known to have been so has not the necessary strength to bear weight in a Court of law. There is a presumption that a man insane, or with insane tendencies, will transmit the same tendencies to his descendants; and it has been found through careful inquiries, that in some families the proportion of insane members is very large. In some of such families in which idiocy, insanity, epilepsy, and other neurosis, are frequent, the only predisposing cause that can be found is that they are all descended from one common ancestor. Sometimes, too, it is found that this ancestor had no symptom of insanity himself. Insanity, therefore, in cousins and other collateral relations forms a presumption of danger of insanity appearing in a family, but such a presumption has more of a pathological than of a legal interest. Dr. Godding observes that, in view of the whole testimony submitted, the jury could hardly avoid the conclusion that the father of the prisoner was a man whose sanity would never have been questioned but for the trial of his son. Nevertheless we are now in a position to bring forward facts bearing upon the question which were not presented to the jury. Dr. M'Farland, of Jacksonville, Illinois, a superintendent of hospitals for the insane, of thirty years' standing, came to testify his opinion that Luther Guiteau was of unsound mind, but he came too late in the trial for his evidence to be heard by the jury.

In a letter, quoted by Godding,[*] Dr. M'Farland writes:—

"The father of Guiteau—a total stranger—visited me in 1864. He came with his second wife and the latter's insane sister. The patient was verging on complete exhaustion, and he proposed staying a few days, remaining part of a week. But he soon seemed to lose all interest whatever in the patient, and devoted all his time, and took up all of mine, to the limit at least of my courtesy, in following me

---

[*] "Two Hard Cases," p. 71.

up with a strain of discourse, the staple of which I perceived to be delusional, though mingled with much fruit of reading, and an intelligence of quite a high order for a man of his standing. It was not the blunt proposition of actual insane absurdities, for his intelligent caution prevented his going so far; but he would state his theory, and appeal to me with some such query as—'Now, is there anything in that contrary to reason?' or, 'Does not the Bible support that view?' or, 'Hasn't your experience proved this or that?' &c. His tone was that of a man who had long brooded in secret over disordered fancies, and who had taken that chance to get some backing. As I now recollect, he believed in the doctrine of metempsychosis; that death was the exchange of the effete and worn-out body for a new-created infantile one. But his great theme was insanity, its nature and causation. His view (as I got it) was that insanity was just what New Testament Scripture makes it, mere diabolical possession, and that superior virtue, such as Jesus Christ possessed, could cast it out now, the same as in that instance. The testimony of John W. Guiteau, in regard to the belief of the whole family on this subject, is substantially what the father unfolded at that time.

"On Sunday, I being at church, he availed himself of the opportunity to visit the ward where his sister-in-law was, to make practical demonstration of his powers in the way of exorcism. I heard ludicrous accounts of his methods over different patients, but was not a witness of them. They consisted, as I learned, in standing in a devotional attitude over the patient, muttering something inaudibly, and making passes with his hands. I don't think it was so much the erratic beliefs of the man that impressed me as it was the complete absorption of all his thought in them, his persistent return to the same topics whenever he caught me for a moment at leisure, and the general *complexion* of the thought as it strikes the observer.

"Now, while the delusions of the father and the son prove the opposite of each other in their tendencies, and especially their results, the fundamental nature of the two is the same—a belief in the power to act by supernatural agency; for this is what C. J. Guiteau's talk amounts to when you sift it out from the chaff of his wild and irrelevant rhodomontade. He has the same fearlessness, defiance, and bombast, the same faith in the final outcome, that all the lunatics have who believe themselves divinely led, and so he will be to his last breath."

There is no doubt that Luther Guiteau's religious opinions had much influence upon the formation of the character of his unfortunate son. Luther Guiteau became a convert to the doctrines of the Perfectionists of Oneida, one of those socialistic communities which have tried to carry out a scheme of society organised on a new basis. One of the most striking tenets of the Oneida Community was the doctrine of free love. Luther Guiteau believed that, through prayer and the laying on of hands, he could give health to the sick, and considered it possible that, through a holy life, he should attain to a union with Christ, which should enable him to live for ever. Nevertheless, he employed a physician when he was ill, insured his life, and made a will. Luther Guiteau believed in direct inspiration. He seemed to have held that any powerful impulse affecting his mind came from Christ.

From all this it appears that the elder Guiteau was a man whose mind by natural proclivity delighted to harbour and cherish chimerical ideas. He accepted the rules of arithmetic and the ways of the world in buying and selling, but out of his office his mind sometimes wandered in a realm of its own, with its own rules of logic ready to defend whimsical conclusions. He might have said with Chrysale:
" Raisonner est l'emploi de toute ma maison, et le raisonnement en bannit la raison."

Quite aware that some of his views might excite comment and opposition disagreeable to himself, he had enough prudence and will power to abstain from bringing them out on ordinary occasions ; but now and then, when away from his usual surroundings, his habitual check was allowed to be relaxed. Whether one would pronounce such a man to be insane depends on whether he is disposed to enlarge and extend the definition of insanity. In any case, Luther Guiteau was not far from the limiting line. Had some illness or unusual distress supervened, his strange ideas might have hurried him across the frontier with delirious force. In his mind there was a brooding neurosis, and some of his mental peculiarities were transmitted to three of his children—John, Frances, and Charles, though in different qualities and proportions. Their mother was a woman suffering from neuralgia. According to her daughter Frances, Mrs. Scoville, she had a brain fever about the time Charles was born, but this was denied by John, who was older than his sister. After Charles, she gave birth to two children, one of whom, a boy, was deformed, and died when two years old; the other, a girl, died, aged twenty months, of consumption.

John Guiteau, the elder brother, took up his father's strange religious notions. He was a manager of an insurance company, and led a respectable life; but his behaviour at the trial made people suspect there was something wrong about his "mental make up."* The sister, Mrs. Scoville, has had repeated attacks of insanity (Spitzka), and was formally pronounced by six jurists, in the State of Illinois, one of them a Doctor of Medicine, to be a fit person to be sent to a State Hospital for the Insane.† The strange book which she lately published,‡ exhibits some of the characteristics of her unhappy brother, amongst others, an inordinate love of notoriety. Facts are mixed up with fictions as in a dream, and the accusation against different well-known politicians, that they instigated and assisted in the murder of the President, do not appear to be better than insane delusions.

The younger sister by the second marriage of Luther Guiteau is said to have exophthalmic goitre, which is a neurosis. About Charles Guiteau's infancy the most notable thing was his extreme restlessness. His grandfather, Howe, said he was the smartest Guiteau he knew of, and by his will left him a thousand dollars. He was, however, slow to learn to speak, and, at six years of age, had a difficulty in pro-

---

* In the "Alienist and Neurologist," October, 1883, Dr. James H. M'Bride writes—" During the trial of Guiteau, I saw much of his sister, Mrs. Scoville, and it was my opinion, as expressed at the time, that she was insane. John W. Guiteau was barely an improved edition of his brother, and I certainly never saw so strange a mixture of sanity and folly as he exhibited. He was frantic, even unreasonable, in his efforts to save his brother, yet he retailed to every chance questioner the plans and secrets of the defence, and was a continual hindrance to Mr. Scoville. He said to me on one occasion that if he knew his father was insane, rather than have the fact proven, he would see his brother hung."

† The certificate is quoted in a paper by Dr. Madigan in the "Alienist and Neurologist," April, 1884, p. 238. The date is not given.

‡ "The Stalwarts; or, Who were to Blame?" By Frances Marie Norton, the only sister of Charles J. Guiteau. London, 1889.

nouncing certain sounds. His father said, that "he knew the child could talk plain, and he was going to make him talk plain." On this theory he punished him, but it never made the least difference.* As Mrs. Scoville put it: "Father would whip him, and after he had punished him he would say, 'Now, say pail,' and he would say 'quail' every time."

This deficiency seems to have passed away shortly after the boy was sent to school. The teacher, David Sunderland,† could recollect that he had a difficulty about articulating or giving the right pronunciation of words. Before he was seven years old his mother died. About six years after his father married again. At about this time the boy ran away, but was found wandering about and brought back. After this he lived sometimes with his grandfather, Howe, and sometimes with his uncle; more rarely with his father. He was boarded in this teacher's house and in that college, and then fell under the kindly care of his married sister. After this he went back to his father, to whom he acted as a copying clerk until the age of seventeen. His father called him the devil's seed, but, by his own admission, he did not look well after him. A man who lived with the family said that Charles Guiteau never seemed to have a friend or associate of either sex, and that "the biggest bump on his head seemed to me to be that of egotism." At his own instance, Charles Guiteau left his father's office, and with the money bequeathed by his grandfather, he placed himself at a preparatory school at Ann Arbor, Michigan, in the autumn of 1859. His father, who never entered the Oneida Community himself, was very anxious that his son should do so, and plied him with propagandist publications of John H. Noyes, and wrote long letters exhorting him to seek salvation by joining that fraternity. In this Luther Guiteau was too successful. In spite of the expostulations of his sister, Mrs. Scoville, the youth ceased attending to his school subjects, and in June, 1860, he entered the Oneida Community. He was then nineteen. He describes himself as taking this step under profound

---

* Mrs. Scoville's evidence. Official Report, p. 463.
† Official Report, p. 854.

religious feelings. On the other hand, John H. Noyes, the chief of the society, said that the real, though concealed, object which Charles Guiteau had in view in joining them, was the free exercise of his unbridled lust for women. His brother John wrote, that* "Charles Julius went to the Oneida Community with both his moral and physical health sadly impaired from previous excesses and wrongs, and he left because he was unable to gratify his lustful desires, and was required to work as the rest did. He had for years before been disobedient, wilful, egotistical, gross, and, I have no doubt, was on the verge of insanity long before father suspected it, for he believed that insanity was the result of sin and Satan's power, and this idea is unquestionably the teaching of the Bible in both Old and New Testaments."

On 10th April, 1865, we find Charles Guiteau writing to his father from Hoboken, New Jersey † :—

"I have left the Community. The cause of my leaving was because I could not conscientiously and heartily accept their views on the labour question. They wanted to make a hard-working business man of me, but I could not consent to that, and therefore deemed it expedient to quietly withdraw, which I did last Monday. I am *one*, however, with them in heart, in faith, and in doctrine, and always expect to be. But I was so certain that I could serve their cause to a vastly better advantage disconnected from any local organisation, that I felt a good heart to try it at all events.

"I came to New York in obedience to what I believed to be the call of God for the purpose of pursuing an independent course of theological and historical investigation. With the Bible for my text-book, and the Holy Ghost for my schoolmaster, I can pursue my studies without interference from human dictation. In the country my *time* was *appropriated*, but now it is at my own *disposal*, a very favourable change. I have procured a small room, well furnished, in Hoboken, opposite the city, and intend to fruitfully pursue my studies during the next three years.

---

* "Letters and Facts not heretofore published, touching the Mental Condition of Charles J. Guiteau since 1865. Submitted to the President of the United States by John W. Guiteau, in the Matter of the Application for a Commission *de Lunatico Inquirendo*," p. 5.

† *Ibid.*, p. 10.

"And here it is proper to state that the energies of my life are now and have been for months, *pledged to God* to do all that within me lies to extend the sovereignty of Jesus Christ by placing at His disposal a powerful daily paper. I am persuaded that theocratic presses are destined, in due time, to supersede to a great extent pulpit oratory. There are hundreds of thousands of ministers in the world, but not a single daily theocratic press. It appears to me that there is a splendid chance for some one to do a big thing for God, for humanity, and for himself. At no time since the creation of the world have mankind been prepared for such an innovation. Everything will soon be auspicious for such a movement. Abolish slavery, close the war, and establish such a press at the centre of national civilisation, and then prophesy the rapid strides that this nation will take in *education*. Conceive of several great theocratic dailies in each of the principal cities of the world, all under the power and magnetism of God."

Here is another passage from the same letter:—

"Do you say that the establishment of a great daily paper is a stupendous work, and only to be accomplished by extraordinary talents and energy? Of course it is. And when I consider the vast work to be done, and my own insignificant attainments, my heart sinks within me; 'but *when* I am *weak*,' says Paul, '*then* I am *strong*,' so that my natural incapacity, after all, may be in my favour, inasmuch as it may enable God the more freely to pour out His grace upon me.

"However presumptuous it may seem, I am nevertheless constrained to confess the truth about myself. Therefore, I say boldly, that I claim *inspiration*, I claim that I am in the employ of Jesus Christ & Co., the very ablest and strongest firm in the universe, and that what I can do is limited only by their power and purpose. I have very little confidence in the *flesh*, but a vast deal in the power and purpose of God; and I know He will give me the requisite energy and ability to do my work *well*. The *favour* of God is vastly more important (in my view) in the pursuit of an object than anything else.

"Whoever edits such a paper as I intend to establish will doubtless occupy the position of target-general to the press, pulpit, and bench of the civilised world; and if God intends *me* for that place, I *fear not*, for I know that He will be 'a wall of fire round about me,' and keep me from all harm."

"To compete with the devil," and so on. The letter is signed, "Your brother and son, Charles J. Guiteau."

Not being able to get enough money on credit to begin the *Theocrat*, he again returned to the Oneida Community. About his behaviour amongst the Perfectionists the accounts are perhaps not quite trustworthy. He left them secretly in the autumn of 1866, with the assistance of his brother-in-law, Mr. Scoville. Mutual recrimination followed. Guiteau endeavoured to extort money from the Oneida Community by threatening to reveal what he had observed in their inner life. A letter has been published from John H. Noyes to Luther W. Guiteau about these doings of his son containing the following passage :—

"WALLINGFORD, 4th *February*, 1868.

"DEAR BROTHER GUITEAU,—Your letter makes all right between us, and I thank God with you for new love and confidence where the devil would have been glad to make a breach. I hear nothing more from the threatened suit, and my impression, like yours, is that Dean has abandoned it. I have reason to believe, however, that Charles is doing his best to stir up hostility against us in the newspaper world, but with poor success.

"It seems to me that the best thing you can do at this time is to write him a kind, fatherly letter, setting before him the folly of his course, and opening to him the door of repentance and return. I am sure I have no ill-will toward him. *I regard him as insane*, and I prayed for him last night as sincerely as I ever prayed for my own son, that is now in a lunatic asylum. I do not wish you to say these things to him from me; but if you feel as I do about him, you can show him, on the one hand that he can gain nothing by war but disgrace, because we are used to exposure, and live in spite of it, but the exposure which he will bring on himself, if he persists in making enemies of us, will ruin him," &c.

Noyes stated again and again his opinion,* that his late disciple was insane, and this statement was repeated by two men who acted as Noyes' secretaries or agents. A lawyer employed by Charles Guiteau raised it as one of the difficulties in coming to a settlement of his client's affairs with the Oneida community that he, Noyes, had admitted that

---

* These statements will be found in the letters and facts already quoted.

Guiteau was insane. Moreover, Guiteau's own father delivered the same opinion in a letter to his son John L. Guiteau, dated Freeport, 30th March, 1873* :—

"As I have viewed him ever since his shameful and outrageously wicked and foolish course with Mr. Noyes and the Oneida Community, as well as his absurd and ridiculous course while at Chicago, and his abominable and deceitful dealings with George Scoville and myself, I have been ready to believe him capable of almost any folly, stupidity, or rascality. The only possible excuse *I can render for him is that he is insane*—indeed, *if I was called as a witness upon the stand I am inclined to think I should testify that he is absolutely insane, and is hardly responsible for his acts. My own impression is, that unless something shall stop him in his folly and mad career, he will become hopelessly insane, and a fit subject for the lunatic asylum.* Before I finally gave him up I had exhausted all my powers of reason and persuasion, as well as other resources in endeavouring to control his action and thoughts, but without avail. I found he was deceitful, and could not be depended upon in anything. Stubborn, wilful, conceited, and at times outrageously wicked, apparently possessed with the devil. I saw him once or twice when it seemed to me he was ready to do almost any wicked thing that he should happen to take a fancy to. You will remember, perhaps, the last conversation we had about him. I told you to keep clear of him, and not to have anything to do with him. Should anybody ask me about him *now*, I should be compelled to say to them I thought he was insane, or at least a monomaniac, and should there leave it and say no more about him. His insanity is of a character that he is likely to become a sly cunning desperado as anything. Could I see him *I might possibly* make another vigorous and desperate effort to change the whole channel of his thoughts and feelings, if I could not do that, I should have no hope whatever of being able to do him any good. I made up my mind long ago never to give him another dollar in money, until I should be convinced he was thoroughly humbled, radically changed. I am sometimes afraid he would steal, rob, or do anything before his egotism and self-conceit shall be knocked out of him, and perhaps even all that will not do it. So you see I regard his case as hopeless, or nearly so, and of course know no other way but to dismiss him entirely from my mind, and leave him entirely in the hands of his Maker, with

---

* See "Letters and Facts," p. 23.

a very faint hope that he can be changed either in this world or the next. Several years ago he, in his stupid self-conceit and wickedness, made a most shameful and wicked attack through the New York newspapers upon Mr. Noyes and the Oneida Community, after they had treated him with all the kindness and love and forbearance of a gentle and loving father and mother. I felt compelled as an honest man and friend of truth and righteousness to expose him through the same channels, the New York papers, by writing a lengthy article, which was published in the same papers defending the Oneida Community from his attacks. I knew of my own knowledge at the same time that his attack upon them was base and mean, beyond belief; but, after all that, I did try by kindness in giving him money to live upon, after he had exhausted some $800 or $900 of his own resources which the Oneida Community had returned to him when he left them."

In his attacks upon the Oneida Community, Charles Guiteau had counted on the assistance of some religious societies with which he had become connected, but finding reason to distrust his character, they withdrew their countenance from him, when he found it expedient to push his claims against the Perfectionists no further than getting back the money which he had paid in on entering their Community. After the murder of the President the worthy leader of the Perfectionists wrote in different terms in a letter to Mr. Scoville, which was sent to the newspapers at the time. It was dated, Niagara Falls, Ontario, 20th October, 1881, and began :—

"I see in the papers that you have named me as a witness, by whom you intend to prove Guiteau's insanity.

"Perhaps it will save you trouble and expense, if I inform you in advance that I do not believe in his insanity, and that I recollect no act or symptom of insanity in his life, while under my observation."

Mr. Noyes thought that his former pupil had been born with a special genius for mischief, but that was not insanity in any legal sense. He wound up in the usual style of professed saints when they are gratifying their vindictive feelings :—

"With the views and the memory of my sore experience with your client, I am afraid I should have to testify strongly against your main plea, and perhaps should be the means of sending him to the gallows, which I should sincerely regret on many accounts, and especially because his father was a dear friend to me and mine. But I must notify you that my regret would be mostly for my personal agency in the tragedy.—Yours respectfully,

"J. H. NOYES."

Judged from his intentions, Mr. Noyes was probably consistent. Though in 1866, he was ready in self-defence to call his apostate disciple insane, he was not willing to do so in 1881, in order to save him from the gallows.

After spending in New York the restored dollars of Grandfather Howe's legacy, Charles Guiteau found his way to Chicago (August, 1867), where he entered Mr. Scoville's office, which he soon quitted for another. A year after he was admitted to the Chicago Bar, and remained in that town three years, trying to gain practice as an attorney. It was difficult to get anyone to remember a case in which he appeared. One lawyer could recall that "Guiteau had to defend a man accused of petty larceny, and though the case seemed too plain for argument, he indulged in a long and rambling speech into which he introduced theology, divinity, and the rights of man."

This was probably the occasion referred to by Dr. Beard.[*]

"I am informed by satisfactory authority—a prominent member of Congress—that about thirteen years ago Guiteau pled the case of a criminal in a court of one of our Western towns. The style of the plea, and his conduct during its delivery, were such as to convince all the lawyers who were present that he was a monomaniac. His talk was as senseless and grotesque as all his talk has been ever since he came before the public, and the whole speech in its matter was adapted best of all to injure his client, was indeed the speech of a lunatic, the manner was even worse than the matter; he talked and acted like a crazy man. There was a bar between him and the jury, he came up to this bar, jumped over it like a monkey, put his fist in the face of a juryman, and talked with great

---

[*] "The Case of Guiteau, a Psychological Study," by George M. Beard, M.D. New York, 1882, p. 32.

vehemence to the amusement of the spectators, and his client was convicted without the jury leaving their seats."

Guiteau got married in July, 1869. He afterwards said that his wife did not suit him, though he had nothing to say against her conduct towards him. They were separated in 1873, and got a divorce in 1874, Guiteau furnishing the requisite evidence against himself by furnishing proofs of incontinence. She got happily married to another man, and had several children. As a witness at the trial, this woman stated that during the time she lived with Guiteau, she had never seen anything to indicate that he was a man of unsound mind.*

The principal work he got in Chicago seems to have been collecting bad debts for merchants. What money he squeezed out of the debtors he spent first upon his own wants, and often he had no superfluity to hand over to his employers.

Guiteau was assiduous in attending the meetings of religious bodies. He haunted prayer meetings as some men haunt public-houses. He was (to use his own phrase) "a high toned gentleman," who neither drank, smoked, nor swore. He was always neat in his dress, and generally had a suave manner, and an air as if he were engaged in some work of great moment. In fact his depravity went much deeper than appearances. He cheated every one with whom he came in touch, even some Israelites, in a manner which extorted their unwilling admiration of his mental acuteness. On one occasion he was arrested at Chicago for debt, and got into the Tombs at New York for a month for some of his fraudulent practices.

From 1870 to 1875, Guiteau was in New York making his living dishonestly or otherwise by soliciting for insurance companies, raising bad debts for others, and evading payment of his own debts. He does not seem to have done anything specially striking during this period, as Godding remarks. Regular occupation, even though it was scoundrelism, seemed to have had a certain controlling influence on his mind. In 1872 he was reported by two witnesses to have said that if

---

* Official Report, p. 1166.

he did not gain notoriety for good he would for evil, "he would shoot some public man," "he would imitate Wilkes Booth." This was thought mere idle talk at the time. Interpreted by after events, it might be quoted to show that he considered the commission of a crime was not too high a price to pay for the gratification of his monstrous vanity.

In February, 1875, he was back to Chicago, and towards the close of the year he is going about trying to persuade people to intrust him with money for schemes out of which he believed he would make an immense fortune. One of these was a plan for telegraphing the bulk of the *New York Herald* every morning, and reproducing it at Chicago. This was afterwards carried out by some one who could command money and credit. He promised to get one man made Governor of Illinois, and another President of the United States, if they would assist him. Mr. Scoville several times rescued him from the misery into which his irregular conduct had led him. When living in his country-house in the spring of 1876, Guiteau, who had become completely destitute, was asked by his sister to split some wood in the shed. As it was very hot in the shed, he took the wood out upon the road, but as the logs blocked the way, Mrs. Scoville told him to remove them, and stooped down herself to take up some of the wood, whereupon he lifted his axe as if to strike her. She mentioned this to a lady in the house, and talked about consulting a doctor. Guiteau, who overheard this conversation, abused her, and said she was insane herself. Dr. Rice, of Merton, U.S., was called in, who gave it as his opinion that Guiteau was insane. Dr. Gray gave a humorous description of the grounds assigned by Dr. Rice in support of his opinion; but it often happens that experienced practitioners in medicine give a shrewd diagnosis of insanity, while stating the facts indicating insanity in a somewhat loose manner. What seems to have struck Dr. Rice most was his exalted emotional feeling, his outrageous egotism, and his pseudo religion. Guiteau, hearing of the project to put him into an asylum, left the house and returned to Chicago.

In the autumn of the same year he took to religious lecturing, and commenced wandering about the States, travelling in the railway cars without tickets where he could, and leaving unpaid bills at boarding-houses. He got one or two of his lectures printed, which he hawked about. In 1879 he was in search of a publisher for his new book, "The Truth, a Companion to the Bible." Not being able to find one, he himself took his manuscript to the printer, and to save appearances, put the name of a publisher on the title-page. The book is said to have been in great part stolen from "The Berean" of his old chief, J. H. Noyes, and similar productions; but he seems to have persuaded himself that it was his own, and called it "a direct revelation equal to anything in the New Testament." His lectures were poorly attended. At the close he sent round a hat. His style of lecturing was abrupt, rambling, and grotesque. A clergyman who heard him said that he thought Guiteau "not so much deranged as very badly arranged." The Deists of the Thomas Paine Hall, whom he threatened with eternal perdition, after the lecture was over, unanimously voted him to be crazy. A few people who met Guiteau on his wanderings suspected that he was of unsound mind, but this was not the general opinion.

In 1872, Guiteau had borne some part in supporting Greeley's candidature for the presidentship. At the election in 1880, there appeared in New York a shabby-genteel, little man, with quick-moving eyes and restless manner, who hung about the committee rooms of the Republican party. He was willing, nay eager to work, but with such a sense of his own importance that he was not contented with subordinate parts. He had copies of a speech in his pocket, Garfield against Hancock, which he had got printed under the auspices of the National Republican Committee. He was only allowed to deliver it once, and that to a coloured audience. He used to give away cards: Charles J. Guiteau, lawyer and theologian. Though the politicians did not give him much work to do, he hung on, lounging about the rooms till he got on speaking terms with the leaders. He evidently considered himself an important agent in the election. The Republican party was victorious, but one section of them called the Stalwarts, headed by General Grant and Senator Conkling, deemed themselves ill-used in the division of the spoils. Guiteau heard a great deal said against the ingratitude of President Garfield, and that he was ruining his party. Guiteau himself first demanded the Austrian Mission, and then the consulship to France, as the reward of his services during the election campaign. He stated in a letter to the President that he was going to get married to a wealthy and accomplished heiress, and that together they might represent the nation with dignity and grace. Getting importunate and troublesome, the Secretary, Mr. Blaine, told him never to speak about the Paris consulship again to him, and the President refused to see him, and took no notice of his letters. Guiteau could neither speak French nor German, and was quite unfitted for these posts. He had rejected with disdain the advice to petition for a humbler place, but there is no proof that he would ever have got any employment whatever from the party now in office. Under these circumstances, the idea of improving the situation by killing the President entered Guiteau's mind like an inspiration, and dwelt there with the persistence of a fixed idea. It was singular that he did not know how to use firearms. He went to a shop to buy a pistol, and somebody coming in showed him how to load it. This was in Washington, where he had gone on the day of the President's inauguration. He went to an open space in the country, and practised with his pistol till he learned how to take aim. It was on the 8th of June that he bought the pistol. Guiteau himself said that he first conceived the idea of shooting the President about the middle of May. On the 12th of June he went to the little church which General Garfield attended, saw where he sat, and examined a window to see if a shot could be fired from that point. A week after, he came up with the President, who was going to the railway station. He was taking his sick wife to Long Branch. He went back to write in his notes that Mrs. Garfield looked so thin, and clung so tenderly to the President's arm, that his heart failed him, and he decided to take him alone. On the evening of the 1st July, he came up with the President walking with Mr. Blaine, and he might have shot them both in the dusk, and escaped. When cross-examined at the trial about this, he said that it was a very hot, sultry night, and he did not feel like it at the time. Whatever might be his motive, Guiteau intended that his crime should be done in public. He had prepared a number of documents and letters to the newspapers justifying his motives, and appealing for protection to his party, the Stalwarts. The danger which occupied his mind was the fear of being lynched by the mob. He had a cab ready to drive him to prison, and a letter to General Sherman asking him to send troops at once to guard the jail, and arrangements for a new issue of his book, "The Truth," which would now be sure to command a sale. The following is his appeal to the American people, dated Washington, D.C., 16th June, 1881 :—

"*To the American People*,—

"I conceived the idea of removing the President four weeks ago. Not a soul knew of my purpose. I conceived the idea myself, and kept it to myself. I read the newspapers carefully, for and against the administration, and gradually the conviction settled on me that the President's removal was a political necessity, because he proved a traitor to the men that made him, and thereby imperilled the life of the Republic. At the late Presidential election, the Republican party carried every Northern State. To-day, owing to the misconduct of the President and his Secretary of State, they could hardly carry ten Northern States. They certainly could not carry New York, and that is the pivotal State.

"Ingratitude is the basest of crimes. That the President, under the manipulation of his Secretary of State, has been guilty of the basest ingratitude to the Stalwarts admits of no denial. The expressed purpose of the President has been to crush General Grant and Senator Conkling, and thereby open the way for his renomination in 1884. In the President's madness he has wrecked the once grand old Republican party; and for this he dies.

"The men that saved the Republic must govern it, and not the men who sought its life.

"I had no ill-will to the President.

"This is not murder. It is a political necessity. It will make my friend Arthur President, and save the Republic. I have sacrificed only one. I shot the President as I would a rebel, if I saw him pulling down the American flag. I leave my justification to God and the American people.

"I expect President Arthur and Senator Conkling will give the nation the finest administration it has ever had. They are honest, and have plenty of brains and experience. CHARLES GUITEAU."

The following document is even more characteristic of the mental peculiarities of the assassin. Though dated the day of the murder, it was said by Guiteau to have been written the day before :—

"WASHINGTON, 2nd *July*, 1881.

"*To the White House*,—

"The President's tragic death was a sad necessity, but it will unite the Republican party and save the Republic. Life is a fleeting dream, and it matters little when one goes. A human life is of small value. During the war thousands of brave boys went down without a tear. I presume the President was a Christian, and that he will be happier in Paradise than here.

"It will be no worse for Mrs. Garfield, dear soul, to part with her husband this way than by natural death. He is liable to go at any time any way.

"I had no ill-will towards the President. His death was a political necessity. I am a lawyer, a theologian, a politician. I am a Stalwart of the Stalwarts. I was with General Grant and the rest of our men in New York during the canvass. I have some papers for the press, which I shall leave with Byron Andrews and his co-journalists at 1140 N.Y. Ave., where all the reporters can see them.

"I am going to jail. CHARLES GUITEAU."

On the face of an envelope he had written :—

"I intend to place these papers, with my revolver, in the library of the State department. The reporters can copy them if they wish to in manifold. CHARLES GUITEAU."

CHAPTER II.

The Assassin in Washington Jail — His Hopes of Assistance — The Trial — The Counsel on Both Sides — The Medical Experts — Theory of the Prosecution — Guiteau's Behaviour in Court — Appears as Witness — His Written Plea — Scoville's Singular Method of Defence — Guiteau addresses the Jury — Mr. Porter's Speech — The Charge to the Jury — The Verdict and Sentence.

After being lodged in jail, Guiteau had slept quietly. He stated his conviction that the President would not recover from the wound, and waited the sequence of events to follow as he had arranged in his own mind. When assured that instead of the Stalwarts trying to excuse and support him, that every party joined in execration of the deed, he was at first quite astounded, but he soon recovered his equanimity. The people had misunderstood his motives, because his declarations had been suppressed. In time the truth would be known, when the tide of popular feeling would be turned, and they would discern the good results of his action, and become grateful to the author of it. Though the leaders of the Stalwart party could not venture at the time to support him openly, but he could not but believe that they were working secretly in his favour. The new President could never be so ungrateful as to forget the man who had made him President. At any rate he had at last attained the notoriety which he had sought all his life, nor did he seem to think that it had come in too repulsive a form.

In jail the assassin slept well, ate well, and gained flesh. He himself said that he prayed that the President might live, but did not believe that it was the Lord's will, and when the tolling of the bells announced that Garfield was dead, he regarded the end as confirming his inspiration.

The following letter might of course have been written to support the notion that he was insane. It was, however, quite in keeping with his other delusions :—

"*President Arthur, my supposed friend (strictly private)*,—

"This will introduce to you my brother, J. W. Guiteau, Esq., of Boston, who wishes to talk with you very privately about my case. He wishes to know how you and your administration feel about me. He will talk with you freely, and I wish you to trust him in the same spirit. I desire you to tell the prosecuting attorneys to go very slow.

"Yours very cordially and with great respect.
"CHARLES GUITEAU.
"IN COURT, WASHINGTON, D.C.,
  Nov. 15*th*, 1881."

Many things combined to make the trial of Charles Guiteau the most memorable which had ever occurred in the United States. The atrocious nature of the crime, the noble character and exalted position of the victim, the prolonged anxiety as to the issue of his illness, the grief of his death, which cast a shadow on every hearthstone in the States from the shores of the Atlantic to the Pacific, as well as the perplexity arising from the plea of insanity, all joined together to seize upon the attention of a people that, more than any other in the world, occupy themselves with public events. Complaints were afterwards made about the eagerness of the Executive to secure a conviction; but it is not unnatural for a Government to show some anxiety to get crime punished, and none the less so when it is directed against the Chief of the State. Nevertheless, this man, hated by a whole people as a noxious miscreant, was allowed the same rights as if he had killed the lowliest member of the community. To use the words of the District Attorney : " Defended by eminent counsel, demanding of right the full benefit of every provision of law and the protection of every guarantee of the Constitution, with the power exercised carefully to see that the jury selected are unbiassed and free from prejudice, every right is extended to the prisoner that would be granted to a criminal charged with the most insignificant offence."

The trial commenced on the 14th of November, 1881.

The presiding judge was Walter S. Cox. There appeared as counsel for the Government—George Corkhill, the District Attorney; Walter Davidge, an eminent jurist; and Judge John Porter of New York. George Scoville and Mr. Leigh Robinson appeared for the defence; but the latter, disagreeing with the line of argument, retired from the case at the outset. It was even found difficult to get a jury together to try the assassin. Of 110 men summoned, 68 declared that their minds were already made up that he should be hanged. After three days occupied with preliminaries, the case for the prosecution was opened on the 17th by Mr. Corkhill in a calm and lucid address, stating the circumstances and the pathetic results of the deed.

Witnesses were then called to prove the commission of the crime; the first was Mr. Blaine, the Secretary, who was with the President. After this, Mr. Scoville made his opening speech for the defence. Rather too long and diffuse, it was nevertheless a clear, sensible, and weighty address. Mr. Scoville (who seems to have honestly believed that the prisoner was insane when the crime was committed) probably thought that the question would be soon decided by sending for several physicians skilled in the symptoms of lunacy, who should examine Guiteau and report upon his mental condition. Had Mr. Scoville been acquainted with the prevailing opinions on insanity, he would have known that the prisoner's case was one on which opinions would be divided; and indeed a man acquainted with the published views of different experts might have made shrewd guesses what their opinions would be. Some of the medical witnesses called for the defence, though they declared Guiteau of unsound mind, also thought him responsible, or qualified their opinion in such fashion that it was of no use in a court of law. Others pronounced him sane, and some had no doubt that he was both insane and irresponsible. Out of these, Mr. Scoville formed a band of medical witnesses, men able and courageous, though somewhat undisciplined. The prosecution on their side, understanding that the plea of insanity would be the difficulty in the way of hanging Guiteau, took measures that the question should be fully met. They therefore wisely chose for their adviser Dr. John Gray of Utica, the medical superintendent of the New York State Asylum, a man of great ability, ripe experience, and imposing personality. Dr. Gray had already gained much practice as medical witness in questions of insanity. As a lecturer on mental diseases and the editor of the *American Journal of Insanity*, Dr. Gray had good means of knowing the particular views of the men who gave themselves to this study. He soon recruited an imposing team of fifteen medical witnesses. To each of them was assigned some particular point in the question, so that their testimony supported one another. Their ranks were swelled by experts summoned by the defence, who, after examining Guiteau, came to the conclusion that he was sane, or at least that he was responsible. Medical men seldom show to advantage as witnesses in courts of law. In any doubtful question they are sure to appear, swearing against one another's testimony with an emphasis which tends to bring what is called "Medical Science" into suspicion.

Those physicians who are called, or call themselves experts, are apt to think that to appear positive on doubtful questions gives them an air of infallible wisdom. While under oath in a court of law they will boldly assert to be certainties what they would only treat as probabilities before a medical society. Some of these experts at the trial deplored the weak judgment of those who had any doubt that the prisoner was sound of mind; others could not comprehend how any alienist could doubt that the prisoner was insane. Nevertheless, the question was an extremely nice one, and a man well versed in the lore of insanity might hesitate a long time what side he would take, or whether the evidence justified him taking any side at all.

A court of law is a poor place to discuss, much less settle, a difficult question of diagnosis. The lawyers, on both sides, try to mislead the jury, and confuse and bully the witnesses, and the medical men, being ostensibly summoned for one party or another, generally end by taking sides as if they were medical advocates, instead of medical witnesses. The universal abhorrence of the crime, and the pathetic descriptions which had appeared in the newspapers of the sufferings of the President during his illness, had aroused an animosity against the prisoner which, with its vast momentum, drifted the medical men whether they would or no. Most of those who appeared as thorough-going partisans had prepared themselves by taking up ground which caused them to view the case in a certain aspect. Those who upheld the sanity of Guiteau were principally men who had viewed with alarm the growing tendency to plead madness as an excuse for crime. These theorists, by their free-handed wide-sweeping definitions, had so augmented the number of the insane, that it included an alarmingly large number of the human race. On the other hand, writers of the same school appeared to hold that mental derangement and irresponsibility were convertible terms, and that it was an enormity to punish, in any way, a man unsound of mind in any form recognised by medical men. Just as the Roman Catholic clergy in the Dark Ages, with their canon laws, their absolutions, and indulgences, and their rights of sanctuary, were continually weakening the precepts of morality, and defeating the claims of justice in favour of atrocious criminals, so these medical speculators were gradually abolishing the groundwork of moral obligations and diminishing the force of the law by taking away the certainty of punishment.

The advocates of the prosecution held that Guiteau was a man who, by yielding to his enormous selfishness, and gratifying his bad passions and impulses, had become a consummate scoundrel; that failing in every way, honest and dishonest, of earning a livelihood, he had taken to electioneering in hopes of bettering his condition, and that through his wonderful self-conceit he grossly overrated the value of his services at the canvass for the presidentship; that being disappointed, he sought for revenge against the supposed ingratitude of the President in a manner which pleased his overgrown love of notoriety. A man's revengeful feelings may be so strong that he is prepared to forfeit his life in order to appease them; but it was pointed out that Guiteau foresaw the immediate dangers of his crime and took elaborate precautions for his own safety. He believed that as through the death of the President his own party would come into power with the Vice-

President Arthur, and calculated that the Stalwarts would manage to save him if he escaped the hasty fury of the crowd. This calculation was a senseless one, but we hear every day the most absurd political forecasts from men who, although foolish and ignorant, could not be properly called insane. Indeed, we know that experienced politicians have often been deplorably in fault as to the temper of the people towards some future action or measure.

Though the gentleman from Chicago worked under the disadvantage of having had little practice in Criminal Law, he had clearly an advantage in having a previous knowledge of the strange mind of the accused.

The first accounts of the trial came to Europe by the telegraph. Naturally, the reporters seized upon every striking feature and made the most of it. Dr. Godding, who was present throughout the trial, assures us that the newspaper statements conveyed an entirely erroneous impression about the laughter and applause believed to be so frequent.

"The Court room was," he tells us, "every day packed with spectators, and during the eight weeks that I was present the conduct was, with rare exception, in the language of the diurnal admonition of Marshal Henry, 'with the same propriety as if they were at church.' Indeed, I have heard laughter and applause in Henry Ward Beecher's church out of all proportion to anything that I observed in the Court room. Deputies, distributed through the room, promptly silenced any whispering or moving about in the crowd.

"The prolonged stillness was sometimes remarkable. It may be thought that the solemnity of the occasion would be, in itself, enough to repress anything like levity. A merciful provision in our organisation is that the deepest grief cannot be indefinitely prolonged; the strain would else prove fatal, or reason would be dethroned. Something dissolves away with the tears, and we have found relief. The sadness of a funeral even could not be prolonged through ten weeks, it would become ludicrous, if not intolerable. We all recall such public funerals. But while the solemnity of the Court room wore off, there was no lack of respectful decorum except on the part of the prisoner."

The advocates for the prosecution stated their belief that had Guiteau got the office he craved for, he would never have dreamed of assassinating the President, whatever might have been the political situation. They were also of opinion that if he had anticipated that his friends the Stalwarts, while profiting by Garfield's death, would never have dared to save his assassin even if they had been so disposed, he would have resisted the murderous impulse and sought revenge in some safer way.

Guiteau himself, though prepared to plead that he acted upon an irresistible pressure from the Deity when he fired the shot, that, to use his own words, "it was God's act and not his," made none of those demonstrative attempts to feign insanity which men accused of serious crimes sometimes get up. His ordinary demeanour in jail was that of a sane man, in fact, he was quick to resent any imputation against his smartness or intelligence. His memory was good, his apprehension keen, and his remarks were often ready and pointed. He had no hallucinations and no extravagant delusions, nor was there any abnormal excitement or sleeplessness. Though one might surmise that there was something wrong about his mental machinery, it was difficult to explain what it was. His own plea was that while he was lying in his bed, the idea had flashed into his mind that all the difficulties of the situation would be put an end to by the removal of the President, and that this idea possessed him night and day. He tried to resist it, and prayed to be delivered from it; but the grinding pressure of the Deity in the end forced him to commit the deed. He himself believed that this was a real inspiration; but if the jury would not admit this, they were bound to hold that it was an insane impulse. He was thus legally insane, though not medically so. Guiteau himself, both before this fixed idea and after the commission of the deed, held that he was quite sane. He called the fixed idea to kill the President "Abrahamic insanity," arguing that any one who believed that Abraham had not a real command from God to sacrifice his son Isaac would treat him as insane. Guiteau said that there were thirty-eight instances in Scripture where people were inspired by God to kill others.

The accused was allowed to sit at the bar beside his counsel. His sister, Mrs. Scoville, and his aunt, sat next him during the whole trial, hoping to cover him from being shot at. His relatives still believed that his life was in danger from a repetition of the two previous attempts to kill him on the spot.

The prisoner said he was confident that the Deity would take care of him. He kept up a desultory series of remarks and comments upon what was said in, and sometimes out of, Court. These interruptions showed the odious features of Guiteau's character, his monstrous egotism, his misplaced vanity, his petulance and ingratitude. His remarks sometimes showed a shrewd view of the bearings of the case in point, and great readiness of retort; at other times they seemed but the expression of wounded vanity and blind anger.

He frequently interrupted Mr. Scoville in an insolent manner, calling him a consummate jackass, who had taken up the case and elbowed out better advocates to gratify his own conceit. The accused freely contradicted the witnesses called for the defence, and now and then assisted the opposing counsel to cross-examine them. Dr. Gray, who thought the prisoner feigning throughout, observes that he never interrupted or insulted the medical witnesses called to prove him insane, and this in general was the case. Probably the reason was that their remarks were not so provoking to him. A mad man, like other people, is less apt to get angry with those who agree with him, than with those who oppose or thwart him. No one ever denied that Guiteau had the sense to perceive that the witnesses for the prosecution were doing something to get him hanged, while those for the defence were trying to save him.

He was especially vicious and abusive against Mr. Corkhill, perhaps because he had expected help from that gentleman, who had been a member of the Stalwart party. He was continually accusing him of suborning witnesses, and threatening him with the wrath of the Deity, much in the style that a little boy threatens his companions with chastisement at the hand of his big brother.

As the interruptions on the part of the prisoner got more and more frequent, the Court ordered him to be removed from the bar to the dock, and as his behaviour there was somewhat worse, it was even proposed to keep him out of the Court-room, and carry on the case in his absence; but this was never put into execution, as the Court was anxious that the accused man should have the full advantage of being face to face with the witnesses, and making suggestions to his counsel.

The prisoner himself as a witness gave an ingenuous confession of what he had done, apparently to support his plea of Divine inspiration. As he complained that Scoville was compromising the case by his awkward cross-examinations, he was allowed another advocate, Mr. Charles Reed. What gave Guiteau more gratification, he was allowed as associate counsel to make a speech in his own defence.

He had previously put in a written plea which he was not allowed to read. It is given by Dr. Godding,* and as he observes is a remarkable document to have been used by a lawyer to preface his plea of not guilty on his indictment for murder. After complaining of being vilified by the press, he wrote:—

"I plead not guilty to the indictment, and my defence is threefold,—

"(1.) Insanity, in that it was God's act, and not mine. The Divine (the word 'Divine' is introduced with a caret in Guiteau's manuscript) pressure on me to remove the President, was so enormous, that it destroyed my *free agency*, and therefore I am not legally responsible for my act.

"(2.) The President died from malpractice; about three weeks after he was shot, his physicians, after a careful examination, decided that he would recover. Two months after this official announcement he died. Therefore, I say, he was not fatally shot. If he had been well treated he would have recovered.

"(3.) The President died in New Jersey, and therefore beyond the jurisdiction of this Court. This malpractice and the President's death in New Jersey are special providences, and I am bound to avail myself of them on my trial, in justice to the Lord and myself. (He first wrote, 'For the Lord's reputation as well as my own,' then drew a line through it.)

"I undertake to say that the Lord is managing my case with

---

* "Two Hard Cases," p. 46.

eminent ability, and that He had a special object in allowing the President to die in New Jersey.

"His management of this case is worthy of Him as the Deity, and I have entire confidence in His disposition to protect me, and to send me forth to the world a free and innocent man. 'He uttered His voice,' says the Psalmist, 'and the earth melted.' This is the God I served when I sought to remove the President, and He is bound to take care of me. (Here he wrote again, and then erased, 'He uttered His voice and the earth melted,'—He, my God.) The Lord and the people do not seem to agree in this case.

"The people consider the President's removal an unbearable outrage, and me a dastardly assassin, and they prayed the Lord to spare the President. For nearly three months the Lord kept the President at the point of death, and then allowed him to depart, thereby confirming my act. The mere fact of the President's death is nothing.

"All men have died, and all men will die. General Burnside died suddenly, about the time the President did. The President and General Burnside were both splendid men, and no one regrets their departure more than I. The President died from malpractice, and General Burnside from apoplexy. Both were special providences, and the people ought to quietly submit to the Lord in the matter. The President would not have died, had the Lord not wanted him to go. I always think of the President's departure as a removal. I have no conception of it as a 'murder,' or as an assassination? I had no feeling of wrong-doing when I sought to remove him, because it was God's act, and not mine, for the good of the American people."

One might have expected that Mr. Scoville would have brought forward witnesses to state that they had seen and examined the prisoner, and to give their reasons for believing him to be insane. Instead of this he propounded a hypothetical question. The witness was to assume that the prisoner had a strong hereditary taint of insanity, that he had several times in his life shown symptoms of insanity, and that during the month of June, 1881, at about the expiration of said term of five years, he honestly became dominated by the idea that he was inspired by God to remove by death the President of the United States; also, that he acted upon what he believed to be such inspiration, and what he believed to be in accordance with the Divine will, in preparation for and in the accomplishment of such a purpose; also, that he committed the act of shooting the President under what he believed to be a Divine command, which he was not at liberty to disobey, and which belief amounted to a conviction that controlled his conscience and overpowered his will as to that act, "and so on." To each of his witnesses Mr. Scoville put the question, Would you believe the man so described to be insane? He reserved himself to prove by other evidence that this hypothetical question contained an accurate description of the prisoner; but this was disputed by the other side; and indeed some of the statements such as the Divine inspiration and pressure rested solely on the prisoner's own assertion. The futility of this strange line of tactics and the withering effect of Mr. Davidge's cross-examination of the medical witnesses are finely described by Dr. Codding. Speaking of the first medical witness for the defence:—

"It was," he says, "apparently a pleasure to Mr. Davidge to converse with this young man. At the second question he drew out the fact that the witness did not believe in a future state of rewards and punishments; and though this was not, strictly speaking, a scientific refutation of the prisoner's insanity, it was in effect to make a Philistine of this witness to the jury, who had stated under oath that they believed in the doctrine of the Christian religion. Dr. Kiernan bore up manfully under the keen questioning of the veteran lawyer, until he drew out the further statement that five out of every twenty-five persons that one would casually meet on the streets were on the road to the insane asylum, which finished this witness with the jury, for, as Mr. Davidge suggested, it would land two of their number there, if it were true. An important non-medical witness followed, and then Mr. Scoville said, 'Call Dr. Nichols.' There was an expectant stir and a feeling of relief in the Court-room. He was not 'an agnostic.' Dr. Nichols had been for twenty-five years superintendent of the hospital at Washington. He was more widely known and respected here than any other expert in the Court-room, probably every member of the jury knew him personally. The judge on the bench had been an official visitor of his hospital for years, and if he was to appear for the prisoner it was Hector taking the field. His testimony had saved Mary Harris, on trial for her life in the same room. And now the lawyers of the prosecution gathered themselves up. In a few words the witness stated his present position, and his length of service in different hospitals; then he replied affirmatively to the hypothetical question, and as the whole Court-room was waiting for the real testimony about the prisoner's state of mind, anticipating an intellectual treat, Mr. Scoville simply said, 'That is all.' There was blank astonishment and disappointment on all sides."

The other medical witnesses had the same question put to them, and made the same answer, indeed the question might be said to contain its own answer. It was like putting the question, "Suppose a man to be insane, is he insane?"

"In my ignorance of law," goes on Dr. Godding, "I supposed that it was merely a shrewd move of the honest gentleman from Chicago to confine his witnesses to the expert opinion on a hypothetical case, and then, if the Government introduced direct testimony from experts in regard to their observation of the prisoner since the 2nd of July to give the experts for the defence an opportunity to testify as to facts observed in Surrebuttal. I now understand the real trouble to have been a lack of positive belief on the part of the experts for the defence in the prisoner's insanity. Some were of the opinion that the man was sane, and so testified later for the Government; and those who doubted his sanity were at a loss where to class him."

Dr. Spitzka of New York came later and delivered some testimony towards the prisoner's insanity based on personal examination. He was cross-examined at great length by Mr. Davidge; but the young physician proved a fair match for the old lawyer.

The witnesses for the prosecution then appeared, eminent physicians and superintendents of asylums; in general they stated that they had examined Guiteau and found him sane, and gave their own views about heredity and the symptoms presented by the prisoner.

A great deal of irrelevant matter was introduced by the medical witnesses. The dogmatic utterances and cross-examinations about hereditary disease, though interesting in some ways, did not amount to much in a court of law; for after all you cannot prove the insanity of a man by proving that his parents have been insane. Some medical witnesses for the prosecution went the length of saying that disease is never inherited; no one, they held, was ever born insane. In fact it is difficult for a new-born child to display symptoms of insanity, or of sanity either. They affirmed that idiocy and imbecility should not be included under insanity. Dipsomania was simply drunkenness; kleptomania simply thieving. On the other side, the attempts to prove Guiteau insane from the asymmetrical shape of his head were quite unwarranted. Perfectly symmetrical heads are perhaps commoner with imbeciles than with sane people, and often men of marked mental power and unquestioned sanity have heads very deficient in symmetry. There was a good deal of fencing about moral insanity, but even granting the existence of this alleged form, it could not seriously be maintained that Guiteau was morally insane. The doctors, when pursued by the lawyers craving definitions, took refuge in the axiom that insanity consisted in disease of the brain, impairing its functions. They had, however, to acknowledge that a man might have disease of the brain without being insane, that in many cases the disease of the brain could only be inferred from the insanity, and that cases were not rare where men had been insane for years, and yet no specific alteration of the brain tissues could be detected on a careful examination after death. Thus the insanity must first be proved through the symptoms, and then the alteration in the tissues sought for, and even though none be found, we may still firmly hold that the man had died a lunatic. The real question was, "Did there exist in Guiteau decided symptoms of insanity?" Dr. Godding tells us that Dr. Gray argued that Guiteau's alleged insanity did not fall within any possible manifestations of insanity, hence, to put it in the clearest form, Guiteau was to be hanged because there was no place for him in the Utica classifications. It is quite true that insanity is the main thing to prove. After that it is of no great consequence how you label the patient. Nevertheless Dr. Gray had a right to ask those who held Guiteau to be an irresponsible lunatic to state clearly the nature and characteristics of his insanity.

What must have been the bewilderment of the twelve wretched jurymen amongst this cross fire of dogmatic assertions and flat denials; one of them, it was said, afterwards went mad under the fear that he had come to a wrong decision. Dr. Spitzka told them that it was very difficult to describe the nature of Guiteau's insanity save to experts; but it would have been easy to have got twelve experts in the Court-house who would have rejected Dr. Spitzka's description as no real portrait of the accused.

Dr. Gray of Utica came at the end of his well-disciplined team. They knew what they wanted, did not fire too high, and made fewer misses than their opponents. Dr. Gray had been called to see the prisoner shortly after the murder. He had examined him again and again, conversed with him, taken notes, conned over them, compared them with notes of other cases. He could find no evidence that the assassin had any derangement of health, even as much as a headache, while he planned the deed.

"During this time, in which he was considering the question, he held in abeyance his own act, his own intention. He controlled his own will; he controlled his own thoughts, reflections, and intentions to do or not to do the act pending the obtaining of the consulship, and the presence in him of reason, judgment, reflection, and self-control in regard to his act, controlled me in forming my opinion; also the fact that he controlled himself as to the time in which he should do this act of violence."

THE PRISONER. "The Lord don't employ a fool to do His work. Please remember that."

A. (continuing). "All of which, in the light of my experience with insane persons who have the delusion that they are controlled or directed, or commanded, or inspired by the Almighty, would be entirely inconsistent. Such self-control, self-direction, and self-guidance is antagonistic to anything I have ever seen in my personal experience in connection with the insane, having such a delusion as a command of God, or a pressure of God upon them, or an inspiration."

Taking into consideration Guiteau's careful preparation for his own safety and protection after the act, Dr. Gray observed, —"In the light of my experience with insane persons of that class, labouring under such insane delusions, there would be no preparation for personal safety, and no thought of personal safety." All those persons whom he had seen afflicted with religious delusions were very deeply insane. Dr. Gray stated his belief that the idea of pleading inspiration was an afterthought, and that he was convinced the prisoner did not believe any such thing, and that his behaviour at the trial was designed to impress the jury with the idea of his insanity.

There is some evidence that Guiteau really fancied from the beginning that the idea of slaying the President was a Divine inspiration.[*] Nevertheless, it did not appear to come with the force of a peremptory order, such as enjoined Abraham to leave the land of Haran and betake himself to Canaan, or called to Moses from the burning bush. It was clear, from evidence given at the trial, that Guiteau's conception of inspiration, which he had learned from his father, was based on the belief of a close communion of God with those who addressed them in prayer. He was apt to refer any new notion entering his mind, or any fixed idea, as Divine inspiration. He claimed[†] that he had been inspired to enter the Oneida Community, and inspired to leave his business to go wandering about as a lecturer on religion. Sometimes a Divine inspiration, which led to unfortunate results, was treated later on as the inspiration of the devil. Such a theory, which Guiteau had worn for twenty years, fitted him loosely. He acted upon it or not as circumstances rendered advisable. He could disobey it or neglect it as he disobeyed the Ten Commandments. He appears to have exaggerated and worked this idea into his mind, just as he exaggerated his natural swagger, irritability, and insolence to make an effect on the minds of the jurors.

A more ungrateful, and a more embarrassing, client advocate never had. He insisted that he had a right to be associ-

---

[*] Dr. Stearns, a witness for the prosecution, says: "From my conversation with Guiteau, and during four interviews, I became strongly impressed with the view that the inspiration idea was a part of his original plan." Dr. Stearns then cites further confirmation of this view, which indeed may be found in the official report of the trial. See "Contribution *in re* Guiteau," by Henry P. Stearns, reprinted from the Archives of Medicine, June, 1882. New York, 1882.

[†] See Official Record, pp. 597-714 and 2341.

ate-counsel, and freely ridiculed the plan of defence, and called the witnesses liars who came to support Scoville's plea. The accused was willing to get off on the open device that the jury should call insanity what he himself called Divine inspiration; but he could not bear being thought really insane during the most of his life. On one occasion, when Mr. Scoville had tried to prove something strange about his conduct, Guiteau broke out :—" I shall be hung if you don't get off this case, as sure as you are a live man. There is no luck where you are. You have been a dead weight on this case ever since you touched it. If you care for my life, get off of it. You are an unmitigated nuisance with your stinking theory. You want to know of every witness that comes on the stand if they don't think I am a fool; and they don't think so. Then you run yourself dry on cross-examination."

In an eloquent and pathetic address Mr. Reed had shown to the jury that the prisoner's conduct was incompatible with sanity, Guiteau did his best to spoil the effect of the speech with his flippant remark, " Mr. Reed is a good fellow, but I wouldn't give a cent. a bushel for his rubbish. If I get a chance at that jury, I will give them the theory to settle this case. My speech will be published in a day or two."

The hour at last came when Charles Guiteau was to deliver the oration which was to correct all Scoville's blunders, to convince the jury, and place him in the same rank with Cicero. It was a stormy day in winter, but the Court-room was crowded. He delivered it sitting, not that he was afraid of being shot, for, as he observed, " this shooting business is declining." He adjusted his glasses, took out his MS., and commenced. His address occupies twenty-four pages in the Official Report. It shows all his senseless conceit, and how little he saw of the real situation. He appeared as a patriot who had saved his country from civil war, boasted of the favour of the Deity, compared his vagabond life to that of St. Paul, and even to Christ, said that his book on " Truth " would " go thundering down the ages whatever became of his body." In one place he tried to be pathetic. After telling the misfortunes of his sad life, his mother dying when he was a child, his father a good man and able one, but a fanatic in religion, his life in the Oneida Community one of constant suffering, his married life the same, his theological life one of anxiety, he wound up, "If it had not been for this, I should have had a far happier life; but let it go. Forgetting the things behind I pressed forward. I have no doubt as to my spiritual destiny. I have always been a lover of the Lord, and whether I live one year or thirty"—and the voice had begun to tremble, and he stopped, the lip quivered, while the chin held it for a moment, the tear was stealing down the cheek before the head dropped, the handkerchief brushed it away, but he stifled it down as a weakness, and completed his sentence with "I am His." "Then," adds Godding,[*] "I allowed that if it was acting it surpassed anything I had ever witnessed. No, it was too real for acting. That religious faith is real, though insane."

He read some passages from senseless letters which he had received. What he had done he was forced to do by the inspiration of the Deity. "Nothing that the Deity directs a man to do violates any law." He blandly recommended the jury to acquit him on the plea of transitory mania. Towards the close of his discourse he denounced Mormonism, and said, that were he President, he would speedily clear out these detestable Mormons. "Perhaps in 1884," he said, "I shall get a chance at them." He reminded the jury that, at the Last Day, they would stand in the presence of God. "As you act here," he cried, "so will be your final abode in the great hereafter. I beg you do not get the Deity down on you by meddling with this case."

"I beg, for your own sakes, and for the sake of the American people, and for the sake of generations yet unborn, that you let this case alone. You cannot afford to touch it. Let your verdict be that it was the Deity's act not mine."

Thus Charles J. Guiteau concluded his last lecture, mightily pleased with the noble figure he had shown to the world.

Having got twelve men forced to listen to them, the lawyers did not let them off easily. Davidge occupied two days with his address; Porter three; Scoville had five days; and Reed

---

[*] "Two Hard Cases," p. 234.

two. Guiteau himself had his address another day. They might be held to present to the jury four portraits; Guiteau crazy from childhood, or from the time he entered the Oneida Community; Guiteau the pious, canting hypocrite, a consummate actor; and then, under this mask, Guiteau the swindler, the disappointed office-seeker, "the malignant, diabolical, cold-blooded murderer, the rattlesnake without the rattle, but not without the fangs;" finally as limned by the assassin himself, the inspired Guiteau doing God's will by removing the President and saving the American people from civil war. What bitterness it must have been to this man, with his irritable vanity, to have the infamy of his whole life rehearsed before him by such a master of invective as Mr. Porter, in presence of an audience who looked on him with loathing eyes. His interruptions were frequent and furious, but only to his own further pain, for the skilful orator easily turned them against the interrupter, like a strong man overpowering a child, grasping his tiny arms and forcing him to belabour himself with his own fists. When Guiteau in his impotent fury threatened his tormenter with the wrath of the Deity, Porter could pay him back in as savage a fashion. Take the following sample:—

The Prisoner. I think the Almighty is stronger than the law.

Mr. Porter (continuing). He will come presently before the Almighty, and had better postpone his argument in defence, if he has any to make, until then.

The Prisoner. You had better postpone yours.

Mr. Porter. He will feel soon what he has never felt before, a Divine pressure, and in the form of a hangman's rope.

With what power of sarcasm does he expose the prisoner's plea of *mania transitoria*.

Mr. Porter. Let us resume the reading. I claim transitory mania.
The Prisoner (interjecting). Yes, sir.
Mr. Porter (continuing to read). That is all there is of the case.
The Prisoner (interjecting). That is exactly it, sir. That is all I claimed from the start.
Mr. Porter (continuing). I don't claim that I am insane any more than you are, except, on—not *before*, not *after*—on the 2nd of July.

When the sun rose on the morning of the 2nd of July, President Garfield was in the full vigour of health and life, honoured and trusted, respected and beloved. When the sun went down that day, General Garfield was in the agonies of a long, slow, torturing, and lingering death. A great calamity had in the meanwhile happened to this swindling Guiteau. When the sun rose that morning he woke from a refreshing night's sleep. He took his bath; he ate his hearty meal; he examined his bull-dog pistol, which he had bought some weeks before; he found it was in working condition; he wiped it to keep it so; he wrapped it up carefully; he arranged the papers which were to be found in his pockets after the murder; he arranged those that were to be hurried off by telegraph that day by the telegraphic wire; he went to the depôt; he completed the arrangements for his own safety; he provided for all the contingencies that might arise. Once more, he thought he had better look at the weapon of murder; he went to a water-closet, examined it, and approved it. He came out and watched the people as they entered, unconscious of the presence of an armed murderer. He waylaid the President. *Just then*—JUST THEN, he was seized with an attack of transitory mania, fired, fired again, and while President Garfield was swaying to the ground, he turned to find his way to that pre-engaged carriage, when he was intercepted by the policeman. His transitory mania was gone.

THE PRISONER (interjecting). I had had it for thirty days.

Mr. PORTER (continuing). This is the insanity which he sets up as a defence. You will remember that he claims he was insane for thirty days from the first of June.

THE PRISONER (interjecting). That is correct, sir.

Mr. PORTER (continuing). But when he saw how that was used against him, when he discovered, by the course of the argument, that this was fatal to his theory——

THE PRISONER (interjecting). It was not fatal.

Mr. PORTER (continuing). He fell back on the Abrahamic theory of transitory mania, and his last utterance before you was one which excluded the thirty days. I read his words:—

I don't claim that I was any more insane than you are, and never have, except on the 2nd of July, 1881.

It is rare that a pious Christian man like Judge Porter has a fit occasion for such choice railing as this:—

"The evidence shows Guiteau to have been cunning, crafty, and remorseless, utterly selfish from his youth up, low and brutal in his instincts, inordinate in his love of notoriety, eaten up by a thirst for money, which has gnawed into his soul like a cancer; a beggar, a hypocrite, a canter, a swindler, a lawyer, who, with many years of practice in two great cities, never won a cause, and you know why; a man who has left in every State through which he passed a trail of knavery, fraud, and imposition; a man who has lived at the expense of others, and when he succeeded in getting possession of their funds, appropriated them to his own private use, in breach of every honourable obligation and every professional trust; a man capable of mimicking the manners and aping the bearing of a gentleman; who bought at pawnbrokers' shops the cast-off clothing, for which he paid, when his credit elsewhere was exhausted; and then, with his plausibility of religious cant, his studied skill as an actor, his unscrupulous self-commendation, drifting about from State to State professing to be engaged in the work of the Lord; a man who, as a lawyer, collected doubtful debts by dogging the debtor, pocketed the money as against his clients, and chuckled over their credulity in trusting him; a man who pawned counterfeit watches as gold to eke out a professional livelihood; a man capable even of endeavouring to blast the name of the woman with whom he had slept for years, and whom he acknowledged to have been a true and faithful wife; capable of palming himself off upon the public, upon Christian associations, upon Christian Churches, from city to city, as a pure and upright man, who had spent six years in shameless fornication; a man who afterwards, when he wished to get rid of his wife, consulted the commandments of God, and reading, 'Thou shalt not commit adultery,' went out and committed it with a prostitute."

While the jury were still under the spell of the eloquent words of the great advocate, Judge Cox gave his charge, very ably put, full of instructive precedents and nice distinctions, which looked as if they would solve any perplexity; but somehow or other in the present case it was difficult to apply them. It did not look as if the calm and subtle judge had himself arrived at a clear decision. He seems to have thought the prisoner hardly sane, but had less doubt about his being responsible. His final summing was in these words:—

"If you find from the whole evidence that, at the time of the commission of the homicide, the prisoner, in consequence of disease of mind, was labouring under such a defect of his reason that he was incapable of understanding what he was doing, or that it was wrong,—

as, for example, if he was under an insane delusion that the Almighty had commanded him to do the act, and in consequence of that he was incapable of seeing that it was a wrong thing to do,—then he was not in a responsible condition of mind, and was an object of compassion and not of justice, and ought to be now acquitted.

"On the other hand, if you find that he was under no insane delusions, such as I have described, but had possession of his faculties, and the power to know that his act was wrong, and of his own free will deliberately conceived, planned, and executed this homicide, then, whether his motive was personal vindictiveness, or political animosity, or a desire to avenge a supposed political wrong, or a morbid desire for notoriety, or fanciful ideas of patriotism, or of the Divine will, or you are unable to discover any motive at all, the act is simply *murder*, and it is your duty to find him guilty."

After their ten weeks' course of law and psychology the jury were now to decide the vexed problem whether the man was sane or insane, whether he should hang or not. The counsel and relations of Guiteau were at the bar expecting an acquittal on the ground of insanity. At the worst, there was said to be one juryman who had doubts, having had experience of insanity in his own family, and a disagreement would entail a new trial. It was a dark, stormy day in mid-winter, the dingy Court-room was packed with spectators all gazing at one little man, ashy pale, with deadened eye, and hunted look. The dusk of evening was setting in when the jury retired to deliberate. After an hour they returned; the foreman gave a verdict of guilty. "So say we all," repeated the jurors. At the request of Scoville the jury was polled. All said, Guilty. The prisoner shouted out, "My blood be on the head of that jury." "Found guilty," was passed along the crowded corridors and down the steps below; passing from mouth to mouth the word fluttered the sea of heads, white and black, that filled the great square. The whole of Washington was waiting for the verdict. The wild shout of gratified revenge for the sufferings of the murdered President ceased for a minute as the condemned man issued out, followed by his sister and aunt, who clung to him still. He shook them off, saying, "I don't want any women folks crying round around me. You needn't worry about me, I'm all right; you'd better go back and look after that judge and jury, the Deity's down on them;" a way was cleared for him—he entered the van. The door was shut to—the black porter stood on the step—the van rattled away to the jail, followed by the mounted guard.

On the 4th of February Guiteau was brought to Court once more. When asked what he had to say why sentence should not be passed on him, the prisoner repeated the old threats. "Those Jews," he said, " put the despised Galilean into the grave, and they had their way for a little time, but at the destruction of Jerusalem, forty years after, the Almighty got even with them. I tell you I am here as God's man. I have no fear of death. Kill me to-morrow if you want to. I am here as God's man, and have been from the start. I care not what men shall do with me."

When the Court in pronouncing sentence of death came to the words, "And may God have mercy on your soul," the condemned man cried out, wildly, "And may God have mercy upon your soul; I am a great deal better off to-day than that jury is."

There were appeals and requests for a new trial, and a petition to have a fresh inquiry into the man's sanity. In the meantime Guiteau kept cheerful and hopeful, selling his photographs and signatures. He had gained notoriety, and was making money at last. All the appeals were in vain. The stream of life was nearing the abyss.

CHAPTER III.

Guiteau's behaviour at his Execution—The Autopsy—The Question of his Insanity—Its Character—Was he Responsible?— Felton and Bellingham.

No doubt many people put the question how would the condemned man demean himself at his execution? Those who thought that he was feigning might fairly presume that, when all hope of a respite was over, the assassin would, in the immediate expectation of appearing before his Omniscient Judge, show signs of fear, if not of remorse. On the other hand, some of those physicians who had averred their belief in his insanity, notably Godding, M'Farland, and Beard, ventured to predict that Guiteau would go on unchanged, to the last maintaining that he was God's man, and claiming merit for his crime instead of forgiveness. And so it turned out. "The Last Chapter in the Life of Guiteau," by Dr. Godding,[*] so finely written that one grudges to abridge any of it. The greater part of Dr. Godding's description is, therefore, given in the following pages :—

"On the 24th of June, 1882, the spiritual adviser of Guiteau, the Rev. Dr. W. W. Hicks, informed him that all efforts for a respite had failed; that President Arthur had declined to interfere with the execution of the sentence on the 30th of June; that his decision was final, and that nothing remained but to make ready for the event. It was thought best for the criminal to disabuse his mind of false hopes, and thus end the pretence, the bravado which had kept him up so long, and by so doing, give him time to make serious preparation

---

[*] Dr. Godding's paper appeared in *The Alienist and Neurologist* for October, 1882. It was reprinted in the same periodical for July, 1884, towards the end of an article by Dr. M. J. Madigan entitled, "Was Guiteau insane?"

for eternity. And the whole community experienced a relief at this, they felt that the farce had gone far enough; and keen eyes watched for the 'weakening,' that, often announced, never came. But still sleep came to him as it comes to a child, his digestion was undisturbed, and to all outward appearance, the sunrise, as it came through the window of his cell on the morning of his execution, was to him the same welcome light that it was when he went to enjoy it in Lafayette Park on the morning of the 2nd of July, 1881. If, as he said to Dr. Hicks, and saying maintained it to the last, 'he had done God's service and had nothing to repent of,' he could well be calm. One year before, he had written, 'Life is a fleeting dream, and it matters little when one goes. A human life is of small value,' and now he was confronted by his own statement. But he really meant this when he wrote it, and he accepted it for himself now. It is too late for me to doubt the sincerity of this man's belief; in his egotism he posed before the world, but he was not playing at a farce with the Almighty. In his religious faith he was as terribly in earnest as John Brown, of Osawatomie, but without the intensity of that old man's devotion.

"I think he was most fortunate in his spiritual adviser. Dr. Hicks, having lived a stirring life in both hemispheres, and having been brought in contact with all kinds of men, knew human nature thoroughly. He found Guiteau sincere in his religious belief. He did not claim to be an expert in mental pathology, but that he was in the pathology of sin is undoubted, and when this criminal bared his inmost soul at the confessional, and the Dr. was convinced that he told him the truth, he did not make the mistake that so many divines would have made, of asking him to turn infidel to the religious convictions on which his life had been staked. With such blind faith, what chance was there for him to repent as the Church sees repentance? The pulpit from the first had been instant in demanding his execution, and now these Pharisees of 'long robes,' hearing his blasphemy, gathered up their skirts and fled from him as from one accursed. This clergyman alone, not attempting to convert, was content simply to 'hold the cross' even to his dying eyes, not daring to assume to limit the possibilities of the Infinite compassion. If this was not bearing worthy testimony to his Master in the face of a frowning Church, I do not know what is. To me this is the one bright spot in all this sad business.

"Winning Guiteau's confidence, Dr. Hicks had great control over him, and I know was thereby able to prevent some steps he was disposed to take which were, at least, unwise. For example, Guiteau had conceived a strange fancy to go in robes of white, and determined that he would be hung in his shirt and drawers alone, and could not be dissuaded from this by his friends. Dr. Hicks told him that the doctors would be sure to point to that absurd costume as conclusive evidence of insanity, and Guiteau was so averse to giving any countenance to the idea that he was really insane that he abandoned his project. He said to Dr. Hicks, 'If you say I am insane I will believe it, but I believe I am sane. I believe I am God's man, I believe I was commissioned to do this work, and I am no more insane than you are.' This was the rock on which he rested, and whatever Dr. Hicks thought, we may be sure he kindly left the word insane unspoken.

"But while Guiteau was ready to leave a world that had grown weary of him, he had still something to say as to the manner of his going. The most egotistic of men was not likely to omit his valedictory, or make it less a gala day because he was the chief actor; the drop scene was merely an unavoidable incident that would only heighten the effect. Nor did he propose to conduct the exercises on an empty stomach—he knew the value of a square meal, though he seldom paid for one. So, after a substantial breakfast, having taken a bath and his usual exercise, both hygienic measures, he sat down to write 'Simplicity,' a poem! Within the last few weeks of his life, Guiteau had taken to writing poetry (?). I here insert two verses from a mystery published in the *Washington Star* newspaper of 17th June, 1882, which sufficiently illustrate his style. It is entitled 'God's Ways.'

"Thou Jehovah!
All things created
Save the evil one!
He being uncreated
Like Thyself.
(See my book.)

* * * *

"The retribution came,
Quick and sharp,
In fire and blood,
In shot and shell,
In endless pain!
Like a jumping tooth,
Lasting for ever and ever!
(A jumping tooth
Gives an idea of hell,
And that is what
Those Jews got!)"

"The parenthesis in each case lets us down from too dizzy a flight, but I think the world was no more ready for his poetry than for his evangel, 'The Truth.'

"But to return, there was much to be done that morning that everything should move off right. Time, for him rapidly merging into eternity, made moments precious, but how could the last half-hour be more profitably spent than in enjoying a hearty dinner, which he had ordered earlier than usual, having requested Warden Crocker to have the procession move at 12 o'clock M. sharp, he knowing how important it was to be punctual and not keep the invited guests waiting. But this wonderful criminal forgot nothing; at the eleventh hour he sent out his shoes to be blacked! It will be remembered that the same office was performed for him at the railroad station on the morning of the 2nd of July, 1881. This was to be another of his field days, and he went to that platform as to a dress parade. At the first step of the gallows he tripped, and said with a smile to Dr. Hicks, who caught his arm, 'I stubbed my toe going to the gallows.' And this was the man they expected would 'weaken'! How little they knew him.

"On the scaffold he stood erect, master of the ceremonies, prepared to conduct his last prayer meeting, assisted by Rev. Dr. Hicks. For twenty years this anomalous being had taken a real pleasure in prayer meetings, it was his privilege to be present at one more. He stood there and looked down into the cold unsympathetic faces, many of them present at a prayer meeting for the first time. But he knew that he was speaking to an audience beyond those dull ears, and that the echoes of his voice would be heard outside the limits of those stone walls which formed his horizon, and past that day's shadows. The clouds of tobacco smoke rolled up like incense from that sensation-seeking crowd; it is but charitable to hope that his prayers rose higher and with a more acceptable savour.

"Dr. Hicks, visibly affected, commenced the services, with a brief but fitting supplication 'out of the depths:' he then held the Bible for the pinioned man to read, and Guiteau, 'cool as an iceberg,' as the *New York Herald* correspondent remarked, said, so distinctly that his voice filled the corridor and everyone heard him, 'I will read a selection from the tenth chapter of Matthew,' naming the verses. Then he opened on that motley audience with a Scripture lesson that they well might heed, commencing, 'And fear not them that kill the body but are not able to kill the soul,' continuing thence for fourteen verses. The *New York Times* correspondent says, 'As he read the verses, sometimes looking on the book and sometimes upon the people before him, he seemed to lose sight of the gallows, and declaimed the words with great earnestness and much dramatic effect.' At that verse which seemed a most precious promise that he applied to himself, 'He that loseth his life for My sake shall find it,' he was eloquent. Then followed that remarkable prayer, which he had written out and had patterned after the seventeenth chapter of St. John. It was delivered in the same firm and, at times, impassioned voice. Then, after a moment's pause, another paper was unfolded before his eyes, and this cool, self-possessed man said, '"Except ye become as a little child ye cannot enter into the kingdom of heaven." I am now going to read some verses which are intended to indicate my feelings at the moment of leaving this world. If set to music they may be rendered very effective. The idea is that of a child babbling to his mamma and his papa. I wrote it this morning about ten o'clock.' He had come to the most trying part of the whole ordeal, the childish babble was to be assumed, and he was to babble to his Father in heaven some of his fearful verses. He humbled himself, this sane man! and thus became as a little child that so he might enter into the kingdom of heaven. This was his new birth; this was that childhood to which he doubtless thought these verses, when set to music, would hereafter afford an effective entrance for other souls, verses written by Guiteau the martyr, like those old hymns that have come down to us from the early Church, hallowed with the blood of the saints, and whose triumphant strains have wafted heavenward many a parting spirit. Here is the hymn that he entitled—

"'SIMPLICITY.'

"'I am going to the Lordy, I am so glad,
I am going to the Lordy, I am so glad,
I am going to the Lordy,
Glory hallelujah! Glory hallelujah!
I am going to the Lordy!

"'I love the Lordy with all my soul,
Glory hallelujah!
And that is the reason I am going to the Lord,
Glory hallelujah! Glory hallelujah!
I am going to the Lord.

"'I saved my party and my land
Glory hallelujah!
But they have murdered me for it,
And that is the reason I am going to the Lordy.
Glory hallelujah! Glory hallelujah!
I am going to the Lordy!

"'I wonder what I will do when I get to the Lordy,
  I guess that I will weep no more
  When I get to the Lordy !
    Glory hallelujah !

"'I wonder what I will see when I get to the Lordy,
  I expect to see most glorious things,
  Beyond all earthly conception,
  When I am with the Lordy !
    Glory hallelujah ! Glory hallelujah !
    I am with the Lord.'

"At last he 'weakened,' he broke down in his recital, not from fear but from genuine emotion. So real to him were his childish pleadings, that the tears came welling up. For a moment all vindictive feeling was gone, the pride of 'God's man' was bowed down, even the egotism disappeared, and he was sobbing like a child as he prattled of the time when he 'would weep no more,' and the heaven where he should 'see most splendid things.' Then proudly he remembered he was master of ceremonies still, and his sobs were hushed and his voice rose, as he closed exultantly with "Glory hallelujah ! Glory hallelujah ! I am with the Lord.'

"And so the end came. Dr. Hicks pronounced the benediction. Guiteau stood proudly erect while the functionary of the law performed his final offices, and as the quickly drawn cap shut from his eyes the last gleam of our sunlight, those orbs turned to watch for the first dawn of the coming brightness, needing no sun to light it, and, master of ceremonies still, he let fall the paper on which his prayer was written as the signal agreed upon with the warden, and saying firmly, 'Glory, ready, go,' he went away.

"Realising how intense must have been the gratification to his mind from all this pageant, even though a momentary pang followed, and, knowing how little the insane man considers bodily pain when controlled by his delusions, I was prepared to admit that this had been euthanasia to him, even though I had been unwilling to avail myself of my ticket to witness his happiness."

The body was examined an hour and a-half after death by Dr. D. S. Lamb,[*] the curator of the army medical museum, in

---

[*] A full account of the autopsy will be found in the *Journal of Mental Science*, January, 1883. Any one who wishes further information should see *The Alienist and Neurologist* for July, and October, 1882, January, 1883, and July, 1884.

Three medical reports were published, the official one by Dr. Lamb, presence of a number of physicians. The principal lesions found in Guiteau's brain were adhesions of the dura mater to the inner table of the skull along the longitudinal sinus, and another signed by Drs. Dana and Morton, and a third by Drs. Hartigan and Sowers. There was also a report of the microscopic appearances of the brain, signed by Drs. Arnold, Shakespeare, and M'Connell.

Writing in the *American Journal of Neurology and Psychiatry*, August, 1882, Dr. Spitzka lays much stress on the asymmetry of the convolutions in either hemisphere, especially those of the island of Riel, in which there were in the right side five fissures and six straight gyri, and on the left side seven fissures and eight straight gyri. As a rule, the right hemisphere seemed somewhat less developed than the left. Unfortunately the two hemispheres were not weighed separately. Asymmetrical brains are not uncommon with quite sane people. Dr. Spitzka states that "aberration in development of the kind discovered in Guiteau's brain has not yet been found in others than persons of unsound mind," and that "the only finding in the brains of constitutional lunatics of monomaniacal tendencies, which promises to establish a relation between the insane and the state of the brain, consists in such architectural anomalies." These statements, if they could be proved, would settle the question; but I doubt whether they can be proved.

While in jail Guiteau suffered from attacks of malarial fever, and the spleen was found to be enlarged.

A piece of the "frontal convex" of Guiteau's brain was sent to Dr. Savage, of Bethlem Hospital. The opinion formed from his microscopical examination is thus quoted by Dr. J. J. Elwell, *Alienist and Neurologist*, October, 1883, p. 645 :—" I should say there is nothing that I have seen which is not compatible with mental health. It is true there are changes about the vessels and their walls, but these and similar changes are commonly found in bodies of persons dying or being killed when past middle age. There are no marked general changes in the nerve cells, and I can only repeat that the specimen examined would not have any weight with me in causing me to reconsider my judgment on the sanity of the assassin."

It is not surprising that those who upheld the sanity of Guiteau should have laid stress upon this statement, for Dr. Savage is an excellent microscopist, and wary in making too much of the import of his findings. Nevertheless, not being present at the autopsy, his evidence was only negative. He may have been served with a piece of brain sounder than other parts.

In reply to a letter about this matter, Dr. Savage writes to me :—" I saw and examined a small piece of Guiteau's brain, and that there was nothing in it pointing to general morbid changes.

" I cannot go so far as to say that, on the strength of that examination, I should be prepared to give a judgment on the sanity of any man. All along I looked upon Guiteau as an unstable person, but I should have been rather astonished if I had found much change in his brain."

adhesion of the dura to the pia mater, and to the brain at a spot on the vertex. There were thickening and milky discoloration of the arachnoid over the sulci in the whole convexity of both hemispheres of the brain. There was unusual paleness of the central medullary matter, which was almost quite anæmic. On microscopic examination of the brain tissue, the walls of the blood-vessels were found to be affected with granular degeneration in numerous minute areas throughout the cortical layers. These layers appeared to the naked eye to be thinner than usual in some places, especially in the frontal lobes. The nerve cells and cells of the neuroglia in the grey matter were found in many places to be degenerated. These appearances indicated the existence of past inflammations; storms within the assassin's brain, which had left their silent traces in adhesions of one tissue to the other, in degeneration of the vascular walls, and in wasting of the nerve cells. Such appearances have been found in persons not insane, in drunkards, and aged people, but no one asserts that they are not proofs of disease. Indeed, brains with fewer and less distinct marks of morbid changes are not unfrequently found in those who have been years in asylums. Thus the examination of Guiteau's brain, though it did not positively demonstrate that he had been insane, must be held to add weight to the arguments of those who sustained that opinion.

It looks like presumption to hazard an opinion where so many eminent physicians were divided after having seen and examined the prisoner, nevertheless, with the space allotted to this paper, it must be written under a certain view; some features of the case must be selected as characteristic, and others rejected as less so. Then, we are in possession of facts which had not come to the jury or to the experts at the trial, new documents afterwards published, the prisoner's behaviour at his execution, and the results of the examination of his brain, all of which throw more light on the question of his sanity. In giving my own views I should not like to be suspected of insinuating a pretension to any superiority of knowledge or judgment; nevertheless, I cannot resist recording the belief that Guiteau had a mind of altogether abnormal character. This indeed was admitted by many who took the side of the prosecution. But then, they urged, every murderer must have something in his mind different from those who obey the laws,—as Mr. Corkhill said in his opening speech, "Crime is never natural. The man who attempts to violate the laws of God and society goes counter to the ordinary course of human action. He is a world to himself. He is against society, against organisation, and of necessity his action can never be measured by the rules governing men in the everyday transactions of life." Assuredly it is often difficult to say where the blackguard ends and the lunatic begins.

Some of the medical witnesses for the prosecution put the question, When did Guiteau begin to be insane? They evidently looked for a disturbing disease which should alter or modify his character,* but we do not think that his form

---

* Dr. Henry P. Stearns, superintendent of the Retreat for the Insane, Hartford, Connecticut, was originally summoned for the defence; but after examining Guiteau in prison, he arrived at the opinion that he was sane, and responsible for the crime. He appeared as a witness for the prosecution. Knowing Dr. Stearns to be a man of great knowledge and calm judgment, I am disposed to lay much weight upon his study of the case. It is, however, to be noted that in a paper already quoted, Dr. Stearns, after showing that Guiteau at the time he fired at the President proved in many ways that he possessed considerable circumspection and self-control concludes that "his act in shooting the President was not the result of a pathological condition of his brain." Dr. Stearns observes that "there is no evidence that Guiteau ever experienced any such marked or particular change in the character of his intelligence, or in his conduct or ability to reason as indicated disease of brain."

It does not, however, follow, Dr. Stearns goes on, "that Guiteau is in all respects like other men, or like other great criminals. On the contrary, it seems to me that his general course in life indicates something quite different and exceptional." Amongst other peculiarities Dr. Stearns mentions: "He has now, and has always had, an unbalanced brain—*i.e.*, one with its faculties unequally arranged or developed. He has always been greatly egotistical, self-reliant, and sanguine in reference to all that relates to himself.

"While he has some faculties well developed, he has a faulty and weak judgment in reference to his own purposes, convictions, and motives; and also as to the motives and probable course of action in other persons. He also appears to be without that common-sense which enables persons to accurately appreciate the conditions of society, and adjust themselves thereto, so as to get on without friction."

"He has had an ambition to be and do more than he has been willing of insanity required such a disturbing force to be proved. We do not think sanity was ever implanted in Guiteau's character. Sanity implies the capability of a man living in such consonance with the society in which he is cast as not to come into continual collision with its beliefs, rules, customs, and modes of life. We doubt whether Guiteau was born with a mind which could attain to this; and unhappily his education was not of a kind to help his congenital tendencies, and his vicious mode of life intensified them. Even amongst the socialists of Oneida, avowed rebels against society, Guiteau was a mutineer. His mind was never rightly balanced, his egotism distorted everything. In relation to himself, he never observed anything truly nor reasoned correctly. He never settled at anything in which he had a chance of succeeding; he never succeeded in anything which he undertook, and never knew why he failed. His intellect was of the kind that is perpetually led astray by fancies and chimeras. He was sharp enough in observing points here and there, but never comprehended a whole situation. He never could take a right forecast of the effect of his own actions, or the course of future events. He could jerk out a pointed remark, which would make people begin to think him clever, but the next sentence would show the radical weakness of his intellect. To find out persons of this sort it is best to let them talk on. In a conversation with well-timed rejoinders they as it were lean upon the person with whom they are conversing, and are kept on towards a straight line by his sensible and coherent replies; but, left alone to themselves, these persons slope away on their fatal zig-zags.

---

or able to qualify himself for doing; he has been inconstant of purpose, partly from lack of mental discipline, and partly from innate quality of mind. His desire to be in some conspicuous position appears to have been so boundless as to lead him to place a false estimate on conditions and qualifications requisite, if, indeed, he ever was capable of estimating them.

"As a consequence of this unfortunate arrangement and development of mental faculties, and still more unfortunate educational influences, and not from disease of brain, he has never been in harmony with the surroundings of his life."

This explains why Guiteau's craziness was oftener recognised by those who heard him make a speech, than by those who held a conversation with him.

My view is, that his mental derangement was of a hereditary character, and of slow growth; that it went on increasing, passing from manifest absurdities into delusions which, had his life not been checked, would have taken more and more the decided and unmistakable hue of lunacy. The process consisted in the overgrowth of some parts of his nature, and the dwarfing of other parts. What medical men would call a general hypertrophy of some mental faculties with an atrophy of others. There was, therefore, no sudden change in his character, but a gradual deformed growth. In my opinion, Dr. Kiernan in treating Guiteau as a case of Primäre Verrückheit,* put him into his right place amongst the insane.

---

* Official Report, p. 758.

In the German Retrospect for the *Journal of Mental Science*, April, 1879, I had the honour of introducing this new division of insanity to the Medico-Pyschological Association. At a meeting of the German Alienists, at Nuremberg, in 1877, the following resolution, proposed by Dr. Meynert, was unanimously adopted: "The members of the German Verein for Psychiatry agree in recognising, besides melancholia and mania, a third original form of mental disease,—primary craziness, or insanity primäre Verrückheit." After giving a description, "I observed that any physician of experience must know cases which might very well be included under this new form."

Dr. Kempster, superintendent of the Northern Hospital for the Insane, in the State of Wisconsin, who had treated above 4000 lunatics, when questioned by the District Attorney about primary insanity, gave the following answer: "I have never seen such a case, sir, and I do not know that there can be such a case; because, before a person can be insane, there must be a change in the natural habits and characteristics of the individual, and if a person was born insane there could be no such change. I do not recognise such a form of insanity."—Official Record, p. 1535.

Now, we can understand that a man's being born insane might interfere with his becoming insane; but if he were so born, there is no need for any change in his natural characteristics, unless to become sane. It is sad that Dr. Kempster did not recognise primary insanity, yet he had been supplied with some of the elements of conviction. A year before the murder of Garfield, Dr. Spitzka described this form under the term of "Paranoia" (in the *New York Medical Gazette*, 15th May, 1860, quoted in the *Alienist and Neurologist*, January, 1889, p. 5).

"Paranoia is based on an acquired or inherited neuro-degenerative

The real difficulty was, it seems to me, that Guiteau's insanity had not reached such a decided stage that it could be

taint, and manifesting itself in anomalies of the conceptional sphere, which while they do not destructively involve the entire mental mechanism, dominate it; that is, there is a permanent undercurrent of perverted mental current action peculiar to the individual, running like an unbroken thread through his whole mental life,—obscured, it may be, for these patients are often able to correct and conceal their insane symptoms; but it nevertheless exists, and it only requires friction to bring it to the surface. The general intellectual status is moderately fair, and often the mental powers are sufficient to keep the delusion under check for the practical purposes of life. While many are what is termed crotchety, irritable and depressed, yet the sole mental symptoms of the typical cases of this disease consist of the fixed delusions. Since the subject-matter of the delusion is of such a nature that these patients consider themselves either the victims of a plot, or unjustly deprived of certain rights and positions, or as narrowly observed by others, delusions of persecutions are added to the fixed ideas, and the patient becomes sad, thoughtful, or depressed in consequence. The patient is depressed logically so far as his train of ideas is concerned, and his sadness and thoughtfulness have causes which he can explain, and which are all intimately allied with that peculiar faulty grouping of ideas which constitute the rendezvous, as it were, of all the mental conceptions of the patient. Nay, the process may be reversed, the patient, beginning with a hypochondriacal or hysterical state, imagines himself to be watched with no favourable eye. Because he is watched or made the subject of audible comments (illusional or hallucinatory), he concludes he must be a person of some importance. Some great political movement takes place; he throws himself into it either in a fixed character that he has already constructed for himself, or with the vague idea that he is an influential personage. He seeks interviews, holds actual conversations with the big men of the day, accepts the common courtesy shown him by those in office as a tribute to his value; is rejected, however: then judges himself to be the victim of jealousy and rival cabals; makes intemperate and querulous complaints or perhaps makes violent attacks on them, and being incarcerated in a jail or asylum, looks upon this as the end of a long series of persecutions which have broken the power of a skilled diplomatist, a capable military commander, a prince of the blood, the agent of a camarilla, or finally, the Messiah Himself."

Dr. Lombroso points out that those alienists who maintained Guiteau's insanity at the trial neglected to refer to his handwriting, which, the Italian professor tells us, exactly reproduces the model given by him of the writing of the insane. Lombroso reproduces the signature of Guiteau, and compares it with the handwriting of lunatics. Guiteau's writing is thick and heavy, as if done with a reed pen.

See Lombroso's interesting book, " L'Uomo di Genio in rapporto alla Psychiatria." Turin, 1888.

recognised without hesitation. It is possible that two alienists, one taking a restricted view of the domain of insanity, and the other a wider view, might be agreed in all the facts of the case, and yet severally hold Guiteau to be insane and sane. The lunacy was not manifested by one fact in particular, but by his view of the whole situation. The belief that his hanging on at committee rooms entitled him to a diplomatic post for which he had no qualifications; that the Republican party would be ruined, or that civil war would take place unless Garfield were removed; that if he were shot the Stalwarts would approve of the murder and screen the assassin from justice; that he would be safe when securely lodged in jail, with the collateral advantage that the notoriety gained by the crime would create a demand for his book and bring its merits into notice, and that the pistol would be an object of attention in a museum; that in the end men would approve of the deed, and that his speeches would stand by the side of Cicero's orations, and his name go thundering down the ages; and behind all, the delusion that God had inspired and sustained the idea to kill the President; his absurd and provoking interruptions during the trial, and his crazy behaviour at his execution;—all these form a totality of symptoms which mark Guiteau as a lunatic. It may be well doubted whether any sane man could have written the childish verses and repeated the blasphemous prayers which he did on that awful occasion. For a sane man to have composed anything like the crazy speech which Guiteau delivered in his own defence, he would have needed to have something like the dramatic genius of Shakespeare. While the prisoner during the trial seemed to have exaggerated his natural insolence and petulance, in my opinion, he was not feigning in any other sense.

This would be like an angry man making the most of his own wrath in order to impress others, or like a sorrowful man nursing his grief. For the same persons to try to show themselves pleased or joyful would be a quite different exertion. Guiteau with his surpassing egotism was not fitted to be a good actor. A man feigning insanity would try to step out of himself, to appear something different. Lunatics sometimes try to feign insanity. I was once sent to see a woman in a jail about whose mental condition there was some perplexity. She had committed a theft, and was afraid of punishment. The opinion I arrived at was that, though the woman was really insane, she was trying to pass herself off as a lunatic to avoid trial. The result was a grotesque imitation of madness, the real insanity behind the mimicry stood out as something quite different. The argument of Dr. Gray, that because Guiteau tried to plead insanity to escape punishment, therefore he could not be insane, was a mere play of words. Guiteau plainly put it that the jury should call his inspiration insanity, and so acquit him. He said in so many words that he did not believe in his own plea; he himself thought the inspiration real, and would have been pleased if the jury had brought him in not guilty, as doing God's will.

Dr. Gray told the jury that in his experience of twelve thousand lunatics of all ranks he had found that "insane persons who have the insane delusions that they are under command of God, or under inspiration, or under any pressure of God to do anything, in every case have been the most profoundly insane persons, independent of the delusion mentioned. That such a delusion is itself a symptom or an evidence of a profound insanity existing and pervading the whole nature of man."*

A few weeks ago I saw at the Morningside Asylum a young man who declared he was Elias. Under this belief he had interrupted a preacher in his sermon, and so had got committed as a lunatic. He talked sensibly and composedly for a little. I reasoned with him about his belief, asking him, How could Elias come down again from heaven, and what proof could he give for his assertion. He did not claim to have heard a voice or seen a vision. He said that God had revealed this to him, and suddenly changing from the ordinary stiff attitude of a Scotchman of the poorer class, he stood erect and threw his arm upwards, his whole frame trembling with excitement, and in a loud voice he delivered an impressioned harangue. He knew that he was here in an asylum because he said that he was Elias; but God had put that con-

---

* Official Report, p. 1617.

viction into his mind, and he would declare it whatever was done to him. Such was the force and thrill of deep conviction in his actions and tones that if his speech had been delivered to an ignorant and impressionable audience, some at least would have been carried away. I observed to Dr. Clouston, "The two other patients you showed me with religious delusions were otherwise obviously insane, but this young man, apart from the belief that he is Elias, seems sensible enough." Dr. Clouston replied that, "if he would abandon that delusion he should at once discharge him." Such cases are not so rare as to escape the notice of superintendents of asylums who are willing to look for them amongst their tens of thousands of patients, unless, indeed, the very number of their patients leaves them too little time to study their individual cases.

Some medical men seem to go on the assumption that no one whose mind is in any degree deranged by disease of the brain should be punished by sentence of a court of law, save, perhaps, by being sent to an asylum. Such an idea, if acted on, would soon put the whole machinery of law and justice into disorder. Medical insanity and legal irresponsibility can never have the same boundary line.

As regards the case of Guiteau, I am disposed to take a position near that of Dr. William A. Hammond,[*] who, while holding that the assassin was insane, quotes a passage written by himself years before the trial :—

"That individuals thus affected are insane, that is, of unhealthy minds, is undoubtedly true; but there is none the less any reason why, when convicted of crimes, they should not be made to suffer the full penalty which the law awards. There is no evidence to show that a crime committed through a morbid impulse, based upon a still more morbid emotion of pleasure, could not have been prevented had the individual chosen to combat the desire of self-gratification. Those morbidly constituted persons who commit crimes because it is pleasant for them to do so, should be treated exactly like other offenders against the laws. The absence of motive is apparent only. The fact that the criminal experiences pleasure from the committal of the act is as strong

---

[*] See his paper on "Reasoning Mania: its Medical and Medico-Legal Relations," with especial reference to the case of Charles J. Guiteau, in the *Journal of Mental and Nervous Diseases*, January, 1882.

a motive as any other that can be alleged, and is entitled to no more extenuating force than the pleasure of revenge, or acquisitiveness, or other passions. 'Lord, how I do love thieving,' said a London vagabond; 'if I had all the riches of the world I would still be a thief.' The plea, 'I could not help it,' is one which every member of the criminal classes can urge with as much force as the subject of emotional morbid impulse, and when it stands alone in an otherwise sane individual should be absolutely disregarded by juries and judges."

I cannot entirely agree with Dr. Hammond that lunatics should in all cases be held responsible, simply because they can make a general distinction between right and wrong, and know when they are breaking the law; but when persons of unsound mind, going free about the world, wish to escape punishment from crime on the plea of lessened will-power, this diminished power of volition should be susceptible of very clear proof. We can judge of a man's knowledge and of his perceptive and reasoning faculties, but to judge of his will-power in a given case must always be doubtful, and in the interests of society it is hardly safe to give the criminal the benefit of the doubt. In medicine, each case may be judged by its own merits; but this cannot be in jurisprudence if we are to live under written law. If Guiteau had failed in his attempt, he would likely have gone into an asylum without any trial; but, as success promotes imitation, it was necessary to do something to render safer the lives of future Presidents. While not agreeing with Dr. Gray that a man possessed with the delusion that the Deity urged him to kill the President would not have taken precautions for his own safety, we think that Guiteau leaned somewhat too heavily upon worldly precautions for escape to have been so thoroughly saturated with the belief that he was God's man as to have his volition paralysed. On this ground alone could he throw off responsibility, and in such a case he would have been acquitted on his own assertion. I am inclined to think that this delusive belief was one of his motives, but I am not satisfied about its intensity. Probably the delusion rather strengthened than weakened after the deed. In considering his absurd hopes of escape through the help of the Stalwarts, we ought to bear in mind that in the United States the law is sometimes strangely lax and dilatory in punishing crimes. There is a prevalent opinion that political influence, popular favour, and sometimes even money skilfully used, occasionally save a criminal, and that the plea of insanity has now and then helped some scoundrels to escape from the halter. Guiteau himself noted in his address to the jury that Sickles, M'Farland, Cole, Hiscock, and other supposed criminals had been acquitted on the plea of transitory mania. Dr. Folsom, who examined Guiteau in jail, was of opinion that in shooting the President " he supposed that he should escape punishment," and that " certainty of punishment would have restrained him from the act."*

Men like Guiteau, at once wicked and wrong-headed, are not so very rare, and they need an example. He seemed to have received scores of letters from sympathisers. Had he been acquitted on the plea of insanity, he would certainly have treated it as a proof of the interposition of the Deity in his favour, and some erratic minds might have thought the same thing. The death of a man like Guiteau was no clear loss either to mankind or himself. He was happier in his exit than maintained at the public expense as a chronic lunatic. Like many who come into the grasp of the law, he was the victim of hereditary tendencies and a bad education. A well-directed and watchful training would likely have turned the bias in a better direction. For the dismal result, Guiteau himself was not without blame. He yielded to temptations till he lost the reins of his own passions and caprices.

Some of the doctors and the lawyers at the trial talked as if insanity and depravity were two parallel lines which might run on side by side, never approaching. In my view, they are two lines which are always slanting towards one another, though they may never meet and blend together in a man's lifetime. The wicked man, the man who gives way to his anger, his spite, his greed, or his lusts, is always

---

* " The Case of Guiteau, Assassin of the President of the United States," by Charles F. Folsom, M.D., reprinted from the *Boston Medical and Surgical Journal* of 16th February, 1882, p. 9.

progressing towards insanity; the insane man towards selfishness and immorality. There are many people in asylums who have become insane through the sheer exaggeration of their own wickedness; they have given way to their passions till the holding anchor of the will is lost. I do not know what the brain disease is in such cases, or whether it ever will be detected by looking at nerve-cells with microscopes of high power, or by colouring nerve-fibres with delicate dyes; yet I doubt not a man's course of life has an influence upon the fabric of his brain, that tracts and lines of conduction are worn in the nervous system through a good life or a bad one, just as surely as the paths people often take are seen on a grass lawn. To live a good, prudent, and temperate life saves a man from the danger of insanity; to lead a vicious and self-indulgent life leads him towards it.

Though political assassination has never been common in England, it has too great a temptation for minds of a certain class to be altogether unknown. Fortunately, the attempt often miscarries, so that to name a reigning king of England who has perished by the hand of the assassin we must go back to the days of the Anglo-Saxons. We can recall only two cases similar to the crime of Guiteau, and those were perpetrated not on kings, but on ministers.

George Villiers, the unworthy favourite of James I., had on the old King's death succeeded in retaining the favour of his successor. As the sole and absolute minister of Charles I., he exercised most of the powers of the executive government, and having nothing but the royal favour to uphold him, he soon came into collision with the prerogatives of the parliament, upon which the King looked with disfavour. Buckingham had been long at variance with the Protestant sentiment of the country, and when he returned with disgrace from the expedition to relieve Rochelle, he was justly held responsible for the defeat which English arms had met with. After a great speech by Sir John Eliot, a remonstrance was carried in the House of Commons which was directed against the Duke. But the King was not prepared to abandon his favourite. A new fleet was fitted out for the relief of the Protestant stronghold. Buckingham had gone to Portsmouth to take command of the expedition, and the King had come to Southwick to see his favourite aboard.

At this time very few people had heard of Mr. John Felton, a lieutenant in the army, who complained that he had been twice passed over for a captaincy. He had also claims against the Government for arrears of pay, amounting to about eighty pounds. He was a short stout man, of dark complexion, and down look, having the left hand maimed through a wound. A woman with whom he had lodged said that he was a melancholy man, much given to the reading of books, and of very few words. She had never seen him merry. He used to borrow many books. This discontented lieutenant used to go to a clerk in Holborn to get his petitions for arrears of pay and other grievances drawn up in proper form.

He found the scrivener in his office hard at work making copies of the remonstrance, for which there were many demands, for it was not yet in print. Mr. Felton, having little money, asked leave to read it. In the end, he got a reading of it, paid for the copy, and carried it away. In this remonstrance the Duke of Buckingham was denounced as the cause of all the evils the kingdom suffered, and an enemy to the public. After brooding for more than a month over this powerfully written protest, a sudden determination came into Felton's mind on Monday, the 18th August, 1628. Next day he prepared to set out for Portsmouth. Before leaving London on the Wednesday, he went to a church in Fleet Street, and left his name to be prayed for on the next Sunday as a man disordered and discontented in mind. Passing a cutler's shop in Tower Hill, he espied a knife in a glass case, which he bought for sixteen pence. It had a cross haft, and was about twelve inches in length. On Saturday, the 23rd, he entered the High Street of Portsmouth a little before nine in the morning. There was a great passing to and fro in the house where Buckingham lodged, and Felton entered the lobby without being challenged. Waiting a little in the shadow, near the issue of the room, he met the Duke coming out of the breakfast-room, talking to an English colonel, "little Tom Fryer," who hardly stood as high as his shoulder.

The next moment Buckingham staggered backwards, flung something from him, cried out, "Villain!" put his hand upon his sword, stumbled forward against a table, and sank on the ground. Felton had struck him in the breast over Fryer's arm, and the knife had entered his heart. Some one heard the words: "May God have mercy on thy soul." While they gathered round what had the moment before been the Duke of Buckingham, Lord High Admiral of England, Felton quietly walked into the kitchen, losing or dropping his hat. No one had seen the blow struck, and some persons who had a little before overheard a lively altercation between the Duke and the Prince of Soubise and the French Huguenot officers, cried out, "A Frenchman, a Frenchman." Upon this, Felton, who fancied they were crying his name, drew his sword and went into the Court, saying, "I am the man, here I am." It was with difficulty he was saved from being killed on the spot. In his hat a paper was found pinned to the lining, on which were written these words, with his name, Jo. Felton:—"That man is cowardly base, and deserveth not the name of a gentleman or souldier, that is not willinge to sacrifice his life for the honour of his God, his kinge, and his countrie. Lett noe man commend me for doinge of it, but rather discommend themselves as the cause of it; for if God had not taken away or harts for or sinnes, he would not have gone so long unpunished."

No doubt Felton wrote these words to justify his motives in the probable event of his being killed on the spot. Had it not been for the loss of his hat and his needless coming forward to avow the deed, the assassin might have escaped.

The Countess of Anglesea, the Duke's sister-in-law, issuing from her bed-room, fell down in a swoon. The Duchess hearing a tumult and wailing, ran out to the gallery in her nightgear, whence she could see the body of her husband lying on the table of the hall, soaking in blood. The hall was already empty. Officers were busy giving new orders, or sending away messengers. Others were examining the assassin. On being told that the Duke was not dead, Felton answered boldly that he knew he was despatched, for it was not he, but the hand of Heaven, that gave the stroke; and though his whole body had been covered over with armour of proof, he could not have avoided it. It was thought by the Court that Felton had been set on to assassinate the Duke by some of his many enemies, and for about three months, while he was in prison, he was ceaselessly questioned, to get the secret from him. It was even proposed by Lord Dorset that he should be put to the torture, when Felton coolly told them that in that case he would probably accuse *them* of having set him on. Felton said that in reading the remonstrance it came into his mind that by killing the Duke he should do his country a great good service. It is said that he afterwards expressed penitence, but it must have been of a qualified kind. Mr. Foster* writes:—

"Examination of the evidence has convinced me that, though he professed at the last a religious penitence for his mortal share in the act, he still morbidly believed the act itself to have had a prompting beyond him, and a design directed to the good of Church and Commonwealth. To the end, we shall find that he bore himself with great composure, and, as he took death when it came, 'stoutly and patiently.'"

The courtiers loudly bewailed the untimely death of the King's favourite. On the other hand, there was no concealing the joy of the people. It was a common thing to drink the health of Felton, both in London and other places; and verses were written in his praise, some of them by no mean hand—witness the following:—

> "For I would have posteritie to heare,
> He that can bravely doe, can bravely beare.
> Tortures may seem great in a coward's eye;
> 'Tis no great thing to suffer, less to die;
> Let the Duke's name solace and crown thy thrall,
> All we by him did suffer, thou for all."

When Felton was brought to London, the people gathered to see him. "The Lord help thee," "The Lord be merciful

---

* "Sir John Eliot," a Biography, by John Foster. London, 1864, vol. ii. p. 359. Besides this work, which gives a pretty full account of the assassination of Buckingham, I have used Clarendon's "History of the Rebellion in England," and "Memoirs of the Reign of King Charles I.," by Sir Philip Warwick.

to thee," came frequently from the crowd. The body of Buckingham was buried late at night for fear the people would openly show their hatred. It was noticed that there was something peculiar about the cast of mind of Felton, but the plea of insanity was not in vogue in those days, or else we might have heard more of his mental characteristics. He was one of those silent, sullen men who feel injustice deeply, and whose pent-up feelings are liable to find vent in a sudden and deadly explosion. Felton resembles Guiteau in the completeness of his preparations for the deed, but was very unlike in his quiet self-reliance and want of ostentation.

Amongst the cases cited by the American jurists at the trial of Guiteau there was one of which the following is a short account :—

The Right Honourable Spencer Perceval was the second son of the Earl of Egmont. He had begun life as a Chancery lawyer, and had held the offices of Solicitor-General, Attorney-General, and Chancellor of the Exchequer. The last step was to become First Lord of the Treasury. He had held this exalted place for about three years, when on the afternoon of the 11th May, 1812, while entering the lobby of the House of Commons, he was shot by a man who had been seen waiting at the door.* The bullet entered the left breast, and Mr. Perceval died in a few minutes. The murderer made no attempt to escape, and acknowledged the action. The Prince Regent appointed a Special Commission to try him, and it cannot be said that any time was lost. He was brought to the bar on Friday, 15th May. He had the day before refused the services of a solicitor appointed for his defence, saying he was competent to manage his own affairs. At an early hour the population had collected in countless numbers, and at nine o'clock the Court was crowded in every corner by members of both Houses and persons of distinction who had known the Prime Minister. As soon as the judges had taken their seats, the prisoner was brought in. "He was heavily

---

* This sketch is mainly taken from an account given in the *American Journal of Insanity*, January, 1882, reprinted from a pamphlet originally published at the time of the murder.

ironed on each leg, and advanced firmly up to the front of the bar, where he bowed respectfully to the Court. He was dressed in a shabby brown duffle greatcoat, buttoned close up to his chin, so as to render his neckcloth, which was dirty, scarcely perceptible. He placed his hands upon the bar, and stooped forward as if to listen with great attention to what was passing." When asked to plead to the indictment the prisoner declared himself not ready to go to trial, as the documents necessary for his defence had been taken from him. On being desired simply to plead, the prisoner said in a firm tone, "Not guilty." Mr. Alley, his counsel, then moved the Court to postpone the trial, upon the ground that the prisoner's friends, who resided at a distance, had not been made acquainted with his melancholy situation; if allowed time, they could unquestionably prove his insanity. He produced two affidavits, one from a male and another from a female relation of the prisoner, stating that his insanity was notorious to all who knew him. Mr. Alley had tried to obtain the attendance of two physicians, but had not time to get them to Court. Sir James Mansfield then pronounced the judgment of the Court, refusing the motion to delay the trial. The Attorney-General then addressed the jury in support of the charge. The prisoner's name was John Bellingham. He had gone some years before to Russia for a mercantile house in Liverpool. He had been imprisoned at Archangel on a charge which he alleged to be false, of giving information to Lloyd's Coffee House regarding the loss of a ship. He complained of the oppression and indignity with which he had been treated, and went to St. Petersburg to lay his case before Lord George Leveson-Gower, the British Ambassador, with a view to getting redress; but he could not interfere with the Russian Government in the case. Bellingham then returned to Liverpool, where he set up a mercantile business. The wrongs which he had suffered in Russia dwelt in his mind. He thought himself entitled to remuneration from the British Government, but could find no one to bring his case before Parliament. He then had applied to Mr. Perceval himself without being able to get him to recognise that he had a just ground of claim. Bellingham had been resident in London for four months, had provided himself with pistols, balls, and powder, and had even, a few days before, got a breast-pocket made in his coat in order to have the pistol ready for use. Being asked what he had to say in his defence, the prisoner thanked the Attorney-General for setting aside the objections made by his counsel on the plea of insanity. He then went at great length into the tale of the oppressive treatment he had suffered in Russia. "He appealed to the jury as men, as fathers, and as Christians, what would have been their sensations had they been so imprisoned, while his wife, who was then pregnant, and his child were compelled to proceed to England from Russia without a friend or protector." He read to the Court a vast variety of petitions, and memorials, other documents to the Prince Regent, the Treasury, the Ministers, the Privy Council, and the Parliament, stating his case, as well as the refusals from all these quarters to grant him assistance. His misfortunes he attributed mainly to Sir G. Leveson-Gower, and he observed that it was an unfortunate thing that his Lordship had not entered the lobby before Mr. Perceval, for with his Lordship's death he should have been better satisfied.

This last statement produced a very strong sensation, more particularly as Lord Gower was sitting but a short distance from the prisoner, who looked him fiercely in the face.

As a last resource he had given information at Bow Street against His Majesty's Government, and he had been told that he might take such measures as he thought right.

"In consequence of this kind of defiance he had resolved to perpetrate the murder of one of the individuals by whom he had been so grievously injured. He had no personal animosity against Mr. Perceval, and would rather have lost his own life than have been brought by circumstances to such a hard necessity; when he reflected upon the act, he could not help bursting into tears. He concluded his defence in these words:—

"'A man who takes a few shillings from another on the highway is adjudged by law to die; but what comparison can there be between his case and that of the British Government, which has robbed me of thousands; and yet the latter goes unpunished. It is no more than a mite to a mountain. I have taken this step, and a dreadful one it is, in order to enable me, after your verdict, to return to my family with some comfort and honour; and I trust that the serious lesson given by me will be a warning to all future ministers. I will not trouble you longer, being convinced that it is unnecessary; and after the law and the fact shall have been stated by the judge, it will, with God's help, remain between you and your conscience to determine upon my case.'"

Three witnesses were then produced who declared Bellingham insane.

"One of them, Mrs. Anne Billet, deposed that the father of the prisoner died mad, and that ever since his return from Russia he had been considered insane upon this subject by all his friends. On one occasion he took the witness and his own wife to the Secretary of State's office, to convince them that he should receive £100,000 from Government. When he arrived he was told positively that he could get nothing; and yet, when he got into the street, he appealed to his wife as to the truth of his assertion, and declared he would buy an estate in the west of England, and a house in London."

Sir James Mansfield in summing up the case, stated the different degrees of mental derangement, and told the jury that if the prisoner at the time of the act knew right from wrong, that they ought to bring in a verdict against the prisoner. After being absent for about a quarter of an hour, the jury returned with the verdict of guilty. During the whole trial, which lasted from ten in the morning to six in the evening, Bellingham remained perfectly calm, and heard the sentence of death without any change of countenance. Seven days after the murder Bellingham was executed, and his body delivered to the dissecting-room of the Royal College of Surgeons. About three months elapsed between the murder of Buckingham and Felton being brought to trial. In the case of Bellingham the unseemly haste in the trial and execution has ever since been considered a disgrace to English jurisprudence. The Court would not even allow time for witnesses living in London to be found and brought forward. A full examination would most likely have proved that Bellingham was deeply insane. It is clear, even from what came out at the trial, that his notions of what was right and what was wrong were so strangely confused and dislocated that the statement the prisoner knew the difference between the one and the other was likely to mislead the jury. The tragical death of the Prime Minister was fresh in men's minds, and no one would listen to any suggestion which would put off for a day the gratification of seeing his assassin hanged.

From Harper's Weekly. Copyright, 1885, by Harper & Brothers.

LOUIS RIEL.

LOUIS RIEL.

CHAPTER I.

The North-West—The Hudson's Bay Company—Manitoba Transferred to Canada—Riel drives back the New Governor, and seizes upon Fort Garry—His Prisoners — The Red River Expedition—Riel is sent to Parliament—Is Committed to an Asylum—His Religious Delusions — Is called from Montana to the Saskatchewan River.

THE great lone land of the North-West of America, between the Hudson's Bay, the Rocky Mountains and Lake Superior, had been held to be the property of the Hudson's Bay Company since the days of Charles II. The principal aim of this Company was to secure a monopoly of the furs of the wild animals which roamed over that wide region.

In all other respects they tried to conceal the resources of the country. The furs were brought to them by the Indians, or by the hunters and trappers whom they kept in their own employment. These were principally French Canadians, or settlers brought from Scotland by way of Hudson's Bay. In the course of time these hardy hunters, taking wives from the Indian tribes, formed a race of metis or half-breeds, who knew no other country.

The Company was at once a governing body and a trading body. All furs must be sold to them, everything must be bought from them. As the country to the south became colonised, and the means of transit got nearer, the half-breeds began to see that they could sell their furs at much greater advantage than by taking them to the Company's stations to give them up at a price regulated by the purchasers. Hence impatience of the rule of the Hudson's Bay Company took the form of a demand for the freedom of trade. A prominent leader in this movement was Louis Riel,* the son of a French Canadian and a half-breed woman. By force of character and power of speech, Riel gained so much influence that when one of their number was arrested for having skins in his possession to sell to some traders from the south, Riel in 1849 organised a committee of opposition, and at the head of an assembly of half-breeds, broke into the Court-house at Fort Garry, and compelled the judges to let the prisoner go, and restore the skins which had been confiscated. The struggle ended in the freedom of trade being gained. This rendered Riel very popular, especially amongst the French-speaking population. From being a hunter in the employment of the Company, Riel became the owner of a mill on the Red River, which he had himself planned. He died in 1864, leaving nine children, the eldest of whom bore the same name as himself. This boy showed such marks of talent that he attracted the notice of a Catholic priest, Father Taché, by whose aid he was sent to study at Montreal.

It was impossible, in the nature of things, that this vast territory, with its fertile soil and varying resources, should remain in the permanent possession of a fur-trading company; and when, in 1869, the Dominion of Canada was formed by the amalgamation of the different Provinces from Nova Scotia to Vancouver, the Imperial Government undertook to transfer the North-West territory to Canada. The affair was transacted at London between the Colonial Office, the Commissioners from Canada, and the shareholders of the Hudson's Bay Company. The rights of the Company were bought up for £300,000, and the promise of one-twentieth of the land. Nothing was said about the inhabitants of the ceded territory; perhaps all the high contracting parties did

---

* "Les Canadiens de l'Ouest," par Joseph Tassé, vol. ii. p. 353. Montreal, 1878.

not know there were any, save the employés of the Company. Nevertheless, there were about 5000 people of French origin and 5000 of Scotch and English, with a mixture of Indian blood, and a few Europeans, Americans, and Canadians, altogether some 14,000 souls, principally dwelling about Winnipeg. This wild region of prairie and forest, with lonely lakes and mighty rivers, was their country. They believed that they had rights and claims and interests which had been forgotten. They had lands, for example, on leasehold, and rights of pasturage which the Company had never formally granted, but which had grown strong by prescription. So, when **surveyors**, sent by the Canadian Government, were seen marking out the land, the people were filled with alarm and **suspicion**. A new Governor, the Hon. Wm. Macdougall, appeared at the frontier at Pembina without an escort, even before all the formalities had been completed which should give his authority due legality. Louis Riel, back from the college at Montreal, and now a freighter on the plains between St. Paul and Winnipeg, had watched the proceedings of the surveyors. He pointed out to the half-breeds that the Canadians were taking possession of their land without the inhabitants being consulted. He told them that their privileges, usages, and rights were in danger. He boldly appeared with seven men to stop the entry of the Lieutenant-Governor, and erected a barricade across the way. A number of halfbreeds soon joined his party, and he drove Mr. Macdougall across the boundary line into the States.

Encouraged by the support he had received from the French metis, Riel now proceeded, step by step, to make his power supreme. He entered Fort Garry with a party of armed men, seized upon the stores, out of which he paid his adherents, and gradually ousted the Governor of the Hudson's Bay Company from the exercise of his power. He then put in prison about forty of his opponents, exercised a censorship over the newspapers, forced them to print what he wanted, and caused goods to be searched for arms at the frontier. He persuaded those friendly to him in the villages around to send delegates to form a council, in which he generally managed to carry what he wanted. About three or four hundred men, principally of British descent, who were dissatisfied with his assumptions, assembled together, and forced Riel to release his captives. The situation was threatening. There were two parties of different nationalities, both bold, hardy, and skilled in the use of arms. A French half-breed, named Parisien, was arrested as a spy by the British party; but he managed to snatch a loaded gun, and to run away closely pursued. Meeting a young man called Sutherland, he shot him either through fear of being stopped, or in order to get his horse. Parisien was overtaken, and so roughly handled that he afterwards died. Under the exasperation caused by this affair, there was danger of a conflict taking place between the two parties; but, as the British gathering had not sufficient provisions to hold together, the men were obliged to return to their homes. Riel, from the outset, had a shrewd appreciation of the value of prisoners, whom he meant to treat as hostages. Observing from the walls of Fort Garry forty men of the opposite party toiling through the snow, he sent out an armed detachment of horse and foot, who captured the whole of them, and brought them into the fort. They were put under an armed guard, and treated with much roughness. Major Boulton[*] tells us he was handcuffed, and chains put on his legs. Riel came to the room where he was confined, and looked in at the door. Without entering, he said:

"'Major Boulton, you prepare to die to-morrow at twelve o'clock.'

"I answered, 'Very well,' and he retired.

"The act he was contemplating," observes Major Boulton, "was for no other purpose than to strike terror to the hearts of the people, and more firmly to fix himself as the autocrat of the country. In this he showed a bloodthirsty spirit as well as a want of tact, which were repeatedly manifested traits in his character. The autocrat himself paid me a visit about ten o'clock in the morning. Riel entered the room in a tragic way, took out his pocket-handkerchief, walked up and down for a while, pretending to weep, and then went out without having spoken a word."

---

[*] "Reminiscences of the North-West Rebellion," by Major Boulton. Toronto, 1886, p. 120. See also "The Creation of Manitoba; or, A History of the Red River Troubles," by Alexander Begg. Toronto, 1871.

Major Boulton's life was spared only by his friends promising to send representatives from the English-speaking settlements to meet in Riel's council.

After the news that his life had been spared, Major Boulton went to sleep. He was suddenly awakened, he tells us, by some one shaking him:

"I looked up, and saw Riel with a lantern.

"He said, 'Major Boulton, I have come to see you. I have come to shake you by the hand, and to make a proposition to you. I perceive that you are a leader. The English people they have no leader. Will you join my Government, and be their leader?'

"The sudden transition from being under sentence of death to being asked to take a position in Riel's Government struck me as serio-comic, but I collected my wits and replied that his proposition was so startling that I could not give an answer at the moment; but, if he would allow me to go back to the Portage to consult with my friends, I would consider his proposition seriously."

After he had given up his intention of shooting Major Boulton, a man, called Thomas Scott, had provoked Riel by openly trying to dissuade his fellow-prisoners from advising their friends to send delegates to Riel's council. Being a passionate man, Scott had exchanged angry words with his guards. Riel got him brought up before a court-martial, who sentenced him to be shot. This was carried out next day at noon. Even the men selected for the office were not prepared to go so far. One of the firing party removed the caps from his gun, and others did not take good aim, so that the unfortunate man was not killed outright. He was thrust into a rude coffin while still alive. Five hours after, he was heard to cry out, "For God's sake, take me out of here and kill me." After a death-agony of ten hours he was despatched with a thrust of a knife.

Major Boulton thinks that Riel hurried his partisans into this cruel murder in order that they should be fairly committed to resistance to the British Government. "At first," he observes, "there did not seem to be any disposition on Riel's part, or that of his people, to oppose the cession of the country to Canada. The opposition he offered seemed to be against the entrance of the Governor or the establishment of the authority of Canada until certain rights had been conceded which he and his supporters claimed to be their privilege, and to have been granted them as inhabitants of the country. As his successes filled him with vanity and ambition, his designs changed, and there is no doubt he conceived the idea of forming an independent government and handing it over to the United States for a good round sum."

It was fortunate that, a few days after the execution of Scott, which took place on the 4th March, 1870, Archbishop Taché returned from Rome, having conferred on his way with the Canadian Government. Through his influence with Riel he was able to dissuade him from extreme measures. Riel held his position in Fort Garry for ten months as head of the Provisional Government till Colonel Wolseley appeared on the 24th August, 1870, with a British regiment sent to restore order. Riel waited till he heard the sound of the bugles, when, with Lepine and O'Donoghue, two of his associates, he fled across the Assiniboine river, destroying the hawser at the ferry to prevent pursuit. In the meantime, the British and Canadian Governments had time to consider the claims of the North-West. They drew up a constitution for the new State, promised to respect the rights of the inhabitants, and assigned one million four thousand acres for the benefit of the families of the half-breeds. Prescriptive tillers were turned into freeholds, and the rights of cutting hay were secured. As most of the residents attributed these measures to the stand which Riel had made, had it not been for the execution of Scott his other high-handed actions might have been condoned. As it was, Riel did not venture to stay to claim the benefits of the amnesty promised by Bishop Taché. Nevertheless, the Canadian minister, who knew his powers to make mischief, sent Riel 4000 dollars at different times through the Bishop's hands, ostensibly as a compensation for the loss of his property.

In 1870, when the Fenians threatened to make a raid across the frontier, Riel and Lepine raised several companies of half-breeds to resist them. Mr. Archibald, the new Lieutenant-Governor of Manitoba, inspected his company, and even shook hands with some of them, if not with Riel himself. In September, 1872, Louis Riel was nominated by the electors of Provencher for the Canadian House of Commons, but he retired in favour of Sir George Cartier, a French-Canadian, who, like himself, had once revolted against the British rule, though he was now a member of the Government. Next year, on Cartier's death, Riel was chosen as member, and in the general election of 1874 he was again returned. In March of that year Riel signed the roll in the clerk's-room of the House of Commons at Ottawa before any one knew that he was in the capital. The House ordered his expulsion by a vote of 124 to 68; but he was again elected by his constituents. In 1874, Lepine was tried before the Queen's Bench of Manitoba for the murder of Scott, and sentenced to death. This was commuted to two years' imprisonment, and finally to five years' banishment.

The same sentence of five years' banishment and life-long forfeiture of political rights, was passed on Louis Riel.* After this, we are told, Riel wandered through the United States for several years, quiet in manners, well behaved, and giving utterance to no delusions. This is the testimony of those who knew him, and met him at St. Paul, Montana, and other places.

In 1876, Riel found his way to Montreal, and one Sunday he interrupted religious services in one of the churches by declaring he was superior to any priests or bishop, and should himself conduct the service. He was arrested, and being examined by two medical men, he was declared insane, and was legally committed to Longue Pointe Asylum, under the care of Dr. Howard. From this establishment he was transferred to the Asylum of Beauport, near Quebec, under the assumed name of Larochelle. Here Riel was detained nineteen months, being discharged in 1878.† It was stated by the superintendent, Dr. Roy, that during his residence in the

---

* "A Psycho-Medical History, Louis Riel," by Daniel Clark, M.D., Medical Superintendent of the Asylum for Insane, Toronto. From the *American Journal of Insanity* for July, 1887.

† The Queen v. Louis Riel, accused and convicted of High Treason. Report of Trial at Regina. Ottawa, 1886, p. 120.

asylum, Riel was suffering from megalomania; that is, delusions of grandeur, with excitement. When conversing on ordinary matters he was reasonable and clever, but liable to be irritable if people contradicted him about his delusions. On several occasions he was so violent that he was placed under restraint. He had a fixed idea that he had from Heaven a mission to fulfil in the North-West, although at that time he could gain nothing from such claims.

Riel afterwards gave the following account of his own delusions about this time:—

"Some persons," he said,* "had known beforehand my supernatural power, but I only knew it myself on the 18th of December, 1874. The last Archbishop of Montreal, Monseignor Bourget, was the first to inform me of this favour of the Saviour. This learned prelate wrote to me, and I have his letter still in my possession, that I had a mission to fulfil. At first I was inclined to doubt it, but later on I recognised my error. On the 18th of December, 1874, while I was seated on the top of a mountain near Washington, in Dacota, the same spirit who showed himself to Moses in the midst of fire and cloud, appeared to me in the same manner. I was stupefied, I was confused; he said to me, 'Rise up, Louis David Riel. You have a mission to fulfil.' Stretching out my arms, and bending my head, I received this heavenly messenger. I have worked for men, and with what success all the world already knows. Events are not finished in a few days or a few hours. A century is but a spoke in the wheel of eternity. I have obtained practical results; but much more still remains to do"

He was discharged apparently cured of his delusions, when he again sought the United States and settled at Montana, where he married a half-breed Cree woman. It is said that he went to Washington in order to get the Government to appoint him to some position over the half-breeds at Montana.† He acted so strangely in the streets that he was arrested. He was soon set at liberty, when he went back to his family.

In the summer of 1884, fifteen years after the troubles in

---

* This passage is translated from an extract from a Montreal newspaper in "L'Etude sur l'état mental de Louis Riel," par le Dr. H. Gibson. L'Encéphale, 1886, p. 54.

† Clark, p. 5.

the Red River, four delegates from the metis on the Saskatchewan, their leader being Gabriel Dumont, appeared to invite Riel to come amongst them to get their grievances redressed. They found him at Montana, at the foot of the Rocky Mountains, "humbly and respectably employed as a teacher in the Industrial College of the Jesuit Fathers," for the instruction of the half-breeds. Riel's term of banishment from Canada had now expired, but he was still deprived of political rights. He returned with the delegates, a journey of seven hundred miles, taking with him his wife and two children.

On the settlement of Manitoba, the half-breeds had been allowed grants of 240 acres for each child of a family, but many of them never entered into possession. Selling their scrip for small sums, ranging from fifteen dollars upwards, they wandered away in their rude waggons across the grassy plains towards the Rocky Mountains. Thus a great part of the one million four hundred thousand acres fell into the hands of speculators, who held the purchased land till it should rise in value with the development of the country.

The metis beyond the bounds of Manitoba on the Saskatchewan River expected similar grants, which the Government was slow to confer, partly because they were doubtful of the policy of turning these wild men, with their hereditary instincts of hunting and wandering, into proprietors; and partly because their attention was occupied by other things. The ministers under parliamentary government in America, as in our own country, have to devote much of their energies to defending themselves from the criticism of opposition and to keeping up their popularity with the electors, hence it is somewhat difficult to spare time for the duties of examining questions of administration.

In any case, the half-breeds believed they had grievances, and welcomed Riel amongst them as the hereditary champion of their rights.

CHAPTER II.

Appearance and Character of Riel — The Grievances of the Metis — Riel Offers to Withdraw — His Artful Policy — His Religious Delusions — Leads the Metis into Rebellion — Defeated and made Prisoner — His Trial — Evidence about his Sanity — Sentence.

Louis Riel was now about forty-one years of age. He was a well-made powerful man, six feet in height. His thick locks of dark hair overhung his forehead. He wore a moustache, but no beard. He had a swarthy complexion, and bright black eyes, restless and searching. The expression on his face was very powerful. Judging from portraits, he had more of the physiognomy of an Indian than his father. His voice has been described by one who had several interviews with him "as capable of any amount of modulation, with a rare charm about it." He manifested in conversation all the characteristics of his race, excitable and enthusiastic. Sometimes his voice was raised in passion, while at other times it was soft, mellow, and sweet. His conversational powers were remarkable, his style of oratory was lively and powerful, full of similes and of impassioned gestures.

Though readily assuming the pleasing hues of sympathy and enthusiasm for the interests of others, Riel proved himself to be wily, self-seeking, and ambitious. He was vain, and had a high opinion of his own powers, but through his genius there ran a strain of insanity which sometimes heightened and sometimes marred his great powers.

Riel appeared at the Saskatchewan river in July, 1884. The metis at once welcomed him as their born leader, who would get all their grievances redressed. A subscription was raised to maintain him and his family, as he was poor.

Meetings were held at which Riel was of course the principal orator. At first his words were quiet and sensible. He told the half-breeds that they were better off than in the States. A correspondent* wrote to the Governor of the North-Western Territory at Regina :—

"There was a mass meeting such as Prince Albert has never seen; people came from the country to meet Mr. Riel from everywhere, and they went back struck with the quiet and gentle way he spoke to them. 'He strongly advocates peace and union among all the several sections of the country. I have not heard a hard word fall from his mouth. What are his purposes?' They are a good many, and require a long time if he wanted to see them all carried out. 1st, He wants the half-breeds to have a free grant to the land they occupy; he wants to agitate to have the three districts of the Saskatchewan, Alberta, Assiniboia, erected into Provinces, or at least to have each district represented in Parliament; he wants the land laws amended to suit more the rapid settlement of the country."

He strongly advised the Governor not to interfere with Riel as long as he kept quiet. "I cannot hide from you," he adds, "that his influence for good and evil is great among the half-breeds, French as well as English; he has a great many admirers even among the white population."

Under Riel's direction, petitions were prepared and forwarded to the Government at Ottawa. The last one seems to have been sent as late as the end of February. The Government replied that they would take the question into consideration. As the agitation gathered strength Riel's orations became more fiery, and were mingled with bursts of prayer, and promises of Divine assistance. Sir John Macdonald, declared in Parliament that Riel offered to leave the country for $5000, and this statement was supported by documents afterwards published.† Riel got Father André,

---

* This letter, which is in the "Epitome of Parliamentary Documents," in connection with the North-West Rebellion, 1885, Ottawa, 1886, p. 388, is dated, Prince Albert, 24th July, 1884.

† The Queen v. Louis Riel. Evidence of Charles Nolin, Riel's cousin, p. 93.

On the 24th December, 1884, Joseph Home, inspector, reports that Louis

a Catholic priest, to use his influence with the Government to obtain this sum for him. Riel said that he would be content with $35,000 then, and that he would settle with the Government himself for the balance of $100,000, which he claimed as an indemnity. He said if he got the money he wanted from the Government, he would go wherever the Government wished to send him; he told Father André, if he was an embarrassment to the Government by remaining in the North-West he would even go to the Province of Quebec. Another time Riel said if he got the money, he would go to the United States to start a paper, and raise the other nationalities in the States. He said, "Before the grass is that high in this country, you will see foreign armies in this country." He also said, "I will commence by destroying Manitoba, and then I will come and destroy the North-West and take possession of the North-West."

On Father André's* representing to him that even if they granted him $35,000, the half-breed question would remain the same, he said in answer, "If I am satisfied the half-breeds will be." He intimated that he would accept a less sum if the Father's influence failed to get him the amount stated.

When he saw that the Government showed no inclination to give way, Riel's language and demeanour became more

---

Riel wished to hold a conversation with Mr. M'Dowell, member for the North-West Council. "He (Riel) stated that he wished representation made to the Government that if a certain sum were paid to him in cash (Mr. M'Dowell seems to think he would accept $5000), he would at once leave the country. He says that he has such influence with the half-breeds that any rights they think they have, or claims upon the Government, would be at once dropped by them if he advised them to do so.

"He says he is very poor, and has actually nothing to live upon, and if he cannot procure means to leave the country, as well as something to settle upon his wife and family, he will starve, which might make him desperate.

"As soon as the Government gives him what he asks for, he will, he says, give up all connection with the other half-breeds, in fact, throw them all over, and pledge himself not to return to this country."

"Epitome of Parliamentary Documents," in connection with the North-West Rebellion, 1885. Ottawa, 1886, p. 383.

* Evidence of Father André, p. 113. These proposals were made on the 12th and 23rd of December.

violent. For the first four months he appeared as a devout Catholic, but in the course of the agitation he advanced pretensions to inspiration which came into collision with the inflexible creed of the Church of Rome. He said that the Spirit of God was in him, that the Spirit of Elias was in him, that he could foresee the future, and that the Pope of Rome was not legally Pope, and that the priests were narrow-minded people. He spoke of making the Bishop of Montreal Pope of the New World.

To excite awe in the minds of these wild and impressionable half-breeds Riel gave out that he would only live on blood,* and got the people who had occasion to butcher cattle to save the blood for him, and from the first day of January he fed exclusively on this instead of flesh, the blood being cooked in milk.

About the 2nd of March Riel completely broke with the priests. He saw that they warned the people not to believe in his claims to inspiration, and were against his proposal to form a provisional government. On the 17th of March he had pushed the French half-breeds into actual rebellion. He took possession of a church, and when the priest protested against his proceedings Riel said derisively, "See, he is a Protestant." He now openly proclaimed the most heretical religious ideas. Vital Fourmond, a French priest living at St. Laurent, near Batoche, said† that Riel told a number of priests assembled together that he had been appointed by the council to be their spiritual adviser. The witness continued :—

"He has extraordinary ideas on the subject of the Trinity. The only God was God the Father, and that God the Son was not God; the Holy Ghost was not God either. The second person of the Trinity was not God, and, as a consequence of this, the Virgin Mary was not the mother of God, but the mother of the Son of God. That is the reason why he changed the formula of the prayer which is

---

* See the evidence of Charles Nolin in "Trials in connection with the North-West Rebellion, 1885." Ottawa, 1886, p. 392.
† "The Queen v. Louis Riel," pp. 117, 118.

commonly known as 'Hail, Mary.' Instead of saying, 'Hail, Mary, mother of God,' he said, 'Hail, Mary, mother of the Son of God.' He did not admit the doctrines of the Church of the Divine Presence. According to his ideas, it was not God who was present in the Host, but an ordinary man six feet high. As to his political ideas, he wanted first to go to Winnipeg, and Lower Canada, and the United States, and even to France, and he said, We will take your country even; and then he was to go to Italy and overthrow the Pope, and then he would choose another Pope of his own making."

Father André said of Riel[*] :—

"He was a fervent Catholic, attending the Church, and attending to his religious duties frequently, and his state of mind was the cause of great anxiety. In conversation on politics, and on the rebellion, and on religion, he stated things which frightened the priests. I am obliged to visit every month the fathers (priests) of the district. Once all the priests met together, and they put the question, Is it possible to allow that man to continue in his religious duties? and they unanimously decided that on this question he was not responsible; that he could not suffer any contradiction on the question of religion and politics,—we considered that he was completely a fool in discussing these questions."

He read, or pretended to read from a book called "The Prophecies of St. Bridget, an Irish saint," who, he said, had foretold hundreds of years ago what was to occur during the years 1885 and 1886. He said that she foretold that all the powers of the world, even the Government of Canada, would be swallowed up in a general whirlpool of destruction. Riel maintained that he himself was the descendant of St. Louis, foretold by St. Bridget, who was to restore peace, morality, and prosperity to the nations. Another witness[†] said that some of his ignorant dupes believed that Riel could make it thunder, and could cure disease without medicines. Riel himself declared that he was once the victim of an incurable disease of the heart, but that on the 24th of May he had

---

[*] "The Queen v. Riel," p. 112.
[†] Vital Fourmond of St. Laurent, Director of Catholic Missions, "Trials," &c., p. 396.

cured the disease by his Divine power. He also declared that should he be killed it did not matter, he would be with them again alive, and that would prove to them his Divine mission. He cried, "It is the Holy Ghost that speaks; who shall dare disbelieve me?"

At the same time, Riel made use of a number of artful devices to drive the ignorant and superstitious half-breeds and Indians into rebellion. He got a few of the leading men to sign their names, pledging that they would support him, and induced an armed crowd to plunder some stores and make prisoners. Some half-breeds were forced for fear of their lives to join with the rest. On a detachment of the police advancing from the nearest fort, Riel announced that the police under Major Crozier were coming to slaughter them all. Going out with his followers to meet the police, Riel attempted to surround them during a parley, in order to take them prisoners. A conflict took place between them and the half-breeds, in which twelve of the police were killed and twenty-five wounded. This affair, which was called the battle of Duck Lake, took place on 26th March. Riel then sent messengers to the Indian tribes announcing a victory, and urging them to rise against the Government. Had he succeeded in arousing their savage nature a great deal of devastation, loss, and misery would have followed. Fortunate it was that the Indian tribes had no crying injustice to complain of from the Canadian Government. The temptations held out by Riel were tried in vain, save at one place, where the Indians set upon the Whites and killed nine settlers. Riel afterwards said that the fight at Duck Lake was sudden and premature. His adherents were not prepared as fully as they expected to be. He had sent messengers to out-lying points to arouse the Indians and his people, and it would take two or three weeks before they were in readiness. Few of the half-breeds of British origin joined with Riel. They did not trust him so fully as the French metis, and disbelieved in his claims to Divine inspiration. Had Riel succeeded in drawing within his fascinations the British half-breeds and the Indians, the loss of life would have been much more serious.

A man detained in the rebel camp gave the following account*:—

"Once Riel had got unfortunate half-breeds into his power he made them believe that their only chance for life was to stay with him, as there would be no mercy shown them by the Government or by the mounted police, and that his intention was so to conduct matters that without any bloodshed he would secure them the full recognition of their rights; by such promises as these, and by resorting to every possible trick of language and action, by pretending to be specially commissioned by God and the Virgin Mary and St. John the Baptist to lead the half-breed people through all their difficulties to a glorious success without shedding any blood, and without any danger; by kneeling down and with his arms spread out like the arms of a cross, his eyes cast up to heaven and his voice raised aloud to God in prayer, and sometimes by throwing himself on the ground shouting to God for directions, and to protect the half-breeds; it was in this way that he kept the poor, ignorant people subject to his power and influence. I heard him harangue the poor people often, and say to them—

"'You know that all power and authority is given to the Holy Father the Pope of Rome, you well know that the Holy Ghost descended from heaven and dwells in the heart of the Holy Father, you know that where that Holy Spirit is there must be all power and authority. Well, the Holy Ghost left Rome in the interest of the poor half-breeds of America, and took up his residence in the heart of the greatest living saint of the world, the Holy Bishop Bourget, of Montreal. Now, dear half-breeds, here is a letter, he cried, holding a paper up towards heaven, from that great saint, Bishop Bourget, written to me, who am to be the saviour of my people, acting under the influence of the Holy Ghost, and that holy saint tells me in this letter that I have a mission to fulfil; that grand mission is to liberate the whole world, but first I have to liberate the half-breed people whom I love so much, who are my own flesh and blood, who are my brothers, and who live in my heart.'

"By such means as these he fascinated a large number of his poor, credulous followers, and by terrorising over and making prisoners of those who, like myself, could not be deceived by his pretended Divine mission, Riel kept under his authority numbers of good, honest, and loyal men who longingly wished for the means of being freed from their disagreeable and false and dangerous position, but who were

---

* Evidence of Charles Nolin, "Trials," &c., p. 394.

powerless in his hands, or under his influence, believing that he was commissioned by God."

There was a widow who had seven sons, quiet and hard-working young men. They had a fine farm, plenty of cattle and horses, and were worth a good deal of money. Riel tried to induce the young men to join him, but without success. He went day after day to the poor widow's, and played on her superstition and credulity. He told her of his holy visions, how he saw himself surrounded by seven glorious stars of extraordinary brightness crowning him with glory. These bright stars, he cried, are your seven glorious sons, who are to achieve the glory of the half-breed nation ; and the poor woman, in her simple faith of his Divine mission, prayed of her fine young sons to go forth and battle under the banner of heaven. The result was, that three of these young men were killed in battle ; another died of a broken heart at the fate of his brothers; another was wounded and crippled for life ; and the remaining two were made prisoners, and tried for their lives. Their mother and their two sisters were reduced to poverty.*

In order to implicate his adherents more deeply Riel was very careful to keep recorded all the proceedings of the council, and had the names of those who accepted this dangerous office engrossed in the minutes, whether they were present or not. Otherwise it is said that the members of his council were mere cats-paws in his hands. He ordered and did whatever he pleased, and threatened death to all who dared to oppose him. It was probably to plunge his followers still more deeply in rebellion that he wished some prisoners delivered over to the wild Indians to be massacred,† but this was prevented by the resistance of the young men who had been induced to join him through the superstitious faith of their mother.

Riel's council, by affixing their signatures to his proclamations, appeared also to lend their credit to the prophetic mission therein advanced. After his name he added the word

---

* "Trials," pp. 377 and 386.   † "Trials," pp. 378-387 and 395.

Exovede, meaning one of the flock; the members of the council were all exovedes, and the council was to be called the exovedate.

The following tirade is taken from the prophecies and revelations of Louis Riel, written in April and May, 1885,* and found at Batoche :—

"The Spirit of God has made me understand the voice of the recruits who sent to me. Fire first. We have never as yet fired first on the enemy. The Spirit of God has told me in English what spirit ought to preside over the movement, *generous, unanimous.*

"The Spirit of God has made me hear the question which should be made to the warriors.

"I have seen a flock of dark geese, they had the appearance of wandering away, but in truth they were hovering in the air. I saw them disperse into two groups. The leading goose, who with the others was directing its course west, suddenly turned to the left, and took an eastward direction. These geese, though they were in the sunshine, did not reflect the light; they were covered with darkness. Oh, warriors, who combat in favour of bad principles, you are these black geese. God will stop you in your flight, and, in spite of all, you will turn back. Understand, hear, obey, and you will escape from the reverses, defeats, and disgraces which overwhelm you! The Spirit of God has made you see the Curé André; he was very small, he turned his back to me, he wished to flee from me, but he could not. The circle of his light was very small.

"The Spirit of God said to me, 'The enemy has gone to Prince Albert.' I prayed, saying, 'Deign to make me know who is that enemy.' He answered, 'Charlie Larence.' The Spirit of God has shown me the place where I should be wounded, the highest joint of the ring finger; pointing to this place with His finger, the Spirit said, 'In this place I think you will be wounded.'

"I have seen a paper written in French, which began in these terms :—'Do you not know some one called Charlie Larence. He wants to drink five gallons in the name of the movement.'

"The Spirit of God has made me understand that we ought to bind the prisoners.†

"I have seen Gabriel Dumont, he was afflicted, ashamed; he did

---

* Translated from the passage given in L'Encéphale, 1886, p. 57.

† Riel had six prisoners whom he kept in a cellar at Batoche. Their hands were bound at night.

not look at me, he looked at his empty table. But Gabriel Dumont is blessed, his faith will not totter. He is firm, by the grace of God. His hope and his trust in God will be justified; he will come out of the struggle charged with the booty of his enemies. Jesus Christ and the Virgin Mary will make him again joyful. My ideas are just, well weighed, well defined; mourning is not in my thoughts. My ideas are level with my gun, my gun is standing. It is the invisible power of God which keeps my gun erect. Oh, my God, give me grace to establish the day of your rest, to bring back in honour the Sabbath day as it was fixed by the Holy Spirit in the person of Moses, your servant,"—

And so on. In fact, Riel wished, amongst his other changes, to restore the Jewish Sabbath.

One of the devices of the leader of the metis was to gain possession of as many prisoners as he could, and to hold them as hostages, to induce the Government to consent to negotiate with him. He wished to raise the Indians in order to increase the difficulties of the situation. He said that the rebellion of 1870 would not be a patch upon this one. One of his proclamations was intended to get the United States to interfere. He pointed out that the North-West Territory was not ceded with Canada by France, and that the States had a right to a share in it. His proposal to divide the North-West amongst seven nationalities,* though a very absurd one, could scarcely be held as a proof of insanity. Failure threw discredit on the wisdom of his plans, but it does not seem to me that success was so improbable as to stamp the rebellion as utterly fatuous, especially when we consider the complete success of the Transvaal Boers in 1881, in throwing off their subjection to British power. It was noted that Riel, while destroying some of the telegraphs did not cut the wire which kept up communication with Ottawa, through which he hoped to conduct negotiations with Sir John Macdonald. One might say that it would betoken some shrewdness in an

---

* Riel himself at his trial mentioned ten—the Bavarians, Poles, Italians, Germans, Irish, Belgians, Swedes, Danes, Norwegians, and Jews. He knew that emigrants from all these peoples could be found in the United States.

enemy to abstain from cutting the telegraphic wires between a capable general and a Cabinet Ministry likely to interfere with his plans. It would have saved much discredit to British arms and British statesmanship had communication been longer and more difficult between Mr. Gladstone in Downing Street and Sir Evelyn Wood in the camp below Majuba Hill.

Fortunately, the Canadian Government was fit to cope with the occasion. The scene of revolt was 2500 miles from the centre of government at Ottawa, but with the help of the new railway to Manitoba, a force of the Canadian militia, under General Middleton, was promptly sent forward, and after some sharp fighting, Riel's followers were driven out of the village of Batoche, on the Saskatchewan river, with a loss on the side of the militia of 51 killed and 173 wounded. At the beginning of the fray, Riel ran about from one rifle pit to another, with a crucifix in his hand, to encourage the half-breeds and Indians; but he seemed soon to have sickened of the fighting, and he showed a disposition to surrender before his brave followers were willing to give up the conflict. He threatened to massacre his prisoners if the militia kept on firing. Two days after the capture of Batoche, Riel was taken and handed over to the civil authorities, who ordered him to be tried.

The Court, which met at Regina, on the 20th of July, 1885, was composed of two judges, one Mr. Hugh Richardson, a stipendiary magistrate, the other a justice of the peace, with a jury of six men. Though exception was taken to the constitution of this Court, it appears that it was in accordance with the law of the country. The prisoner was provided with counsel sent from Quebec, to defend him. The proceedings were conducted with temper and decorum, and Riel himself acknowledged that he had a fair trial.

As the plea of insanity was put in by the prisoner's counsel, three witnesses were summoned to report on his mental condition—Dr. Roy, of the Beauport Asylum, Quebec; Dr. Daniel Clark, of the Asylum at Toronto; and Dr. Howard, of the Longue Pointe Asylum. The last gentleman did not appear, as he refused to come alone, owing to his state of health.

Dr. Clark, who saw Riel before the trial, at the prison in Regina, observes:—

"His movements were nervous, energetic, and expressive, as are so characteristic of the French. This was evidently a normal condition, and not from apprehension as to his fate. He was very talkative, and his egotism made itself manifest, not only in his movements, but also in his expressed pleasure in being the central figure of a State trial, which was likely to become historical. The writer told him that his lawyers were trying to save his life by proving that he had been insane. At this statement he got very much excited, and paced up and down his cell like a chained animal, saying, with great vehemence and gesticulation, 'My lawyers do wrong to try to prove I am insane; I scorn to put in that plea. I, the leader of my people, the centre of a national movement, a priest and prophet, to be proved to be an idiot! As a prophet, I know beforehand the jury will acquit me. They will not ignore my rights. I was put in Longue Pointe and Beauport Asylums by my persecutors, and was arrested without cause when discharging my duty. The Lord delivered me out of their hands.'"

Dr. Roy, called in as witness for the defence, well remembered the prisoner's case, when under his charge, at Beauport. He believed Riel to be insane and irresponsible during the late rebellion, because he had a fixed belief in his divinely inspired mission in the North-West, which no reasoning could overcome. Dr. Roy's view was connected and logical; but its full effect was somewhat marred by his giving up speaking in English, and thus requiring his ideas to be transmitted through a French interpreter.

Dr. Daniel Clark, of the Toronto Asylum, stated his belief that the prisoner was insane, though he admitted that he might be simulating madness. To be sure that this was not the case, he would require much longer opportunities of observing the prisoner. Dr. Clark assigned as a proof of Riel's insanity, the hopeless character of the revolt of five or six hundred metis and Indians against the whole power of Canada, with that of Great Britain behind, and also his absurd scheme to divide the North-West into provinces peopled by seven nationalities.

It scarcely ever happens that medical witnesses are produced at an important trial without other medical witnesses being brought forward in the opposition. In the present case, two rebutting doctors were employed. Dr. Jamens Wallace, medical superintendent of the asylum at Hamilton, had examined the prisoner for half-an-hour in the jail at Regina. He believed Riel to be quite sane, although he admitted that he had patients in his own asylum for weeks before he found any symptoms of insanity. Dr. Jukes, senior surgeon of the mounted police, who had been in practice thirty-five years, had been in the habit of seeing the accused almost daily for about two months during his imprisonment. He said :—

"I have never seen any thing to make me question his mental condition, and therefore I have never led the conversation, under any circumstances, to draw out any possible insane notion. I have never made any effort to do so, because my duty was otherwise."

He never spoke to Riel on religion, nor on his mission with reference to the North-West territory. In short, Dr. Jukes had never approached the peculiar delusions of the prisoner. This would be as absurd as a surgeon called in to testify that a man had no fracture or dislocation of the leg who admitted that he had not asked the man to stand or walk, or examined the limb. General Middleton was then called, as he had held some conversation with Riel the day he was taken. Captain Holmes Young, in whose charge the prisoner was until handed over to the civil authorities, also gave his opinion. Both these officers considered Riel a man of sound mind, shrewd, and intelligent. Captain Young, with somewhat malign generosity, said that he thought Riel was cleverer and better educated than himself, and paid a compliment on the arrangement of the line of rifle pits, which seemed to give much pleasure to the accused. The Rev. Charles Bruce Pitblado gave some evidence about Riel's plan, showing that his hopes principally rested upon the probability of the Ottawa Government being willing to enter into negotiations should he be able to make a number of prisoners to hold as hostages.

The evidence of insanity was of course clouded by confusing cross-examinations and demands for definitions. It would have required to have been clearly stated by a powerful speaker in order to reach the minds of the jurors, but in place of an address of this kind, Riel was called upon to speak in his own defence. His address was ill arranged, without logical connection, and full of repetitions, as if uttered on the spur of the moment. But though he had to speak in English, a language he did not habitually use, his speech contained passages of great power of expression, simplicity, and pathos, which showed how he was capable of carrying away an audience who would lend him their sympathy. Viewed as a defence it was nothing, but then the fact of rebellion was undeniable, and the Court would not listen to any justification of it. He said that he did not wish to be acquitted on the ground of insanity:—

"To-day," said the accused, "when I saw the glorious General Middleton bearing testimony that he thought I was not insane, and Captain Young prove that I was not insane, I felt that God was blessing me and blotting away from my name the blot resting on my reputation on account of having been in the lunatic asylum of my good friend Dr. Roy. I have been in an asylum; but I thank the lawyer for the Crown, who destroyed the testimony of my friend, Dr. Roy, because I have always believed that I was put in an asylum without reason; to-day my pretension is guaranteed, and that is a blessing, too, in that way." Then a little after, "The nineteenth century is to be treated in certain ways, and it is probably for that reason I have found the word 'Exovede.' I prefer to be called one of the flock. I am no more than you are; I am simply one of the flock, equal to the rest. If it is any satisfaction to the doctor to know what kind of insanity I have, if they are going to call my pretensions insanity, I say, humbly, through the grace of God, I believe I am the prophet of the New World.

"I wish you to believe that I am not trying to play insanity; there is in the manner, in the standing of a man, the proof that he is sincere, not playing. You will say, What have you got to say? I have to attend to practical results. Is it practical that you be acknowledged as a prophet? Is it practical to say it? I think if the half-breeds have acknowledged me, as a community, to be a prophet, I have reason to believe that it is beginning to become practical. I do not wish for my satisfaction the name of Prophet. Generally that name is accompanied with such a burden, that if there is satisfaction for your vanity, there is a check for it. To set myself up as Pope.

No, no; I said I believed that Bishop Bourget had succeeded the Pope in spirit and in truth. Why? Because, while Rome did not pay attention to us, he, as a bishop, paid attention to us."

Throughout the whole speech we see his sensitive vanity:—

"I know," he said, "that, through the grace of God, I am the founder of Manitoba. I know that, though I have no open road for my influence, I have big influence concentrated as a big amount of vapour in an engine."

He seeks to give a better explanation of statements made by the witnesses about his demeanour and want of self-control:—

"If you take," said he, "the plea of the defence, that I am not responsible for my acts, acquit me completely, since I have been quarrelling with an insane and irresponsible Government. If you pronounce in favour of the Crown, which contends that I am responsible, acquit me all the same. You are perfectly justified in declaring that, having my reason and sound mind, I have acted reasonably and in self-defence, while the Government accuser, being irresponsible and consequently insane, cannot have acted wrong, and if high treason there is, it must be on its side and not on my part.

"For fifteen years I have been neglecting myself; even one of the most hard witnesses on me said that, with all my vanity, I never was particular as to my clothing; yes, because I never had much to buy any clothing. The Reverend Father André has often had the kindness to feed my family with a sack of flour, and Father Fourmond. My wife and children are without means, while I am working more than any representatives in the North-West, although I am simply a guest of this country—a guest of the half-breeds of the Saskatchewan. Although as a simple guest I work to better the condition of the people of the Saskatchewan, at the risk of my life to better the condition of the people of the North-West, I have never had any pay. It has always been my hope to have a fair living one day. It will be for you to pronounce."

The jury were of opinion that the prisoner was sane, and unanimously pronounced him to be guilty of high treason. At the same time, they recommended him to the mercy of the Crown. It was afterwards stated by three of the jurors that this recommendation was based upon a misgiving of the soundness of mind of the prisoner. On being asked if he had anything to say why the sentence of the Court should not be pronounced on him, Riel delivered another address, in which he gave a version of the history of the troubles in 1870 on the Red River and the recent rebellion, justifying his conduct. We reproduce the opening and concluding sentences of his speech, in which he touched on the plea of insanity :—

"Up to this moment I have been considered by a certain party as insane, by another party as a criminal, by another party as a man with whom it was doubtful whether to have any intercourse. So there was hostility, and there was contempt, and there was avoidance. To-day, by the verdict of the Court, one of these situations has disappeared.

"I suppose that, after having been condemned, I will cease to be called a fool, and for me it is a great advantage. If I have a mission, —I say 'if' for the sake of those who doubt, but for my part it means 'since'—since I have a mission, I cannot fulfil my mission as long as I am looked upon as an insane being—human being; at the moment that I begin to ascend that scale, I begin to succeed."

He closed with the following words, which showed a disposition to shift his ground, and a willingness to save his life by availing himself of the plea of insanity :—

"I ask that a commission of doctors examine me. As I am declared guilty, I would like to leave my name, as far as conscience is concerned, all right. If a commission of doctors sits, and if they can examine me, they can see if I was sincere or not. I will give them the whole history; and as I am declared guilty of high treason, it is only right I should be granted the advantages of giving my proofs whether I am sincere, that I am sincere. Now, I am judged a sane man, the cause of my guilt is that I am an imposter, that would be the consequence. I wish a commission to sit and examine me. There have been witnesses around me for ten years, about the time they have declared me insane, and they will show if there is in me the character of an impostor. If they declare me insane, if I have been astray, I have been astray not as an impostor, but according to my conscience."

CHAPTER III.

Variance about Riel's Sentence—The Question of Insanity—The Medical Reports—Riel's Execution and Burial—Debate in the Canadian Parliament about the Death Sentence—The Degree of the Responsibility of the Insane.

The sentence of death pronounced on the leader of the rebellion was looked upon with very different feelings by the two races who share the territory of the Dominion. Those of French origin were generally favourable to Louis Riel, as the champion of the just rights of the metis, and as a man whose faults were to be excused on account of partial derangement; while the British regarded him as an artful and mischievous incendiary who had abused the lenity of the Government by leading the half-breeds for the second time into a dangerous insurrection, which had called away the flower of the young men of Upper Canada on a distant and toilsome expedition, in which many lives had been lost. In Quebec they wished Riel to be pardoned; in Toronto they wished him to be hanged. As many as sixty-three petitions were sent to the Governor-General praying for commutation of the sentence, or a medical inquiry into his sanity, principally it may be presumed from the French Canadians. On the other hand, resolutions were sent from some Orange lodges asking that the law should take its course, and threatening to withdraw their support from the Conservative ministry if Riel's life were spared.

In order that the different appeals put in by Riel's counsel should be heard, it was necessary that a reprieve should be granted. In the meantime the prisoner was confined in a narrow cell, and very strictly guarded. It was asserted that his mental condition was getting worse. In a letter to M. Lemieux Riel's advocate, Father André said :—

"I have just been visiting him, and during an hour he spoke of extraordinary revelations made to him by the Spirit the previous night, and that he has been ordered to communicate to me and to all the Catholic clergy—'The great cause of sin in the world is the revolt of the body against the Spirit. It is because we do not chew our food enough, and by this want of mastication, it communicates animal life only to the body; while by masticating and chewing it well, it spiritualises the body.'

"He has been searching for this secret since fifteen years, and it had been communicated to him but the previous night; and he was in a state of great joy for having discovered this means, which will prove to be a powerful agent to communicate spiritual life in bodies gradually leaving this world to rise to heaven."

While he was speaking, he suddenly stopped, showing me his hand—

"Do you see," says he, "blood flowing in the veins; the telegraph is operating actively, and I feel it; they are talking about me, and questioning authorities in Ottawa about me.

"It is of similar fantastic visions he speaks with me every day. I am convinced that he is not acting a part; he speaks with a conviction and a sincerity which leave no doubt in my mind about the state of his mind; he has retracted his errors, but he believes himself to-day to be a prophet and invested with a Divine mission to reform the world on the day he has spoken to the Court; and when I reprove him for his foolish and extravagant ideas, he answers that he submits, but that he cannot stifle the voice that speaks to him and the Spirit that commands him to communicate to the world the revelations he receives."

The opinion of his old friend, Archbishop Taché, is even more noteworthy :—

"For many years I have been convinced beyond the possibility of a doubt, that, while endowed with brilliant qualities of mind and heart, the unfortunate leader of the metis was a prey to what may be termed 'megalomania' and 'theomania,' which alone can explain his way of acting up to the last moments of his life."

An appeal that the prisoner had not been tried before a competent Court was heard before the judicial committee of the Queen's Privy Council, but was not sustained. In answer to the petition for inquiry as to the prisoner's sanity, Dr. Jukes, of the Mounted Police at Regina, was again asked to report; and two medical men, who had never before seen Riel, were sent to examine him—Dr. Michael Lovell, Warden of Kingston Penitentiary, and Dr. Valade, of Ottawa. They reached Regina on the 7th of November, and immediately commenced to make inquiries about the prisoner, and held long conversations with him.

In considering the reports of these gentlemen, to which all will be prepared to allow great weight, it ought to be borne in mind that the scope of their inquiry was confined by the instructions of the Government who sent them. "As the inquiry could not go behind the decision of the Courts, the examination was necessarily limited to the period subsequent to the verdict of the jury and sentence of Court." Nevertheless, there is not the smallest reason to doubt that these gentlemen made a most careful and painstaking examination of the prisoner. The first report was from Dr. Jukes, who stated :—

"Louis Riel has been under my special care medically, as surgeon of this force, for upwards of five months, since his arrival here as prisoner. During that time I have visited him with few exceptions every day, have studied him closely, and conversed with him long and frequently. I have personally a strong aversion to punishment by death. I believe that, failing to establish his insanity, his death is near at hand, but, after careful and continuous examination of him under varying circumstances from day to day, I cannot escape the conviction that, except upon purely religious questions having relation to what may be called the Divine mysteries, he was when first entrusted to my care and still continues to be perfectly sane and accountable for his actions. Under these circumstances my duty, though a painful one, is clear, and my opinion, not hastily formed, equally so, namely, that Riel's peculiar views upon religious subjects, which so strongly impress the ignorant and unreflecting with an idea of his madness, cannot rightly be regarded as interfering with, or obscuring in the slightest degree his clear perception of duty, or as rendering his judgment less sound in the affairs of everyday life. I therefore record my opinion that, with the reservation above made, Riel is a sane, clear-headed, and accountable being, and responsible for his actions before God and man.—I have, &c.

"(Signed) A. JUKES,
"Senior Surgeon.

"To the Hon. Edgar Dewdney,
"Lieutenant-Governor of N.-W. Territories."

After having finished his examinations, Dr. Lovell, sent on the 8th November, the following report in cypher by telegraph to Sir John Macdonald, at Ottawa:—

"I have the honour to report that having given conscientious consideration to the case of Louis Riel now confined here under sentence of death, and fully appreciating the trust committed to me, and the consequences involved, I am of the opinion that the said Louis Riel, although holding and expressing foolish and peculiar views as to religion and general government, is an accountable being, and capable of distinguishing right from wrong.

"(Signed) M. LOVELL, M.D."

The same day the other medical man sent transmitted the following report:—

"REGINA, 8th November, 1885.

"SIR,—After having examined carefully Riel in private conversation with him and by testimony of persons who took care of him, I have come to the conclusion that he suffers under a hallucination on political and religious subjects, but on other points I believe him to be quite sensible and able to distinguish right from wrong.

"(Signed) F. X. VALADE, M.D."

On receiving the opinions of these three medical men the Government at once ordered the execution of Riel. It took place within the precincts of the jail on the morning of the 16th of November, 1885. Riel had been reconciled to the Catholic Church and had given up his peculiar views in religion.*

---

* This statement is twice made in documents in my possession on the authority of Father André. Dr. Clark quotes the *Toronto Mail* to prove that Riel took advantage of the presence of Father M'Williams on the Friday night before his execution, to affirm his Divine mission. "I am," he said, "a prophet; I have been ordained, not as a priest but as the prophet of the North-West, to preach a reformation to you and every minister of the Church, and will continue to fulfil my mission till I mount the scaffold. Then pointing towards the scaffold and fixing

He received the sacraments of the Church, and Fathers André and M'Williams followed him to the scaffold. He was dissuaded by the priests from delivering a last address. He met his fate with courage and composure. After death the hair was cut off one side of the head and face, the buttons were torn off the coat, and the moccasins cut in pieces to obtain relics of the deceased. The body was placed in a deal coffin to await the directions of the Government.

Dr. Clark says he was so sure that some changes indicating insanity would be found in Riel's brain that he represented to the Government to have a *post mortem* examination held, but this was refused. The body, after being kept for four weeks, was given to his relations for burial.

The controversy about the responsibility of the leader of the Metis did not end with his life. Resolutions blaming the Ministry for carrying out the sentence were passed at large meetings at Montreal and Quebec; and in March, 1886, a motion was proposed in the Dominion Parliament calling on the House to express its deep regret that the sentence of death was allowed to be carried into execution. This motion, supported by the Opposition, led to an interesting debate, in which great rhetorical ability was shown on both sides. The chief speakers in favour of the motion were Mr. Laurier, C. Cameron, and the Honourable Edward Blake, the leader of the Liberal party. They blamed the Ministers for their inattention to the just claims of the Metis, who only asked what was granted to them after the suppression of the insurrection. They insisted that the leader of the rebellion was not tried before a proper tribunal, and that the recommendation to mercy should not have passed unheeded. Their strongest plea, however, was that Riel was not responsible for what he had done, his mind being influenced by delusions

---

his eyes upon the priest, he shouted, To that scaffold will I walk boldly, preaching the mission of Church reformation so much needed throughout the world."

Dr. Clark also tells us that a few days before his execution, he wrote to a clerical friend in Winnipeg a long farewell letter, in which he repeats his principal religious delusions. *Op. cit.*, p. 15.

on religion and politics, which swayed his conduct during the period the alleged crimes were committed. Legal and medical authorities were cited, and the difficult question, How far insane delusions exempt a man from responsibility? was argued in the most exhaustive manner.

No doubt there were people ready to blame the Government for letting the leader of the rebellion escape with a lesser punishment than his dupes; while there were others ready to blame them for hanging a lunatic. It is not easy even for one out of the range of political interests and passions, to judge what alternative they should have preferred, for on each side there seems to be considerations which nicely balance one another. We admit that there are many living in our present state of society who are really insane, but who, nevertheless, manage to discharge their usual employments, to do their duty as citizens, and to pass unsuspected through the world. But, while we allow these people to live without seeking to deprive them of their liberty, or the right of managing their own affairs, while we suffer them to make contracts and to draw up testaments, it will scarcely do to pretend that these people should escape all punishment when their conduct brings them within the grasp of the law. The law treats a man as either mad or not mad; but between the sanity that is beyond question and the insanity that is sure to be recognised, there are many gradations. Some delusions may affect the conduct, others not. Some delusions may weaken the will to resist temptation in one direction, and even strengthen it in another. A man may be insane in one direction, and wicked in another. Sometimes it is difficult to say where the villain ends and the lunatic begins, hence some physicians well acquainted with the many forms of lunacy have proposed that there should be varying degrees of responsibility, and corresponding grades of punishment. It might be objected to this, that as a man's mind approaches insanity, the punishment to have a deterrent effect would in many cases need to be rendered more severe instead of less so. Naturally the plea of insanity rarely comes in save where all other defence fails; it is seldom urged save to excuse great crimes, as the punishment and collateral disqualifications the very admission of lunacy entails, would generally bear more severely on an offender than what the law would pass upon anything less than a very grave offence.

The new definitions of Sir James Stephens and others were no doubt an improvement over the tattered axioms of the old jurists, but define and generalise as cleverly as you may, there will always arise cases of insanity which have bearings that have not been foreseen. Towards the close of a masterly speech Mr. Blake said:—

"My conclusion is clear that Riel was so disordered in mind as not, within the accepted rule, to have been a proper subject for the capital sentence. It is impossible, in cases of serious delusion or so-called monomania, to be sure how far the flaw has affected the conduct in question. It may not have affected it in some cases, though whether it did or not is very frequently a question beyond the wit of man to determine. But here we know it did, because we know that the flaw had regard to these very two points of religion and politics, upon which this rising and these events turned. Criminal responsibility then, for public security, there may and must be, though there may be some mental disorder, but not responsibility unto death; and here again comes in the political nature of the offence, the general rules relating to these offences and the special circumstances of the conduct of the Government in this matter; and my belief, therefore, is that the maximum sentence for the same crime of which Riel was convicted, had he been tried under the milder procedure of the modern law under which his colleagues were tried—namely, imprisonment for life—would have been the proper and adequate disposition of his case."

The task of replying to the orators of the Opposition devolved upon the Honourable S. D. Thompson, the Minister of Justice. He answered the questions of jurisdiction, and vindicated the fairness of Riel's trial. Without asserting that the man was perfectly sane, or that he was merely acting a part, Mr. Thompson blamed the unworthiness of the tricks which Riel had used to push the Metis and Indians into revolt, and pointedly asked, What was the character of the Divine mission which the prophet had offered to abandon on the receipt of 35,000 dollars? The honourable gentleman showed considerable ignorance of the lore of lunacy when he argued that Riel, had he been insane, could not have influenced his sane followers, and that it was proof of his soundness of mind that he put under restraint one of the half-breeds who had become mad. The conclusion of Mr. Thompson's speech was well calculated to have a powerful effect on the minds of practical politicians. He said :—

"With regard to what might have been done in this case, I would like to invite the reflection of the House for a moment as to what must have followed if executive clemency had been exercised. One section of hon. gentlemen opposite hold that this man ought to have been condemned to imprisonment as a criminal, a great criminal, although not so great as to be outside the executive clemency; another class on that side say, No, he was totally mad, and he simply should have been put into an asylum. Had either course been taken, how long would his confinement have lasted? If the executive ought to have acted on the broad principle that this was only a political offence, and that, therefore, the executive clemency should have been extended to it, it would have been inconsistent with that view that Riel should have been long detained in prison. If he were confined in a lunatic asylum, how long, I ask, with the power the evidence showed he had during the outbreak, of controlling his own conduct and of getting possession of his senses when he wanted them—with the power of controlling his action and recovering his balance when he wanted it— how long would it have been deemed just by the humane sentiment of the country to keep him in confinement? He would have been set at liberty, under the report that he was cured and no longer mad, and he could have established a cure whenever he chose ; and what then would have been the security for life and property in the North-West? I think that Louis Riel's next exclamation would have been, not that the rebellion of 1869-70 was not a patch upon that of 1885, but that both together would not be a patch on the rebellion he would raise the next time. I think that to have exercised the executive clemency in a case like that would have been, in the words I have quoted from Mr. Justice Stephen, 'not benevolence, but cowardice.' But let me ask attention to another point connected with this branch of the subject. Let me call attention to the fact that the Indians, who this man incited to rise, perpetrated some very cruel murders at Frog Lake, which called, in every sense of the word, loudly for the execution of the supreme penalty of the law against the Indians concerned in that massacre, not only because they committed great crimes, but on other grounds on which it is deemed proper to inflict capital punishment, namely, that it is absolutely necessary, by making a great example through the infliction of such punishment, to deter people disposed to crime from committing it. How could the perpetrators of the Frog Lake massacre have been punished, if the man who incited them to rebel—and the massacre was to them the natural result of the rebellion—had escaped? How could the punishment of the law have been meted out to them, or any deterrent effect have been achieved, if 'the arch-conspirator,' the 'arch-traitor,' if the 'trickster,' as he had been called by men who did him their best service, was allowed to go free or kept in a lunatic asylum until he chose to get rid of his temporary delusions? It was absolutely necessary, as I have said, to show to those people, to those Indians, and to every section of the country, and to every class of the population there, that the power of the Government in the North-West was strong, not only to protect, but to punish."

There are occasions in which the safety of the State is the supreme law, but the expediency of statesmen will be most sympathised with by statesmen themselves. The Canadian Ministry seem to have regarded the grave as a strong prison, to whose gates there is fortunately no key for the weakness and mercy of popular assemblies. It is difficult to reconcile oneself to the idea that the penalty of death should have been exacted because the Crees and Sioux did not understand the plea of insanity, or might think it unjust that their own chiefs should be hanged for murder while Riel should only be sent to an asylum for life.

In the case of Guiteau the published evidence was so full that one can see all the grounds of the judgment, but then this was at Washington. At Batoche and Regina there was no one accustomed to study the symptoms of insanity, and the information given to the world is by no means complete enough to enable one to say that he has gone over all the material facts of the case. Experts came from a distance, had a short time to stay, were required to give a round opinion, and then go away. Thus one is induced to lay considerable stress upon the opinion of Dr. Roy, who had treated Riel for months in his asylum, and recognised the same symptoms again. Dr. D. Clark [*] believes that Riel had several successive attacks of

---

[*] Dr. Clark writes:—"There is no doubt that Riel was responsible for some years, up to the time of the Duck Lake fight. The excitement of

insanity. One appeared when he was studying for the Church, during which time he wrote letters full of insane delusions, another when he was sent to the asylum at Longue Pointe, probably a third when he was at Washington, and a fourth paroxysm was brought on by the excitement of the Duck Lake fight.

Under this admission, however, it might be held that Riel was, when still a sane man, guilty of treason, for the first count in the indictment against him was the levying of war on the Queen's forces at Duck Lake. He had already got the half-breeds to plunder the stores, he had them assembled with arms in their hands, and though he afterwards recognised that the fight was somewhat premature, a man who prepares a conflagration cannot be excused because his explosive materials go off a little too soon. Nevertheless, we should certainly like to have more evidence about Riel's mental condition after this fight. Dr. Clark says :—

"I spoke to some of the half-breeds who were in all the engagements with Riel, and they uniformly said he was not the same man after the first fight. He seemed to have changed entirely, and became frenzied. He organised no opposition after this time. did no fighting, but was looked upon as inspired by his deluded followers, and ran about from rifle-pit to rifle-pit, holding aloft a crucifix, and calling upon the Trinity for aid. The military organisers, leaders and fighters, were Dumont and Dumais. These sane, shrewd, and brave rebels have been amnestied by our Government, but the mental weakling was hanged."

Certainly this is not confirmed by the published evidence in the Parliamentary Reports, but then the depositions at the trial are mostly made by witnesses who were willing to get their friends off by throwing the blame on Riel. Moreover, after an unsuccessful undertaking, there are always recriminations. No one whose opinion is worth quoting seems to dispute that Riel's religious delusions were genuine, though he probably made the most of them for the purpose of helping his ambition, and resorted to some mean artifices, for Riel was

---

that fight caused another attack of insanity, and from that time there is no evidence that he was accountable for what he did."—p. 16.

selfish and indifferent to human life and suffering when his ends were to be served. Firm religious faith does not always lead a man to fair dealing.

There is one other point on which we have to be satisfied. It seems to me that Riel's delusions bore directly upon his conduct in raising the rebellion. He thought that he had a Divine mission to help his brethren, the half-breeds, to establish different States in the North-West, and to found a new religion ; granting this, it seems to follow that he had a right to take up arms to carry out these beliefs. The law may hold that a man is responsible to the full, or not at all. In this case it would seem imprudent to have held Riel not responsible, and to have sent him to an asylum to be set free on being declared recovered. On the other hand, if he sincerely entertained these delusions, it is difficult to see how they did not diminish his responsibility. With all respect to the medical men to whom was intrusted the painful and onerous duty of reporting on Riel's mental condition, I should like, before treating their verdict as conclusive, to know the logical process by which they arrived at their opinion ; others may be more quick-witted and sagacious, but I cannot rehearse it in my own mind.

Without pretending to know all the facts, and see clearly the whole question, it appears to me a matter of regret that the full punishment of death was carried out on Louis Riel. He was clearly too dangerous a man to be let go, and if he had been kept in prison, any future Government would have committed an act of deplorable weakness in setting him free ; but it was surely enough for the Ottawa Ministers to bear their own responsibilities without shutting the door on the possible temptations which they thought their successors might be too weak to withstand. At the same time, it is impossible to go over this passage in the history of the Dominion without recognising the great ability, courage, and patriotism which the Canadian Government displayed throughout these trying events.

GABRIEL MALAGRIDA.

GABRIEL MALAGRIDA* was born at Mercajo, near Milan, on the 18th of September, 1689. At the age of twenty-two he was admitted into the Society of Jesus, and in 1722 he set out as a missionary to Brazil. Here he laboured at the conversion of the Indian tribes on the Maragnon. The Jesuits were at this time engaged in forming a number of States on the frontier of the Portuguese and Spanish colonies in South America, taking the entire direction of the temporal and spiritual affairs of their converts. In this work Malagrida showed that daring and activity which did not leave the Jesuit missionaries even in their degenerate days. He went about on the hot ground with bare feet, and lived on roots and wild fruits. On his body there were scars which bore tokens of wounds from arrows and the bites of wild

---

* The principal authorities used in writing this sketch are—" Memoirs of the Marquis of Pombal, with extracts from his writings, and from Despatches in the State Paper Office," by John Smith, Private Secretary to the Marquis de Saldanha. London. 1843.

Nouvelle Biographie Générale. Paris, 1860. Art. Malagrida, by A. de Lacaze.

Griesinger's "History of the Jesuits," translated by A. J. Scott, M.D. London, 1885.

"Anecdotes du Ministère de Sebastien Joseph Carvalho, Comte D'Oeyras, Marquis de Pombal." Nouvelle édition, à Varsovie. 1784.

"Anedoti del Ministero, di S. G. Carvalho, Marchese di Pombal," &c. 1787.

These last two books are written in defence of the Jesuits. The one seems a translation of the other, some passages being missed out in the Italian version. I have been obliged to depend entirely on them for the account of Malagrida's life in South America.

beasts, received during his wanderings amongst the Indians. They said that he never kept money about him, and when he wished to go to any distant expedition, he would enter the first vessel which would receive him, and live on alms. He was unwearied in his religious duties. Sermons, confessions, catechising visits, nothing was neglected; but he was especially zealous in practising the spiritual exercises of Loyola, which had such a powerful effect in deepening religious impressions. Malagrida got several houses founded for orphans and young girls, and was unwearied in pushing the work. The father himself might be seen amongst the labourers bearing stones and mortar. Twice he crossed the ocean to go to Lisbon to complain of the oppression of the Portuguese against the native Indians. The father gained the title of the Apostle of Brazil, the Francis Xavier of his age. After labouring as a missionary for twenty-seven years, Malagrida was induced by Marianne of Austria, the Queen of Portugal, to become her spiritual adviser. On his landing at Lisbon in 1754, Dom José, Prince of Brazil, afterwards King of Portugal, fell at the father's feet to receive his blessing; and the reigning monarch, John V., practised spiritual exercises under his direction. Through a mixture of austerity and mystic piety, Malagrida soon acquired a wonderful deal of influence at the Court of Lisbon. He lived solely on bread and beans, half-starving himself through his frequent fasts; he applied the scourge to his bare shoulders, and only allowed himself a few hours' sleep on a plank, or on the bare ground. He had a house of retreat in Lisbon, where he took in penitents to perform religious exercises, and was a favourite confessor among the nobility. Malagrida was also an eloquent and persuasive preacher, and wrote several dramatic pieces. So great was his reputation for holiness, that the Pope, Benedict XIV., in a letter about the death of John V., wrote that it was a happy augury for his salvation that the King had died in the arms of Father Gabriel. John V. had been an indolent and luxurious ruler who, while given to the pleasures of the world and neglecting his duties, yet felt the terrors of the Church. For several years before his death, he had been in a state of fatuity. At the accession of his son, Joseph I., in 1750, the state of the country was at its lowest. The laws were feebly observed, feared only by the weak; commerce gone from the people, what remained was in the hands of the Jesuits, the finances in confusion, corruption and embezzlement everywhere, the army and navy and civil establishment existed mostly in name, for the benefit of functionaries whose function was to draw pay. The nobles were insolent in their claims of privilege, and all classes plunged in ignorance and superstition. The clergy had gained an exorbitant share of the wealth of the kingdom. For more than a hundred years, since Francis Xavier and Simon Rodriguez had come to Lisbon, the Jesuits had been powerful in Portugal. Teachers of youth, favourite confessors of the great ladies at Court, the holders of much wealth and far-reaching social influence behind the scenes, they directed the affairs of State, and ruined every one who opposed them. Fortunately for Portugal, the new King, Dom Joseph, called to his counsels one of those great and gifted men who now and then appear to save a State from ruin, Sebastian Joseph de Carvalho e Mello, Count d'Oeyras, best known in history as the Marquis of Pombal. As the son of a simple country gentleman, he could scarcely expect a high career as a statesman amongst the haughty and exclusive nobility of Portugal. But his tall and handsome figure, noble countenance, and persuasive manner, had gained him the hand of a lady of high rank and great wealth. In 1739 he was sent as an ambassador to London, where he remained fourteen years, after which he became ambassador to Vienna. For his second wife he married the daughter of Marshal Daun. Like Cavour, he carefully observed the working of the British Constitution, and inquired into the causes of the commercial prosperity of Great Britain. He took Sully for his model, and his work in Portugal had much similarity to what was done in France by the great Huguenot Minister. Pombal at once set himself to take measures to revive trade, to regulate the government of the colonies, to correct the abuses of the revenue, to diminish the multiplicity of offices, and put an end to the waste in the royal household, as far as waste in royal households can be put an end to. These reforms excited the hostility of the nobility and the dangerous resentment of the Jesuits, who would fain have governed the new king as they did the old one. They used their myriad arts to ruin the Minister in the opinion of the sovereign, and freely denounced his reforms from the pulpit. The Marquis was not slow in retaliating. He got the Jesuits expelled from the palace, and persuaded the King to take a Franciscan for a confessor. He induced the Pope to issue a bull to prohibit the Jesuits making slaves of the Indians, took measures to break up the independent States they were forming on the Maragnon and in Paraguay, and got the Cardinal de Saldanha to be made nuncio for Portugal, with powers to bring the clergy into better discipline. As the Jesuits still continued talking against the new reforms and stirring up disorders, the Cardinal caused them to be prohibited from preaching and confessing in Portugal. Moreover, the Marquis sent an energetic message to the Pope that the order of the Jesuits should be recalled to their original purity. On this the indignation of the holy fathers arrived at such a height, that they considered the earthquake which threw Lisbon in ruins on the 1st November, 1755, as quite an appropriate manifestation of the Divine displeasure. It was remembered at that dreadful time, when the King was trembling with religious terror, that he cried out to his Minister, who had just entered the palace, "What is to be done to meet this infliction of Divine justice?" "Bury the dead, and feed the living," was the calm reply of Pombal. The able measures taken to give help and restore security raised the great Marquis still more in the estimation of the King. But the Jesuits naturally did not lose their claim to the earthquake without some exertion of their accustomed eloquence. Father Malagrida wrote a little book pointing out the absurdity of attributing the earthquake to spiritual causes, or anything else than the indignation of God at the innovations of Carvalho. Copies of this sagacious production were sent to the king and queen and great persons of the Court, and even to the Marquis himself.

Malagrida also wrote a dramatic piece called Haman, in which the satrap of Ahasuerus was described in terms which looked very like the Minister of Joseph I. Enraged at this,

Pombal got the cardinal to order Malagrida to be sent across the Tagus to Setubal. About this time the Jesuits got a prophecy spread abroad that there was to be another earthquake, and even had the imprudence to fix a date for it on the same day of the following year. The non-fulfilment of the prophecy only strengthened the hands of the Minister. Despairing of ruining Pombal in the favour of the King, it was determined to assassinate Dom José in order to have an end of Dom Sebastian. The principal instigator of the conspiracy was the Marchioness of Tavora, to whom Malagrida acted as confessor. The young Marchioness, her daughter-in-law, had become the King's mistress, and this no doubt exasperated the family of Tavora, for all the male members of it were engaged in the plot. On the night of the third of September, 1758, as the King was returning from the house of his mistress in a carriage the Duke of Aveiro and John Miguel rode up and directed their guns at him; one did not go off, the other missed its aim. Two more horsemen pursued the carriage and fired slugs into it, by which the King's arm was lacerated. Joseph had the presence of mind to order the carriage to be turned round and driven to the house of his surgeon, who stopped the bleeding and dressed his wounds. The injury was not announced, and the King was kept in seclusion in order that inquiry should better be made about the authors of the murderous attempt. Nothing broke the quiet surface of society; nobody stirred; nobody fled; no one was arrested. Pombal suffered no word to escape him that might betray his intentions. In a letter afterwards found amongst the papers of the Marquis of Tavora, the writer says:—" The silence of this man alarms me. He appears perfectly easy about what has occurred." It is said that one of the measures of Pombal to gain a clue to the conspiracy was to order a ship to sail from Lisbon to Brazil. Several Jesuits took their passages, and the captain had sealed instructions to search all the passengers' papers, and then to return with what word he could collect. On the 9th of December, three months after the attempt on the life of the King, a proclamation was published giving an account of the affair, and offering a reward for the apprehension of the criminals.

"Four days afterwards, on the 13th of December, the work of retributive justice commenced by the arrest of the Marquis of Tavora, his two sons, his four brothers, his sons-in-law, the Count d'Atouguia and the Marquis d'Alorna, together with Dom Manoel de Souza Calhariz; all of whom, with some of their servants, were conveyed to the prisons at Belem. The Marchioness of Tavora was sent to a religious house. Other members of the Tavora family were likewise imprisoned or immured in convents. In the meanwhile, the Count d'Obidos, Antonio da Costa Freire, the Solicitor-General, and the Count de Ribeira, were also arrested, and the Jesuits were forbidden to leave their homes."*

The Duke of Aveiro was also arrested; his valet, who had been engaged in the affair, escaped. Ten Jesuits were also seized. Amongst them was the Provincial, the Procurator-General of Portugal, and that of Brazil, and the former confessors of the King and Queen.

According to the Marquis Pombal, Malagrida had written letters to different parts of Europe predicting that the King of Portugal would not survive the September of 1758. The father was conveyed from Setubal on the 11th of December, and on the 13th he was taken by the Cardinal Saldanha to the house of the Minister, by whom he was examined, especially about a letter which he had written to Donna Anna de Lorena, one of the ladies of the palace, warning the King of the danger which hung over him. Malagrida himself said that the letter was rather written as a warning of the danger to which the King exposed his soul, than to save his life. Probably the letter was of a vague character, for it had been returned to Malagrida without being shown to the King, and was found amongst his papers at Setubal.†

A tribunal was appointed to try the accused, most of whom

---

* Smith, *op. cit.*, vol. i. p. 194.

† In the Anecdotes published at Warsaw, the fact of the letter is admitted:—"Tout ce qui en a transféré, c'est qu'il y fut question d'une lettre qu'il avoit écrite dans son exil à Setubal pour prevenir le Roi du danger auquel il s'exposait. Cette lettre que sa Majesté ne vit point, fut trouvée parmi les papiers de ce père."—p. 164.

In the Italian Anedoti all mention of this inculpatory letter is passed over.

confessed their guilt. The sentences against them were carried into execution on the following day. Here is the description given by Mr. Hay, the British Minister, of this dreadful spectacle :—

"Saturday, the 13th of January, being the day appointed for the execution, a scaffold had been built in the square of Belem, opposite to the house where the prisoners were confined, and eight wheels fixed upon it. On one corner of the scaffolding was placed Antonio Alvares Ferreira, and on the other corner the effigy of Joseph Policarpo de Azevedo, who is still missing—these being two persons who fired at the back of the King's equipage. About half an hour after eight o'clock in the morning, the execution began. The criminals were brought out one by one, each under a strong guard. The Marchioness of Tavora was the first that was brought upon the scaffold, where she was beheaded at one stroke. Her body was afterwards placed upon the floor of the scaffolding, and covered with a linen cloth. Young José Maria de Tavora, the young Marquis of Tavora, the Count d'Atouguia, and three servants of the Duke of Aveiro, were first strangled at a stake, and afterwards their limbs broken with an iron instrument. The Marquis of Tavora and the Duke of Aveiro had their limbs broken alive. The Duke, for greater ignominy, was brought bareheaded to the place of execution. The body and limbs of each of the criminals, after they were executed, were thrown upon a wheel, and covered with a linen cloth. But when Antonio Alvares Ferreira was brought to the stake, whose sentence was to be burnt alive, the other bodies were exposed to his view. The combustible matter which had been laid under the scaffolding was set fire to; the whole machine with the bodies was consumed to ashes, and then thrown into the sea."

The name of Tavora was abolished, and the young Marchioness, whose conduct had aroused the anger of her family against the King, was sent to a convent, "not a very strict one, it is said, where she lives very much at her ease."

As from the explanations made, and the documents discovered, the Jesuits were believed to be the contrivers of the conspiracy, the King issued a decree for the sequestration of all their property, real and personal, which turned out to be very large. The Jesuits denied complicity in the plot, which they attributed to the desire of two noble families,* to revenge a private injury. Nevertheless the Jesuits tried to excuse the conduct of the conspirators. They then got the Pope, Clement XIII., to take their part, but the resolute Marquis collected all the fathers and brothers of the order together and sent them away in ships. It is said that in all 1200 Jesuits were landed at Civita Vecchia. They were at the same time expelled from all the foreign dominions of Portugal. This order had got incorrigibly corrupt and intriguing, and the exposure to which they were subjected by the Marquis of Pombal was one of the blows which hastened their downfall. The order was abolished by Clement XIV. in 1773.

One hundred and thirteen of the Jesuits were kept at St. Julian, a rock in the sea about three hours' sail from Lisbon. Thirty-nine of them died there. Thirty-six were deported to Italy in 1767, and the rest set free after the death of King Joseph.

But to return to Malagrida, he, along with two other Jesuit fathers, Alexander and De Mattos, were kept in prison, as being implicated in the conspiracy. But in Portugal there was still a difficulty in trying ecclesiastics for secular offences, so, instead of committing Malagrida for high treason, it was thought preferable to accuse him of heresy. No doubt the case of that eccentric Jesuit caused the authorities some perplexity. He was now, we are told,†

"either a perfect hypocrite, or he laboured under a most extraordinary religious hallucination. He passed many hours a-day in prayer in the most painful postures, sometimes with his head touching the ground, at others, in positions still more difficult and painful. He believed that he heard a voice continually calling him, a delusion which Mattos and many others of his companions declared was Divine inspiration."

During his confinement he wrote a book, in Portuguese, entitled "Heroic and Wonderful Life of the glorious St. Anne,

---

* "Histoire Genérale de la Naissance et des Progrès de la Compagnie de Jesus." Amsterdam, 1761. Tome quatrième, pp. 236 and 239.

† SMITH, vol. i. p. 206.

Mother of the Holy Virgin Mary, dictated by this Saint, assisted by and with the Approbation and Help of this Most August Sovereign, and of her Most Holy Son." This book swarmed with absurdities. Amongst other things, Malagrida revealed—

"That St. Anne had been sanctified in her mother's womb, in the same manner that the holy Virgin had been sanctified in that of St. Anne.

"That the privilege of being sanctified in the womb of her mother was granted only to St. Anne, and to Mary, her daughter.

"That St. Anne, in the womb of her mother, heard, knew, loved, and served God, like all the saints elevated to glory.

"That St. Anne, in the womb of her mother, did shed tears, and excited tears of compassion in the cherubim and seraphim, who were in her company.

"That St. Anne, while yet in her mother's womb, made her vows; and in order that neither of the Divine powers should have cause of jealousy by the appearance of more affection towards one than towards another, she had made her vow of poverty to the Eternal Father, her vow of obedience to the Eternal Son, her vow of chastity to the Eternal Holy Ghost, &c.

"That he (Malagrida) had heard the Father Eternal speak with a clear and distinct voice, as also the Son and the Holy Ghost. That St. Anne married to be more of a virgin (*per essere più vergine*).

"That the family of St. Anne, besides the masters and some other persons, consisted of twenty slaves—twelve men and eight women.

"That St. James followed the trade of stone hewer or mason, and that he lived in Jerusalem with St. Anne; that she was the strong woman of whom Solomon had spoken, but that this King had made a mistake, since it was from among his own people, and of his own blood, that this blessed woman was to be born.

"That St. Anne had built a sanctuary at Jerusalem for fifty-three devout girls; that, to complete the buildings, angels had disguised themselves as carpenters; and that for the support of these girls, one of them, named Martha, bought fish, and sold it again with profit through the city; that some of these devout girls of St. Anne had married solely to obey God, who had decreed from all eternity that these blessed girls, brought up under the inspection of St. Anne, should become mothers of saints, male and female, and of several apostles and disciples of Jesus Christ; that one of them had married Nicodemus; that another had married St. Matthew; another, Joseph of Arimathea;

T

and that from the marriage of another, St. Lin, the successor of St. Peter, was born.

"That the holy Virgin, in the womb of her mother, had spoken these words:—'Comfort you, my well-beloved mother, for you have found grace before the Lord; here you shall conceive, and you shall bring forth a daughter, whom you shall call Mary. The Spirit of the Lord shall rest upon her, and shall cover her with His shadow. He will conceive in her, and by her the Son of the Most High, who shall save His people.'"

Malagrida affirmed that the Virgin had made this revelation to him, and that she had added thereto:—

"That rejoicings were made in Paradise during eight days for this event and these miraculous words. Moreover, that God had told him not to hesitate raising the grandeur of the Virgin Mary above all bounds—*usque ad excessum et ultra;* that thus he was not to fear to appropriate to her, and to make her participate in, the attributes of God Himself, of immensity, infinity, eternity, and omnipotence."

"That the sacred body of Jesus had been formed from a drop of blood from the heart of the holy Virgin; that it had grown by degrees, by virtue of the nourishment taken by her mother, till such time as it was perfectly organised, and capable of receiving the soul which had been united to it; but that the Divinity and the Person of the Word had already united themselves to this last drop of blood, at the very instant that it left the heart of the Holy Virgin to enter her most pure womb; that the three Divine Persons had had many deliberations and consultations together; that there had been many propositions and many opinions on the title and rank which should be given to St. Anne; and that at last they had taken the resolution to give her a superiority over all the angels and all the saints."

Malagrida also wrote in Latin a treatise on the "Life and Empire of Antichrist," in which he said there were to be three Antichrists—a father, son, and nephew. The last of these personages was to be born at Milan in A.D. 1920, the child of a nun and monk. He was to take for his wife Proserpine, one of the infernal furies. We do not learn what was to be the result of this imprudent marriage.

From all this we have no difficulty in coming to the conclusion that the old priest was affected with delusional insanity, but we are told that he was mad only on one subject, though much given to melancholy. Before the Inquisition, which treated him as a heretic, Malagrida persisted to the last in maintaining the proof of his prophecies, nor would he deny any of the miracles attributed to him, the visions he had seen, or the supernatural revelations with which he had been favoured. Not being accustomed to deal with lunatics, the Inquisitors could make nothing of the old priest, and being Dominicans they were no friends to the Jesuits. Father Gabriel Malagrida was convicted of the crime of heresy, in having affirmed, written, and defended propositions and doctrines opposed to the true faith. He was convicted of hypocrisy, and of obstinately professing the same errors. He was deposed and degraded from his order, and delivered up, with the gag, the cap of infamy, and the label of arch-heretic, to secular justice, "praying earnestly that the said criminal may be treated with kindness and indulgence, without pronouncing against him sentence of death or effusion of blood." This recommendation to mercy was not attended to.

Mr. Hay records that Pombal had told him that if Malagrida had not suffered from heresy, he would have undergone another trial for high treason. "The political intrigues in which this artful and designing man had been engaged, the estimation in which he was held by many bigoted and superstitious individuals, and the influence he had acquired as confessor to so many noble families, rendered him a dangerous ally and an implacable enemy, two characters which reconcile us to the severity of the sentence which the necessities of the times rendered imperative."

Malagrida was sentenced on the 20th September, 1761, three years after his arrest, to be strangled and burned. This was executed at the auto-da-fé, held on the 21st, in the Plaça da Rocio at Lisbon. He was now seventy-two years of age.

Fifty wretches figured in the procession; fourteen of them were baptised Jews, suspected of relapsing; there were also some sailors convicted of bigamy, and two Pietist nuns. Malagrida was the only one of them all who suffered the pain of death. Dressed in a tiara and long robe, he was preceded by a crier, who, in a loud voice, proclaimed his iniquities. A pitying eye in the crowd saw the old priest cast a deprecating glance on the figures of devils pictured on his robe. His Jesuit friends recorded that when near his end he said, "I confess that I am a sinner; and as to my revelations, it is not expedient to say what I think of them."

The execution of Malagrida made some sensation in the Catholic countries of Europe, and was the cause of some heated controversy amongst the religious orders in Italy. The Jesuits denied the accusations against him, and treated him as a martyred saint.

It is curious to observe that Malagrida was a contemporary of Swedenborg, and had the latter lived in the Spanish instead of the Scandinavian Peninsula, he might have had a similar fate. In his "Siècle de Louis XV.," Voltaire wrote, "Malagrida was condemned to be burnt without being brought to question about the assassination of the King, because that was only a fault against one of the laity and the rest was a crime against God. Thus the excess of the ridiculous and the absurd was joined to the excess of the horrible. The culprit was brought to judgment as a prophet, and was burnt, not for having been a regicide, but for having been mad."

It seems strange that the Jesuits should have allowed a man obviously deranged to occupy a position in which he might compromise their order. Perhaps they were slow to distinguish excess of religious zeal from mental derangement.

THEODORE, KING OF ABYSSINIA.

THEODORE OF ABYSSINIA.

ABYSSINIA, a country unique in Africa, is a wide table-land fully 6000 feet above the sea-level. It is separated from the coast of the Red Sea by a belt of low and almost waterless desert. This beautiful country of high mountains and fertile valleys, enjoying from its elevation a temperate climate, is inhabited by a peculiar race of the white family of men, whose affinities are lost in prehistoric times. While all around adopted the creed of the Arabian prophet, the Abyssinians remained Christian, following the rites of the Coptic Church, and preserving some old sacred books and traditions. For the last three centuries, the once powerful empire of Ethiopia had been in a state of decay. Suffering from the encroachment of the Gallas on the south, shut out from the sea-board by the Turks, with anarchy, civil war, and feudal oppression within, the people had all the vices, and endured all the miseries of semi-civilised nations. About the year 1865, Abyssinia, almost forgotten by the rest of Christendom, suddenly became the object of attention and interest through the crimes and follies of its ruler, who had provoked the resentment of the only European power that could get within striking distance of his remote dominions. The strange character and deplorable career of this man is all the more deserving of study that such another is not likely again to appear even in Abyssinia.

There is some obscurity about the early history of Theodore.*

---

* My information about Theodore is principally derived from the following works :—

From what appears the most trustworthy accounts, he was born in 1822, others say 1818, in the province of Quara, on the north-west frontier of Abyssinia. His father is said to have been Hailu Weleda Georgis, brother to Dejatch Confou, governor of the north-west province of Abyssinia.

According to Stern, his father died while the boy was still very young, and the property left by the deceased noble was seized and squandered by dishonest relatives. His mother, thus rendered destitute, repaired to Gondar, where she eked out a poor living by the sale of kosso, a medicine much in use owing to the habit the people in Abyssinia have of eating raw flesh. Kasa, as he was then called, was from childhood passionate, impatient, and proud. He was sent* to a convent at Tschangar, near the northern shores of Lake Dembea, to be educated for a scribe. Here Kasa was taught to read and write, learned the Bible history, and had his mind imbued with the religious traditions of Abyssinia, which exercised an enduring influence upon his thoughts and actions. He was not suffered to remain long in this peaceful abode, for a fugitive rebel chief, thinking the

---

"The Captive Missionary: being an account of the Country and People of Abyssinia, embracing a Narrative of King Theodore's life, &c.," by the Rev. Henry A. Stern. London, 1869.

"A Narrative of Captivity in Abyssinia, with some account of the late Emperor Theodore, his Country and People," by Henry Blanc, M.D. London, 1868.

"The Story of the Captives, a Narrative of the Events of Mr. Rassam's Mission to Abyssinia," by Dr. Blanc, one of the Captives, with a Translation of M. Le Jean's articles on Abyssinia and its Monarch. London, 1868.

"Narrative of the British Mission to Theodore, King of Abyssinia," by Hormuzd Rassam. In two volumes. London, 1869.

"The British Captives in Abyssinia," by Charles T. Beke, Ph.D., F.S.A. London, 1867.

"A History of the Abyssinian Expedition," by Clements R. Markham. London, 1869.

"The Abyssinian Expedition, with Engravings from the *Illustrated London News*," by Roger Acton. London, 1868.

* The Rev. Mr. Stern, who is valuable for giving details, tells us that, "Impatient, passionate, and proud, he (Kasa) disdained the humble vocation of his mother, and in a fit of anger left her poor hut and took refuge in a convent in Tschangar, near the northern shores of Lake Tzana." This is perhaps the only instance on record of a wild boy running away to school.

convent to afford a safe prey and an easy vengeance on the fathers of those who had defeated him, broke into the building and killed some of the boys and the aged priest who acted as their preceptor. Kasa fled for his life, and sought refuge in the stronghold of his uncle Confou. This was the resort of some of the most warlike of the Amhara chiefs. Confou took his nephew with him on his plundering forays, and while only fifteen years of age, Kasa began to gain a reputation for bravery and skill in arms. On his uncle's death, Confou's sons, Gared and his brothers, fell to fighting about the succession. Woisera Menin, the ambitious wife of Atze Johannes, the puppet king of Abyssinia, who governed for her son Ras Ali, took advantage of the quarrel to seize on the north-western portion of Confou's principality, while the chiefs of Godjam conquered the districts near Lake Dembea. Kasa, who had taken the side of the eldest son, was compelled to flee, and was glad to accept the hospitality of a peasant's hut near his native province. Kasa organised a band of seventy freebooters, who infested the borders of the western lowlands. But these ferocious men became impatient of the imperious command of their young leader. They fought amongst themselves till one half were killed. Kasa, not thinking his life safe from the vengeance of the rest, fled to Matamma, the advance post of the Egyptian dominions on the Atbara, where he worked as a grass cutter for the stables of Sheikh Shuma.

In a few months he was at the head of a new gang of bandits. Tired of this life, he returned to his native province, waiting for an occasion for more honourable adventures, and brooding over dreams of future aggrandisement. In the convent at Tschangar, Kasa had learned the old legend that there would appear a great king called Theodore, born of poor parents though of Solomon's royal line. For a time he would remain in retirement, then his exploits and feats of arms would bring him into notice. He would revive the old glories of the Ethiopian empire, drive away the Turks from the Holy Land, plant the Cross on the site of the ancient temple, make Jerusalem the metropolis of the world, and bring princes and rulers, nations and tribes, in homage before his throne.

These ideas were listened to by the irregular soldiers whom

Kasa gathered round him, and he was soon at the head of a force which enabled him to defy the King of Abyssinia. Several generals were sent against the daring young rebel; but he either defeated them or baffled their pursuit. Force failing, Ras Ali thought to attach Kasa to him by calling him to his court under safe conduct, and giving him his daughter Tawawitch (she is beautiful) in marriage. It is said that the Abyssinian princess was instigated by Woisera Menin to compass the ruin of the upstart soldier who had gained her hand by successful rebellion against her father; but she proved a true wife and a faithful adviser to her husband, who, though sometimes unfaithful, loved her to the last.

The queen mother next got Kasa sent on a dangerous expedition to harry the Mussulman tribes under the rule of Egypt. He left with an army of 16,000 men, and was met at Egyptian outposts at Kedarif by a detachment of 800 Bashi Bazouks. The Turks, who knew something of military strategy, awaited the tumultuous host of Abyssinia behind a stockade from which they poured a murderous fire of musketry and artillery. Kasa is described by an eye-witness as galloping about on a superb charger over the dead and dying, shouting out his orders to push on till a bullet brought him down from his saddle. The would-be destroyer of Mahomedanism was borne away, leaving three-fourths of his matchlock men and spear-men to feed the jackals, the crows, and the vultures. He himself sought refuge in the monastery of Tsangar, where the monks received him kindly, and Tawawitch came to tend him. An Abyssinian surgeon promised to extract the bullet from his side if he got as fee a cow and a jar of butter. Kasa sent a message to Woisera Menin asking for a cow to be sent to him. The proud old queen thought this a good opportunity to revenge the humiliations she had suffered from the upstart soldier. Instead of a cow, she sent him a piece of beef, saying, that "men of low birth were not entitled to a whole cow." The insulting message was delivered to the wounded warrior while lying on his couch with his wife beside him. The princess said she would remain no longer with him, if he tamely submitted to this insult. Kasa waited with what patience he could, till he was able to mount his horse, when he hastened to Quara, gathered his adherents together and pressed forward to Gondar to demand, as he said, the respect due to him.

Menin sent a body of troops against him, who were defeated by the daring rebel. Amongst Kasa's prisoners was Dejatch Wauderad, a chief who had loudly boasted at Gondar that he would bring back the son of the kosso-seller, dead or alive. Kasa, who had heard of this unlucky speech, sent for Wauderad in the evening after the battle, and forced him before the rebel chiefs to drink a hornful of the infusion of kosso, with the biting words,—" My mother did no business to-day ; you will therefore accept this humble fare for your evening repast."

The ceaseless energy of Kasa, his untiring activity on the march, his reckless daring in fight, his great skill in the use of arms and horses, his winning manners, manly eloquence and lavish promises, fascinated his soldiers. After every victory a portion of the vanquished army passed over to his side, and so in spite of all the exertions of Menin and the valour of Ras Ali, at the end of a furious civil war Kasa came out the victor of many hardly fought battles. He drove the legitimate king, Ras Ali, into exile, and defeated and made prisoners of Biru Goshu, the chief of Godjam, and Oubié, the ruler of Tigré.

Kasa had some difficulty in persuading the Aboona, or Patriarch of the Abyssinian Church, to sanctify his usurped power ; but by dexterously playing off the rival claims of a Catholic bishop against that of the Abyssinian primate, and through the solicitations of the military chiefs, the dislike of the Aboona was at last overcome, and amidst the chanting of priests and the shouts of the army, Kasa was, on the 8th of February, 1855, crowned Negus, or Emperor of Ethiopia, in the church of Mariam Deresgie at Axum. After the coronation, Theodore marched off his army to complete the subjection of the old feudatories of the kingdom of Abyssinia, who had in the loose reigns of his predecessors become well-nigh independent. Unable to persuade Oubié, whom he held in chains, to order his sons to surrender the inaccessible stronghold of Amba Hai, above 11,000 feet high, Theodore cunningly made use of a noted devotee, and through the persuasions of the holy man, which were rewarded by a handful of dollars, the two lads were induced to surrender their fortress to the camp below, where they hoped for kind treatment for themselves and their old father.

"So you trust a monk and not a king," were the cutting words addressed to the amazed princes on the departure of the recluse, by the man who had sworn to shelter and protect them. "Well, you were right, and if the chains in which you will be fettered are ever taken off, you will afterwards be more cautious and prudent." In fetters they remained until the day when the British flag of liberty fluttered to the breeze, on the ramparts of Magdala.*

As the fruit of this treachery, Theodore gained possession of the store of treasures and arms collected in the mountain fortress.

Without losing any time, Theodore then attacked the Shoans, whose army he defeated and compelled to surrender. Gathering together a mighty host of his old followers and vanquished enemies, he now swept down upon the Gollo-Gallas, tribes of Mussulmans who occupied the rich plains to the south-west of the sources of the Blue Nile. A fanatic in his religious faith, Theodore regarded the massacre of unprepared Mussulmans as the duty of a good Christian. He laid waste the country, drove those who escaped to take refuge in the mountains, and led away crowds of weeping boys and girls, and countless herds of cattle. To secure his hold of the Galla country, he occupied the mountain fortress of Magdala, leaving a garrison with two of his most trusted chiefs in charge. Here he fixed his arsenal and state prison.

Theodore was a man of middle height, with broad chest, small waist, and firm and sinewy limbs. His complexion was dark for an Abyssinian; the face thin, cheek bones rather high, the nose aquiline and finely traced, with a low bridge. His forehead was high, with a peculiar furrow along the arched eyebrows. When in good humour, there was a soft

---

* Mr. Stern, whom we quote, adds in a note :—" The two princes, Kasai and Quanquoul, who were my companions in chains for sixteen months, gave me this account of their capture." *Op. cit.* p. 21.

expression in his dark eyes, but when angry his glance was fierce and terrible. The lips were very thin, the chin sharp. His features were expressive and mobile, and he was a consummate actor. His hair was generally arranged in thick plaits; the beard and moustache scanty. At the height of his power, Theodore used sometimes to appear in splendid costumes; but in general he was plain in his attire, wearing a cotton shama or embroidered toga, a European white shirt and native-made trousers, no shoes, no covering for the head, or in battle a soldier's helmet. He always carried loaded pistols in his belt, and bore a lance in his hands. On the march he carried a soldier's buckler, while a man followed bearing a splendid shield covered with blue velvet. Theodore's tents were plain, and without useless luxury. He preferred being in camp to living in houses. He rarely took more than one meal in the day, and was an early riser and diligent in discharging business.

Theodore always employed secretaries for his correspondence. His memory was so good that he could recall the contents of a letter written months before, and dictate an answer without hesitation. He was a good speaker, and was boastful and fond of effect, understanding well the people with whom he had to deal. His household, camp, and army were all well regulated; his directions were precise, and he saw that his orders were duly executed, if not the culprit was in danger of his ready lance. He was generally courteous in his demeanour, and could when he wished be both kind and condescending. Though deeply selfish and indifferent to the suffering of others, he occasionally amused himself with acts of benevolence, such as taking charge of orphan children and providing for them.

In his intercourse with women Theodore at first made great pretensions to continence. He sincerely loved his first wife, the Princess Tawawitch, and years after her death was seen to shed tears when reminded of his loss. His fidelity to her was, however, never complete, and he gradually become looser and more promiscuous in his amours. Passing his youth among freebooters and robbers, Theodore could scarcely be expected to have much regard to human life.

From the beginning he was strict in his punishments, and terrible in his wrath. While he was rising to power, he was, for an Abyssinian, merciful to his defeated adversaries and was even praised for his clemency and generosity, and other virtues by Mr. Plowden, the British Consul, in dispatches, which the same functionary would have been very ready to correct a year later.

Theodore made a great pretence of religion, and professed a belief in his divine mission, as a descendant of Solomon, to destroy the Turks, and reclaim the heritage of Constantine, another of the ancestors whom he had assigned to himself. A chapel, with a number of priests and deacons, always went with his camp.

The Aboona, or patriarch, and a few bold priests now and then ventured to reprove him for his misdeeds. Sometimes he was seized with a fit of remorse, when he would make atonement to those he had wronged, or perform a public penance, forcing his chiefs and officers to do the same. For a while he would be severe and continent, and then again fall into his besetting sins. While he sometimes talked with derision of the legends of the Abyssinian priests, in other things Theodore rose little above the superstitions of his country. He believed in magic, and had always with him astrologers, whom he consulted on perplexing occasions.

Theodore had certainly the gift of gaining faithful and enduring followers, and enthusiastic admirers. Amongst these was an Englishman, named John Bell, who had been led to Abyssinia through the attraction of an adventurous life. He married an Abyssinian lady by whom he had four children. Bell had taken service under Ras Ali, and fought against the insurgent army at the battle of Djisella in 1853. As the day went against Ras Ali he had taken refuge in a church. Theodore induced him to leave the sanctuary on promise of good treatment. He took the Englishman into his service, treated him like a friend, ate out of the same dish, and spent much time in listening to what Bell told him of the history, politics and arts of Europe. On the other hand Bell showed great fidelity to the Abyssinian ruler, slept at the door of his tent, and fought by his side. Bell had the title of Likamankuas, one of the four officers who, in battle, wore the same costume as the Emperor to lessen his danger by sharing in it. Theodore had the sense to value the friendship of Bell, and listened to his bold and sincere advice. A striking proof of the influence which the Englishman had over this extraordinary man is given by Le Jean, the French envoy:—

"Bell had one day asked for justice from his royal friend for some grievance, of the nature of which I am not aware, and, not obtaining what he asked for, remembered an old feudal custom which permitted an Abyssinian gentleman, while armed and mounted, to speak to his sovereign with the most absolute impunity. Without loss of time he takes his sword and buckler, mounts his horse, and goes to seek the Emperor, who is seated in the midst of his chiefs at the door of his tent, and reproaches him sharply for his caprices, tyranny, and ingratitude. Theodore says nothing; in the evening the two friends sup together as usual; the Negus goes out for an instant, he re-enters, carrying a large stone on his neck, and bows himself before Mr. Bell. By the law of the country the injured party has a right to this reparation on the part of the offender, whatever may be their respective ranks; and the Negus, a restorer of old customs, was not inclined to withdraw from them. Mr. Bell, surprised and confounded, threw himself before him, took the stone in his hands, and begged, with respectful bluntness, that the Negus would not forget he was the sovereign."

Such freedoms were not without danger from the irritable despot. Once Theodore threw a spear at Bell because he interposed when the Negus rushed upon the powerful chief of the Lastas,* who supported the clergy in their refusal to alienate the revenues of the Church. On another occasion,† Bell received a blow when he interposed in a quarrel between Theodore and his wife, the proud Terunish. In the beginning of 1860, Theodore saw in a church a young girl praying. Struck by her beauty and modest demeanour, he asked who she was, and was told that she was the only daughter of Oubié, the Prince of Tigré, whom he held as a captive. The young girl was with some difficulty induced to become the wife of Theodore

---

* STERN, p. 25.
† BLANC: "The Story of the Captives," p. 151.

in hopes of bettering the condition of her father. But though Theodore thought highly of her beauty, grace, and intelligence, he missed the warm affection of his first wife. Terunish, while she accepted her fate, was cold and proud. One day when he came in to see her she pretended not to notice him, and remained reading a book; and when Theodore asked why she did not answer his greeting? she replied, "Because I am conversing with a greater and better man than you, the pious King David." Theodore sought to mortify her by publicly consorting with several concubines. Terunish had not even the consolation of bettering the condition of her kindred, for though Theodore at first set her father at large, in a short time, on some pretext, he again put the poor old man into prison; and though he repeatedly promised to liberate her brothers, they remained in captivity at Magdala till set free by the British. The death of his wife, Tawawitch, and of his friend, Bell, removed the only two councillors who had a restraining hold on Theodore's irritable and suspicious mind. In 1860, Mr. Plowden, in failing health, on the way to return to his own country, was made prisoner near Gondar by Gared, Theodore's cousin. Though ransomed a few days afterwards, the consul died of a wound from the spear of his captor. Bell never rested till he got the Emperor to set out to avenge Plowden's death. While Theodore and Bell were riding a little ahead of the troops, through a small wood, they suddenly came face to face with Gared and his brother. Bell threw himself in front of the Emperor, and, taking aim at Gared, shot him dead. A moment after Gared's brother shot Bell; and Theodore revenged his friend by slaying his cousin on the spot. Furious at the loss of his faithful friend, he caused the wood to be surrounded. Though Gared's followers surrendered, they were all butchered, to the number of 1600, and their wives and children condemned to perpetual slavery. For this exemplary punishment of the murderers of Plowden and Bell the Emperor received, through Earl Russell, the thanks of the Queen.*

---

* See BEKE, *op. cit.* p. 61.

About the same time a formidable insurrection broke out under the leadership of Negusye, a chief of Tigré, who was recognised by France. Abyssinia remained in suspense while two powerful armies approached one another. Theodore sent emissaries with promises and threats to act upon the minds of the revolted troops, and on the night before the expected battle, a herald shouted out in the darkness from a neighbouring height, that those who would desert from Negusye and betake themselves to the Emperor's camp or the churches of Axum or of Adona would be pardoned; but those who should be found next day under arms could expect no mercy. In the morning Negusye found himself deserted by the greater part of his host, and had no other resource than to take to flight with a few faithful followers. He was soon captured, along with his brother; their right hands and left feet were cut off, and they were left to die; every one being forbidden to give them any relief. Negusye lingered for three days. Dishonouring his own promises, Theodore put to death or sent away in chains the chiefs who had by his own directions sought refuge in the sanctuary at Axum. To a trembling deputation of the clergy of that town he indulged in vainglorious boastings, amongst which these foolish words were kept in memory: "I have made a compact with God; He has promised not to descend to the earth to smite me, and I have promised not to ascend to Heaven to strive with Him."

Though he seemed now at the pinnacle of his power, Theodore might have reflected that this insurrection, at one time so formidable, showed the existence of a wide-spread discontent.

It is not surprising that men like Plowden and Le Jean might have indulged in glowing hopes when Abyssinia, so long torn with the strifes of warring chiefs, seemed again united into one state, under an able, firm, and just ruler. Recalling some bright pages in history, they hoped that the reforms which Theodore talked about would soon pass into realities; that the Emperor's magistrates would replace the power of the feudal chiefs; that the peasant would be protected, trade flourish, and peace and prosperity appear.

Unhappily, though Theodore possessed sufficient daring, address, and military skill to overcome all the rival candidates for power, he neither could cast away the vices which had helped him in the struggle to rise, nor could he resist the new temptations which unlimited power brought along with it. The expected regenerator of Abyssinia had no capacity for civil government. He never rose above the height of a robber chief on a large scale; for though a brave and keen leader in the field, he was no general.

He talked much of his divine mission to destroy the Turks, and threatened that soon all the Mussulmans in Abyssinia would need either to be expelled or submit to be baptised, but he never ventured to repeat his attack upon the Egyptian outposts. Unwilling and afraid to disband his huge army of 150,000 men, which, with camp followers, amounted to half a million of souls, he tried to support this wasteful multitude on the taxes wrung from a population of three millions. When dollars became scarce, he led them from one fertile territory to another to eat up everything. Originally temperate in his diet, he gradually yielded to indulgence in liquor. At last he became drunk every evening. Once the Aboona, abandoning all fears for his own safety, had the courage to resist him and denounce him openly. Theodore, alarmed at the superstitious uneasiness of his troops, sent as an apology for his atrocities, that he had been drunk for a month. Unable to break the high spirit of Terunish, he took as a second wife a Galla woman named Tamagno, who never showed any jealousy and encouraged Theodore in his debaucheries. She rose so high in his favour that he publicly proclaimed that he had discarded Terunish, and that Tamagno should in future be considered by all as the queen.

Theodore's hostility to the Abyssinian chiefs, and his attempts to strip the Church of some of its wealth, might have, in the beginning, been justified by reasons of state policy, for the chiefs had gained too much power, and the Church had accumulated too many possessions for a well-governed state, but his capricious and tyrannical method of acting outraged all sense of justice. In the end, nearly all the powerful chiefs whom he forced to accompany his camp were put to death in his fits of suspicion or passion, or were sent in chains to his prison ambas or rock fortress, where they were treated with the vilest cruelty. Aware of the hatred which he had excited, the tyrant took great precautions against poison. The hillock on which his tent was pitched was always surrounded by a guard of musketeers, and he slept with loaded fire-arms at his side. Even his most faithful followers fell victims to his fits of fury and unreasonable suspicion. The executioner of to-day became the victim to-morrow. The least contradiction, the slightest gesture of dissent, or what he imagined to be such, aroused his murderous fury. At times his guards knew that it was dangerous to approach him, and they would warn those to whom they were well disposed to keep away. His consuming egotism gradually passed all bounds of reason. At last his enemies, his subjects, his most faithful servants all believed that he had periodical fits of madness. The long-suffering peasants to whom oppression was not new, despairing of saving any of the fruits of their toil from the greedy hands of the tyrant and his host of robbers, in many districts sought refuge in the heights and secluded valleys, where, under some scion of their old chiefs, they threw off all obedience to the Negus. Thus province after province passed away from his rule, while Theodore vainly tried to quell the ever increasing tide of disaffection by new cruelties and treacheries. When he advanced with his hosts into the revolted districts, the people drove away their cattle, burnt their dwellings, and fled to the mountain fastnesses. The insurgent chiefs, although they never dared to meet him in the field, hovered round his army, cut off stragglers, and rendered foraging very difficult. Theodore's soldiers, once pampered and gorged with plunder, were now ragged and half starved. Their ranks were thinned by losses, pestilence, and desertion. At last he could only support his troops by plundering the provinces round about Lake Dembea, which still remained subservient.

Both Britain and France had sent envoys to open friendly relations with the new Emperor of Abyssinia, but the officials had soon reason to regret coming within the power of the petulant and unreasonable despot. The French envoy,

M. Le Jean, was put in chains for some imputed offence, and was glad to get leave to depart from Abyssinia.

Having a great admiration for the mechanical arts of Europe, Theodore had enticed by lavish promises a few workmen to enter his service. They went and settled, with their houses and workshops, at a place called Gaffat, near Debra Tabor. At first these European mechanics were treated with kindness and liberality, and induced to marry Abyssinian women. The Emperor soon tired of them making pick-axes, doors, and utensils, and ordered them to fabricate cannons, mortars, and shells, which they were forced to do as well as they could.

On the 13th of October, 1863, the Rev. Henry Stern, a missionary well acquainted with the language and customs of Abyssinia, unluckily presented himself before Theodore at the end of a carouse. It afterwards turned out that the European workmen had complained to the Negus about some passages contained in a newspaper, attributed to Mr. Stern, which reflected upon their Abyssinian marriages, and had told him of some passages in a book published in England by Mr. Stern censuring his severities. Theodore was also displeased with Stern on account of his intimacy with the Aboona, whom he much disliked. The interview with the vindictive tyrant is thus described by Mr. Stern:—

"The last jar of hydromel had at last, as a royal page, *en passant*, assured me, been quaffed, the last reeking joint had been devoured, the last batch of rioters had at last vanished, when the folds of the tent were thrown aside, and his Majesty, surrounded by half-a-dozen officers and several pages, strutted out into the open air. My companions quickly prostrated themselves into the dust, whilst I, without imitating their servile obeisance, made a humble and deferential bow. 'Come nearer,' shouted the attendants. I obeyed, and advanced a few steps. 'Still nearer,' reiterated several stentorian voices. I complied, and made another forward movement. 'What do you want?' sharply demanded the flushed and drink-excited Negus. 'I saw your Majesty's tent,' was the response, 'and came hither to offer my humble salutations and respects to your Majesty.' 'Where are you going?' 'I am, with your Majesty's sanction, about to proceed to Massowah.' 'And why did you come to Abyssinia?' 'A desire to circulate the Word of God among your Majesty's subjects prompted the enterprise,' I rejoined. 'Can you make cannons?' 'No,' was the reply. 'You lie,' was the laconic retort, and then, turning with a withering glance towards Negusee, one of my companions, and a servant of Consul Cameron, he imperatively demanded to know the name of his province. 'I am from Tigré,' tremulously responded the poor man. 'And you are the servant or interpreter of this white man?' 'No, your Majesty, I am in the employ of Consul Cameron, and only accompany him down to Adowa, whither I am bound to see my family.' 'You vile carcass! you base dog! you rotten donkey! you dare to bandy words with your king. Down with the villain, and *bemouti* (by my death), beat him till there is not a breath in his worthless carcass.' The order was promptly obeyed, and the poor inoffensive man, without a struggle, ejaculation, or groan, was dashed on the ground, where, amidst the shouts of the savage monarch, that the executioners should vigorously ply their sticks, the animated and robust frame was in less than a minute, a torn and mangled corpse. 'There's another man yonder,' vociferated the savage king, 'Kill him also.' The poor fellow, who stood at a considerable distance, was immediately dragged to the side of his motionless companion, and, without having breathed a word or syllable that could possibly have irritated the sanguinary tyrant, doomed to share the same unhappy fate. In my agitation I might, unconsciously, have put my hand or finger to my lips. This the cruel tyrant construed into an act of defiance, and, without one warning or reproof, he rushed upon me with a drawn pistol, like a lion baulked of his prey. For an instant I saw the glittering weapon sparkling in the rays of the sinking sun, and then, as if checked in his fell design by an invisible power, it disappeared again in the case suspended round his waist. 'Knock him down! brain him! kill him!' were the words which rung appallingly on my ear. In the twinkle of an eye I was stripped, on the ground, insensible. Stunned, unconscious, and almost lifeless, with the blood oozing out of scores of gashes, I was dragged into the camp, not as my guards were commanded, to bind me in fetters, but as they thought—and I heard it from their own lips—to bury me."

In his affecting book, the captive missionary describes the privations, chains, and tortures, which he had for three years and a-half to endure from the vindictive tyrant. He was not to suffer alone. On the 22nd of November, 1863, Mr. Lawrence Kerans, an Irishman, not yet twenty years old, came from Nubia to Gondar to become Secretary to Consul Cameron.

He brought with him a beautiful carpet representing Jules Gerard, the lion killer, in the dress of a spahi or irregular cavalry soldier. Instead of being pleased with this gift, Theodore said it was intended to insult him. It represented a Turk firing at a lion, which could be no other but the Emperor of Abyssinia, who had a lion on his seal. The attendant behind supporting the infidel, was a Frenchman, but he added, "I do not see the Englishman who ought to be by my side." As the victim of this perversion of the meaning of his present, poor Karens had to suffer four years' imprisonment in chains.

Theodore now became very inquisitive about what the Europeans in his country wrote concerning him. He caused informers to relate what they said; got their letters opened and their papers searched; in this way he heard of some reflections upon his conduct, which, though only private notes, provoked him mightily.

Theodore was much disgusted that no answer came to a letter which he had sent to the Queen of England, and Consul Cameron had reason to regret that the clerks at the London Foreign Office never found time to attend to the missive of this distant potentate, which Earl Russell did not remember ever having seen. Theodore also felt aggrieved that the Consul seemed to be on friendly terms with the Turks, whom as a good Christian, he held in abhorrence. He wrathfully asked where was the answer to his letter, and on the 4th of January, 1864, he ordered Cameron to be imprisoned, saying that he would see if he were really an accredited envoy or not. Theodore had always a pretext for every act of cruelty or treachery, but these it would be idle to repeat. About this time he had also in confinement the Patriarch of Alexandria, and a Mahomedan ambassador who had been sent, the one after the other, by the Viceroy of Egypt. As nothing followed these breaches of the law of nations, the boastful tyrant now thought he might do anything he pleased with the foreigners in his power.

In the year 1864 Theodore was still at the head of a powerful army, and his rule acknowledged over a great part of Abyssinia; but his senseless doings were working out his ruin. In 1865 he made an inroad into Shoa, and had to retreat, much harassed by his old enemies the Gallas. Instead of taking any lesson from his reverses, his cruelty, caprice, and treachery became worse and worse. He kept his army almost continually on the march, their way marked by ruined homesteads and burning villages, more dreadful to the subjects who had trusted to him than to the enemies who fled at his approach. He plundered and levelled with the ground the populous town of Zagé, and on some hardly specious pretext gave up the city of Gondar to be spoiled by his ruffianly soldiery. The meanest huts were ransacked, the forty-four churches hitherto left inviolate in all civil wars, were stripped of their treasures, and only four were left standing. The houses were set on fire, and hundreds of aged priests and helpless women were thrown into the flames. He plundered the fertile district of Begember, which had up to this time remained faithful, and forced the men, whom he had reduced to starvation, to enlist amongst his troop of robbers.

But all his cruelties could not prevent large numbers of his soldiers deserting, though the lash and the mutilating knife were freely employed on the victims of his ever wakeful suspicions. Rassam tells us that he inflicted 150 lashes with a whip of hippopotamus hide upon the wife of an officer who had quitted his camp, although there was no proof that the unfortunate lady knew of the meditated desertion of the man who had left her behind.

"On the 7th of June, 1867," writes Stern,* "upwards of six hundred and seventy of Wadela, Yedshou, and other troops, under the false pretext that they were to receive their pay, appeared unarmed before the tyrant. 'Aha, you vile slaves,' was the address, 'I hear you want to join the rebels and fight against me. I will feed the hyenas with your foul carcases before you execute your designs. Off with the traitors.' In an instant they were in the grasp of friends, companions, and kinsmen, who, strange as it may appear, readily performed the executioners' work."

On the day of this massacre, Ras Adalou, the chief of the Yedshou troops, mounted his horse, and gathering together all

---

* *Op. cit.* p. 311.

his retainers, with their wives, children, and followers, marched out of the stockaded camp. Theodore saw their backs turned upon him, but did not dare to make an effort to prevent them.

As the Patriarch told him to his face, Theodore in his fits of rage became a complete diabolos, a demoniac. Dr. Blanc calls him "a homicidal monomaniac." In his passion his black visage acquired an ashy hue, his thin white lips were compressed, and he struck the rocks around him with his spear, and his whole frame showed the excitement of savage and uncontrollable fury. In one of his last plundering expeditions into Begember, he drove away to Debra Tabor thousands of cattle. At night the peasants came and implored him to have pity on them, for without their oxen they could not till the ground. Theodore seemed disposed to restore the cattle, when some of his officers said :—

"'Does not your majesty know that there is a prophecy in the country, that a king will seize a large amount of cattle, and that the peasants will come and beg him to return them; the king will comply, but soon afterwards die.' Theodore replied, 'Well, the prophecy will not apply to me.' He then ordered all the cows in camp to be shot. The order was obeyed, and nearly a hundred thousand cows were killed and left to rot on the plain not far from the camp.

"The next day,* Theodore, seated outside his hut, perceived a man driving a cow into the fields, he sent for him, and asked him if he had not heard the order. The man replied in the affirmative, but said that he had not killed his cow because his wife having died the day before on giving birth to a child, he had kept that one for the sake of her milk. Theodore told him, 'Why did not you know that I would be a father to your child? Kill the man,' he said to those around him, 'and take care of his child for me.'"

On his last march to Magdala, Theodore, on one or two occasions, called his soldiers around him, and thus addressed them :—

"'I know that you all hate me! you all want to run away. Why

---

* BLANC, *op. cit.* p. 336.

do you not kill me? Here I am alone, and you are thousands.' He would pause for a few seconds, and add—'Well, if you will not kill me, I will kill you all, one after the other.'"

Theodore said at first he thought his mission was to give peace and prosperity to the Abyssinians, but he found that in spite of all the good he had done, more rebels rose against him than ever rose in the time of the worst tyranny; he now saw that his true role was to be the Flail of the Wicked—the judgment of God upon Abyssinia. He got engraved upon his gun carriages and howitzers, "The Flail of the Wicked, Theodore." At other times he could still be courteous, and was thoughtful about the welfare of his soldiers and the multitude of camp-followers that moved about with him, stopped when he stopped, and yielded obedience to the terrible force of his character. Though all Theodore's proceedings were not equally unreasonable, it does seem surprising that so many were left to obey his capricious commands; but his tyranny was not without its method. Through his informers he was often aware of what men said of him. This enabled him to weed out the disaffected, and to detect plots against his life, and to inflict savage punishments upon the conspirators. The rest were thoroughly cowed, wretches who made a practice of directing the tyrant's suspicions against one another, to gratify their spites and jealousies, and who dreaded their master's fall as the day of retribution for the cruelties he had made them commit. Everywhere he went, the revolted chiefs hovered round his host of robbers, getting bolder every day, attacking his followers in the passes, and hurling stones and maledictions upon the tyrant from the cliffs. No mercy was shown on either side. Those whom he took were beaten to death, or burned alive, and Theodore's soldiers, if caught beyond the bounds of his camp, were slaughtered without mercy. Even deserters were in danger of being killed by the enraged peasants, and were generally stripped of all they had.

By the close of the year 1867, Theodore's once mighty host was reduced to five or six thousand fighting men, and his rule did not extend beyond the ground on which he was encamped, besides Magdala and another amba, in which he had garrisons, that still remained faithful.

The British Government anxious about the dangerous position of Consul Cameron and his seven companions in captivity, sent Mr. Rassam, Dr. Blanc, and Lieutenant Prideaux, on a mission to Abyssinia, with a letter and presents from the Queen in hopes of persuading the savage to let his captives go free. This mission, which reached Theodore's camp near Lake Dembea in the beginning of 1866, seemed at first to please him. He accepted the presents, gave Mr. Rassam $5000, and went through the ceremony of a mock trial with the captives, who had to acknowledge that they had done wrong. Then Theodore begged their forgiveness, and released them from their chains. His good humour did not last long. One day while inspecting the works near Debra Tabor, an old beggar asked the Emperor for alms, adding that the European lords, meaning the European artificers, had always been kind to him.

Theodore instantly turned upon the beggar, crying out, "How dare you call anyone lord but myself? Beat him, beat him, by my death." Two of the executioners at once fell upon the poor old cripple who in a few minutes expired under their blows. Theodore then fell upon the members of the mission with abuse and reproaches, and imprisoned them along with the former European captives in a store-house built of stone without windows and only one door. After they had been a little time in this dismal stifling abode, the prisoners were startled by a message from his Majesty informing them that he could not rest before comforting his friends, and that he would come and see them. He soon afterwards appeared, bearing a horn of arrack over his shoulder, and with some wax candles in his right hand and a servant behind carrying mead. He said :—

"'Even my wife told me not to go out, but I could not leave you in grief, so I have come to drink with you.' On that he had arrack and tej presented to all of us, himself setting the example. He remained with them an hour conversing on different subjects, in the course of which he said, 'My father was mad, and though people often said that I am mad also, I never would believe it; but now I know it is true.'"*

No improvement in the captives' condition followed on this royal condescension. They were kept close prisoners for two days and then sent to Magdala, where chains were hammered on their hands and feet, which they had to wear for twenty-one months, in constant dread of their lives, vilely lodged with Theodore's other prisoners, and in danger of starvation.

The British Government had now no choice but to try to deliver its ambassadors and subjects. It was a costly and difficult undertaking. General Napier, to whom the command was given, asked for 16,000 troops, and spoke of a two years' campaign. Counting camp followers and those employed by the commissariat, 32,000 men were engaged in this expedition. Had Napier been aware how much Theodore's power had sunk, a smaller force, pushed on more quickly, would likely have been used. The army was landed at Annesley Bay, near Massowah, on the Red Sea, from which they made an undisturbed, though toilsome, march of about 400 miles over the mountain ridges to Magdala. Warkit, the widowed Galla queen, whose son, held as a hostage, had been cruelly murdered by Theodore, brought all the help of her people to push on the invading force, whom she knew to be her avengers.

Magdala was surrounded by Theodore's enemies, but greatly through the exertions of the ill-used queen, Terunish, the garrison still remained faithful. Theodore, who was in the neighbourhood of Debra Tabor when he heard of the landing of the British army, could soon have reached Magdala, if he could have made up his mind to leave behind him his heavy pieces of ordnance. He had fourteen gun carriages, ten

---

* That Theodore was actually insane seems accepted by all who have written on the events. See especially BLANC, pp. 178, 317; STERN, p. 357; MARKHAM, p. 290; ACTON, p. 60; Rassam writes:—"My own sincere conviction is that this antagonism (of the chiefs and people), perpetuated and intensified by the unwise measures which he took to repress it, so unsettled the mind of the haughty monarch, that at times he was decidedly mad. On no other supposition can I account for his extraordinary conduct towards the Mission from first to last," vol. ii. p. 335.

waggons, and some huge mortars, which he forced his people to haul up the steep ascents. In some places new roads had to be cut for them over the mountains with steep gradients. Sometimes he could only advance at the rate of two or three miles a-day. His troops, ragged and hungry, living upon the unripe corn which they cut, could not venture to go far to plunder, for the whole country was against them. Theodore's army was treated by the Abyssinians as hostile invaders, and Napier's as friendly deliverers. Sometimes Theodore talked despondently, and said openly that his troops could never contend with the English, but that he would be glad to have the sight of a disciplined army before he died. He even talked as if he would be able to make an alliance with the British to recover his lost dominions. At other times he would boast, in his old vainglorious strain, that he would go to meet the British in battle, and enrich his troops with their spoils. He reached Magdala on the 26th of March, a fortnight before Napier. Though Theodore's ruin now seemed certain, he held in his hands the stake for which Napier was playing, the lives of the eight captives, besides the European workmen and their families, whom he had with him. His last proceedings showed the derangement of his mind. He wasted five months in bringing over the mountains his cumbrous artillery, which he did not know how to use, and which did not serve him in the struggle.

Magdala is a plateau of about a mile and a-half long and a mile broad on the top of a mountain about 9000 feet high. Its lofty and steep crags of columnar basalt only allow of approach at two points by narrow ascending roads commanded by fortifications. Even with the great superiority of the British troops in arms and martial skill, the place could only have been stormed at a great loss of life. Had Theodore disputed the ridge of Fala, and then thrown himself into the fortress, Napier's task in dislodging or blockading him would have been a hard one. As it was, Theodore, in a reckless mood, sent three thousand musketeers, matchlock men, and spear men, down the heights to attack the first brigade of about 2000 British and Indian troops in a plain a few miles from Magdala. In this crisis of his fate Theodore did not even lead his troops as of old. The day before he had released the women and children amongst his Abyssinian prisoners, 186 in all. He ordered the chains to be struck off the male captives, and thirty-seven chiefs and ninety-five other men were set free; but, as knocking off the fetters was a slow process, few smiths being employed, some of the prisoners grew very impatient and cried for food, as none had been given them for two days. This Theodore overheard; he got angry, and his clement mood passed away for a fit of homicidal mania. He shouted out: "I will teach them to ask for food when my brave soldiers are starving." He ordered the guards to bring out the prisoners, and hacked the first two to pieces with his sword. The third was a young child, who was hurled alive over the precipice. As each prisoner was brought forth, his name and offence were called out. Three hundred and seven were hurled over the precipice, at the foot of which was a party of musketeers to despatch those who still showed signs of life. Only thirty-five of these unfortunates are said to have been guilty of any serious crime. Some had been put in prison for trivial offences, such as daring to laugh when the King was in bad humour, or loading a gun for him which failed to go off. Amongst those dragged before Theodore on that dreadful afternoon were two boys imprisoned along with their father, who was accused of having taken liberties with one of the royal concubines. The King shouted, "Away with them," when the innocent boys forthwith were hurled over the precipice; but when the father of the two boys was produced, Theodore's fury was somewhat exhausted, and, after hearing the man's crime, he cried out, "Open his chains and let him go." It is said that he commanded the European captives to be led forth; but one of his officers suggested that it would be better to reserve them for next day to be burned alive.

Next day, Good Friday, the 10th of April, the attack was made on the British advanced guard, who gained an easy victory over the brave but undisciplined and ill-armed Abyssinians. Only about one-third of his soldiers returned to the heights of Fala. That night, the humbled despot sent a message to Mr. Rassam asking his captive to reconcile him with the man who was stronger than he. Next morning, two of the Europeans, with Theodore's son-in-law, were sent to the British camp to sue for peace. Lord Napier demanded that all the Europeans should be sent in, and that Theodore should come and give himself up as a prisoner, when he should receive honourable treatment; for several hours, the fate of the captives depended upon the hesitating thoughts of Theodore, who, during this time, was drinking heavily. Some of his chiefs advised him to kill his captives, and fight to the last. In his rage and despair, he pointed a pistol at his own head, but his hand was seized by those around. After writing a defiant and incoherent letter to Lord Napier and then apologising for it, Theodore sent the captives into the British camp on the evening of the 11th, and next day, sent in all the European artisans and their wives and effects. Some of Theodore's officers now came into the British camp, and on the 13th, Lord Napier ordered an advance to blow in the gates of Magdala. Theodore's soldiers, remaining in the place, now refused to fight or even to accompany him in his flight. He shot two of them with his pistols, but the rest only fell back without yielding to his orders. With about a score of his old officers who still stuck to him, Theodore now tried to escape by the Kafir Bir gate, but was scared back by the Gallas, watching for their old enemy to deliver him into the hands of the Mahomedan princess, whose son he had slaughtered. With his scanty band of faithful adherents, Theodore turned back to defend the Koket Bir gate, upon which the British were now advancing. Most of his companions fell dead under the fire of the storming party, and seeing the British soldiers had got through the second gate and were advancing upon him, in his despair, he put a pistol to his mouth and sent a bullet through his head. The remaining prisoners had broken loose, and ran down in their fetters to meet their deliverers. They recognised Theodore lying dead by a broken finger from an old wound, and set up a shout of joy. Our soldiers then entered the place and set all the prisoners free. Magdala was burned and dismantled. Alamayo, the only son of Theodore by a marriage recognised as legitimate, with his mother Terunish, was led away with the returning army. Terunish fell ill on the way to the coast; she said that she knew that her days were numbered, for which she was not sorry, and then added, "Mine has been a miserable existence since childhood, and I am now looking forward to that happiness which is promised me by our Saviour." She died, and was buried in her own country. Her son was taken to England, but soon after died. Theodore left five other children by different wives or concubines, who, in the complete ruin of their father's house, had to seek refuge amongst the kindred of their mothers.

Theodore was able to command an army, but not to rule a country. He does not seem to have had any good quality, save bravery in battle. The energy, daring, power of dissimulation, and unflinching will, which helped to raise him so high, were in their overgrowth the cause of his downfall. Absolute power always depraves its possessor, and with the Negus, the depravity passed into insanity. From what he himself said it appears that the mental derangement was hereditary, and it was no doubt increased by his drunken habits.

It is a reproach to Abyssinia that this man's cruelties lasted so long, and that, though many rose against him, he found willing tools to the end. His insanity seems to have been of an intermittent character, and to the hour of his death, he struggled with vast energy against the fate which was the sure Nemesis of his misdeeds.

THEBAW, KING OF BURMA.

THE founder of the latest Burmese dynasty was a hunter who gained the fame of a hero in the war which ended by his countrymen throwing off the yoke of the Talaing conquerors. In 1752 he became King of Ava, under the name of Alompra. He extended the Burmese Empire from China to Siam, and founded the city of Rangoon. Alompra died in 1760. His successors had frequent wars with the Chinese, who were only got rid of by the Burmese kings consenting to be numbered amongst the feudatories of the Celestial Empire. Within his own dominions the King of Burma was absolute monarch, the lives and property of the people were wholly at his mercy, and a marked inclination for ruthless acts of cruelty seemed to characterise the dynasty. Commencing with a man of humble origin, but possessed of great bodily strength and much energy and mental power, the race was sure to degenerate in the Golden Palace, which royal etiquette scarcely ever allowed them to quit. To hasten the decline of the family, the Kings of Burma, in order to keep up what they called the purity of their blood, preferred marriages with the female descendants of Alompra, marrying with even their half-sisters.

Bodau Phra, the third son of Alompra, put to death his predecessor and caused his women and children to be burned alive. This king in his ruthless energy reminds one of Mohammed Toghlak. On a plot being discovered in a village, he caused it to be surrounded and all the people, young and old, were driven together and burned alive. The village was razed to the ground; the trees cut down and burned, and the site turned up with a ploughshare. He ordered all the inhabitants of Ava to remove to a new capital to which he gave the name of Amarapura. As a missionary priest wrote, no words can express the sufferings, the fatigues, the exactions, and the oppressions which were brought about by the change of capital. Bodau Phra conquered Arakan and invaded Siam, but his army fled in a panic, and he made a disgraceful failure. This king wished to be regarded as an incarnation of Buddha, and in imitation of Sakya Muni, the great founder of Buddhism, he left his palace and wives and took up his abode in a monastery. Failing to convince the monks that he was Buddha, he became disgusted, returned to his palace, and for the rest of his reign was bitterly hostile to the priesthood. He died in 1819. His grandson and successor, Phagyi-Dau, inherited the arrogance of Bodau without his ability. We know something of this prince from the accounts of Adoniram Judson, the celebrated American missionary.* Ignorant of the strength of the white strangers who ruled in Bengal, and encouraged by the predictions of his astrologers, the Burmese prince provoked a quarrel, and sent some troops across the frontier. The British landed, took Rangoon, and marched up the Irrawady, easily chasing the Burmese before them, but suffering much loss from the unhealthiness of the country. Their victorious army was within forty miles of Ava when King Phagyi-Dau began to comprehend the situation, which he quaintly described by comparing himself to a man who had taken hold of a tiger's tail, and found that it was equally dangerous to hold on or to let go. The vanquished monarch could only purchase peace by paying a crore of rupees, one million of money at the old exchange rates, and ceding the provinces of Assam, Arakan, and Tenasserim.

The Burmese did their best to forget this severe though wholesome lesson. In their secluded ignorance both king and people had worked themselves into the belief that they were the bravest and sturdiest race in the world, and they looked down upon the puny and unwarlike people of Lower Bengal, not clearly comprehending that their English rulers had great

---

* See "Memoir of Dr. Judson," by Wayland, vol. ii. p. 350, and also "An Account of the American Baptist Mission to the Burmese Empire," by Ann K. Judson, p. 227. London, 1823.

resources in their own country, and in the sepoys of Upper India. The Burmese drama from which all classes derived many impressions, flattered them with its fictions till they forgot realities. Their only history, "The Great Chronicle of Kings," stated everything in a way flattering to Burmese vanity. The following is their account of the war of 1825[*]:—

"The kula-pyro, or white strangers of the West, fastened a quarrel on the Lord of the Golden Palace. They landed at Rangoon, took that place and Prome, and were permitted to advance as far as Yandabo; for the king, from motives of piety and regard to life, made no effort whatever to oppose them. The strangers had spent vast sums of money upon the enterprise, and by the time they reached Yandabo, their resources were exhausted, and they were in great distress. They petitioned the king, who, in his clemency and generosity, sent them large sums of money to pay their expenses back, and ordered them out of the country."

Phagyi-Dau fell much under the influence of his queen, a woman of low rank, but possessed of cunning and address. As she was plain-looking, her influence over the king was ascribed to sorcery, in the latter years of his life.

Phagyi-Dau suffered from hypochondria, and in 1837 he became insane,[†] when he was deposed and placed in confinement by his brother Tharawadi. He died in 1845.

Before his accession to the throne Tharawadi had been a favourite with the people, and had shown a fondness for the society of Europeans, but in gaining absolute power he became morose and cruel. He put to death his brother's favourite queen, and his only son with his whole family and household, on a false charge of treason. He compelled Phagyi-Dau's old ministers to work as labourers on the roads. He soon came to quarrel with the British residents, and threatened war. He indulged freely in strong liquors, and got so ferocious that he would shoot or stab a minister or favourite with his own hands. Having become clearly insane, in 1845 he was placed in con-

---

[*] CRAWFURD's "Embassy to Ava," vol. i. p. 304.
[†] See "Burma, Past and Present," by Lieut.-Gen. Albert Fytche, C.S.I., &c. Vol. i. p. 83.

finement never more to be seen. It is said that he was smothered in the recesses of the palace.* Tharawadi was succeeded by his son Pagan-Meng. "He was a slave to low pleasures such as cock-fighting, ram-fighting, gambling, and debauchery." He was in constant fear lest he should share the fate of his father Tharawadi, and put to death two of his own brothers, with their wives and families.

Having explained away all their reverses to their own satisfaction, the new generation of Burmese were now ready to provoke the British power, which brought about the war of 1852. The Burmese were beaten as before, and the whole of Pegu annexed by Lord Dalhousie. The blame of their defeats was thrown upon the king, who was deposed, and his half-brother, Meng-Don, was called to the throne from a Buddhist monastery. For an Oriental prince, Meng-Don was a liberal and humane ruler, fond of learning, and averse to the shedding of human blood. He could not be brought to sign any treaty ceding Burmese territory; but the new boundaries were traced out by British engineers and tenaciously kept. The kingdom of Burma had now lost all its maritime provinces. Meng-Don died on the 1st of October, 1878. He left about thirty sons. The King of Burma has the right to determine which son is to succeed him; but the late king, fearing that the selection of an heir, if prematurely proclaimed, might be dangerous to his own life, postponed the performance of this duty to the last. It is said that he frequently indicated his intention of making the Nyoungyan prince his successor, and on his death-bed the king sent for this prince. In the meanwhile the mother of Prince Thebaw had made herself mistress of the palace, and the Nyoungyan prince, fearing treachery, delayed compliance with the king's summons. Shortly afterwards the mother of the sovereign, with the principal ministers, proclaimed the regency of the Thebaw prince, and subsequently they announced the king's death, and the prince's accession. "The Nyoungyan prince and his younger brother sought refuge in the British Residency. The ministers tried in vain to induce Mr. Shaw

---

* FYTCHE, *op. cit.* p. 118.

to surrender them."* The princes were sent to Calcutta, where they were maintained by the British Government, who knew their value as possible substitutes to the reigning king. Even under the protection of the Government, the prince stated that he was in danger of his life; and emissaries, no doubt sent to assassinate the prince, were noticed by the police, and returned to Upper Burma on being told that their motions were watched. Thebaw, at his accession, was twenty years of age. Some accounts say that he was the only son of royal blood on both sides, and that he had been the favourite of his father; others that there was doubt concerning the paternity of the Thebaw prince, and that his father had said that he would never allow him to succeed to the throne. Thebaw's wife, called Soo-pay-alat, was his half-sister. It is generally said that Thebaw himself was weak and good-natured rather than cruel, and that the subsequent atrocities and follies were owing to his wife, who had a complete influence over him. If so, he must have been weak indeed, and she must have been cruel indeed. His reign began by the arrest of his principal relations; and on the 15th, 16th, and 17th of February, he ordered the massacre of all his brothers and their families. It is said that eighty persons were put to death, though some reduced the number to thirty-two. As it was not thought decorous to spill the blood of the royal family of Alompra, their necks were stretched with a cord, and then broken with repeated blows from a bludgeon. "Infants were taken from their mother's arms and their brains were dashed out against the wall. Others were struck on the head, and thrown, only half-dead, on to the heap of bodies in the pit. The queens and princesses were stripped in order to search their clothes for secreted jewels. Some, it is said, were dishonoured before being killed, though this is perhaps untrue. All was effected under the superintendence of the personal

---

* My information about these and subsequent events, is mainly derived from the Blue Book entitled "Correspondence relating to Burmah since the accession of King Thebaw in October, 1878." London, 1886. I have also derived useful information on doubtful points from the letters of some officials of rank at present in Burma, procured through the kind exertions of my friends.

followers of the king."* By the direction of the Indian Government strong remonstrances were made by the British Resident, to King Thebaw's foreign minister. The Resident received a reply in which was asserted "the right of the King of Burmah, as an independent sovereign, to take such measures to prevent disturbance in his country as might be desirable without regard to the blame of others." The Resident, supported by the Italian Consul, interceded for the lives of those objects of the royal jealousy or hatred, who were still alive in prison. It was ascertained that the mother and sister of the Nyoungyan prince, and two of the late king's wives, were confined in a close and narrow cell, with irons on their legs, and wretchedly fed. There have always been difficulties about intercourse between the Burmese king and the British Resident. The sovereigns of the East and of the West have different methods of getting their subjects to acknowledge inferiority, for that is the meaning of court ceremonial. In general society Europeans show their respect by taking off their hats, the Orientals by taking off their shoes. On this matter the Burmese Court had always decided views. The first Burmese War with China was caused by the Chinese Ambassadors refusing, or delaying, to take off their slippers before the Master of the White Elephant. British residents had repeatedly demurred, and brought up the shoe question, which, when the Prince of Wales visited India in 1875, was discussed in an exhaustive manner. On this occasion, "His Excellency the Viceroy received the Burmese Mission, who were wearing hats and shoes, and were permitted to sit on chairs 'in the same manner as his Excellency himself.' 'It was impossible,' his Excellency said, 'that the custom observed at the Court of Mandalay should continue any longer.' The matter was not to be pressed in a manner distasteful to the king, 'still it would be carried through.'" But as the King of Burma would not grant reciprocity, and as the Resident would not take off his boots, the golden-footed king had no more of the Resident's visits, for which he was probably not sorry, but the Government of India seemed rather to have regretted declaring their

---

* Burma Blue Book, p. 21.

resolution that the Resident should stand on a new footing "before they were prepared to insist effectively upon the substitution of another form of reception." Not only were the remonstrances of the Resident unheeded at Thebaw's Court, but he was completely isolated. No official dared to be seen speaking with him, and his influence was insufficient to protect British subjects residing in Burma from oppression and maltreatment. He occasionally received private letters and messages from the captive princesses, in chains and in terror of their lives, begging for help from the strong arm of Britain. From time to time our Resident sent news of cruel executions in the palace or the jails, and of Thebaw's war preparations.

As Thebaw's reign began, so it went on. Dismissing the old ministers of his father's, and surrounding himself with other counsellors, laconically described by the Resident as "hardly rational animals," Thebaw indulged in acts of ferocity which created a reign of terror in Upper Burma. The Queen-Dowager, his mother, tried to restrain his follies, and interceded and wept for his victims, but his wife, Soo-pay-alat, was his evil genius. Her cruelties were especially shown towards any one whom she feared might prove a rival to herself. It was said that she caused a poor girl who had attracted Thebaw's attention, and who was *enceinte* by him, to be beaten to death.

The Chief Commissioner in Lower Burma, Mr. Charles U. Aitchison, considered a reinforcement of troops was necessary for the safety of the province, and when the troops came it appeared a good time to insist that the remonstrances of our Government against the King's wanton massacres should be attended to, and that the commercial engagements between Upper and Lower Burma should undergo revision. The Governor-General, while very determined upon the shoe question, was not willing to expose the lives of her Majesty's subjects "in an unprovoked war" with the King of Burma, because the prince, whilst at peace with the British Government, had barbarously taken the lives of his own subjects. The time was not opportune for pushing the matter to a practical issue with Burma, for, during our difficulties with Cabul, it was not expedient to have a war on the other side of India, so our Resident was entirely withdrawn from Mandalay, and the ignorant, arrogant, drunken king went on in his follies and cruelties for five years longer. During this time many of the inhabitants of Upper Burma fled to the lower province for safety. The continued misrule and occasional massacres in the native state were recorded in the Rangoon papers, and the British merchants sent remonstrances to the Government about the injury which commerce was suffering from the cruel and incapable despot in Mandalay.

At that time the French had views of founding an Indo-Chinese Empire, and had been extending their territory in Cochin till it seemed, as M. Jules Ferry observed to Lord Lyons, that "The French and Burmese were about to become neighbours." In 1884 a Burmese embassy was sent to Paris, and a commercial treaty was concluded. It was plain that the King of Burma was anxious to throw himself into the arms of our powerful neighbour, and there seemed danger of an arrangement being made by which the Burmese might claim the support of France, and perhaps open for the French a trade route with the southern provinces of China.

When, in 1885, King Thebaw subjected the Burma Bombay Company, trading in timber in Burmese forests, to what was nothing less than an arbitrary fine, the crisis was reached. An ultimatum was sent demanding that Thebaw should receive a British envoy at his Court, allow the commercial treaties to be revised, and consent to the reception of a British resident who, with his boots on, should regulate all the foreign diplomacy of Burma, and give advice, not to be disregarded, about the conduct of internal affairs. The king replied in a proclamation to his subjects that he was going to appear in person "with large forces of infantry, artillery, elephantry, and cavalry, by land and water, and with the might of his army efface these heretic Kalas, and annex their country."

Towards the end of 1885 a British force was ready to advance on the Burmese capital. As usual there was much bombast and defiance and little resistance. French and Italian officers had been engaged to teach the Burmese drill, but they were not allowed power enough to force the troops to go through distasteful exercises. Rifles and cannons had been purchased, which the Burmese had never been taught to use properly. There was no head, consequently no action. The British flotilla soon silenced the forts at Ava, and threading its way amongst the boats which had been sunk in vain hopes of blocking the river, the invaders came in sight of the pagoda roofs and spires of Mandalay. Here they were met by the Minister of the Interior begging for an armistice, and announcing that the forts had been ordered not to fire upon them. When they came to the capital there were crowds to witness their arrival, and nobody seemed displeased. The British regiments landed peaceably on the morning of 28th November, 1885, took possession of the gates of the city, and then of the gates of the palace, and summoned the king to surrender. The Burmese troops gave up their arms, and most of the officials fled. Nobody thought it worth while to fight for Thebaw. Next morning General Prendergast, with Colonel Sladen as his interpreter, walked up the grand central staircase of the palace which, up to that hour, only princes of the royal blood had been allowed to use before. After passing through the palace buildings, they reached a little raised house where they came in sight of King Thebaw, the Queen Soo-pay-alat, and the king's mother. The king's dress was plain without any jewels. In person he was short and stout, but though he looked heavy and unintelligent, he had an air of quiet dignity. The queen who wore a magnificent diamond necklace, sat crouching behind the king eagerly whispering to him suggestions which he adopted. She looked young and clever, and had bright eyes, but her lips were thin, and gave a hard look to an otherwise pretty face. To the right the Burmese ministers, who had followed the English officers, lay prostrate on the ground, it being thought a great crime even to look at the king. Thebaw, king no longer, hoped that the English would spare his life. Colonel Sladen reassured him upon that point. He then complained of the ingratitude of his servants who had run away the night before, and left him even without food, and said that he was afraid of his life from his own people, who would blame him for his tame surrender. He stipulated for a proper guard. He begged to be allowed to live in Mandalay, at any house the English might assign to him; but he desired to reign no longer. His ministers, he said, had grossly deceived him, and kept him in utter ignorance of what was going on in the world; and for weeks he had been almost a prisoner. He was told that he must prepare to leave the capital that day. After some delay in getting ready, the king with his wife and mother entered a bullock carriage. They were followed by a train of attendants, mostly girls on foot carrying bundles. The melancholy procession of fallen greatness then started for the river. They passed through many of the streets. The people looked on with indifference; in the most places, indeed, even the customary attitude of respect was not shown, though now and then there was some display of feeling. It was dark before they reached the river, when Thebaw and his suite, consisting of the queen, queen mother, and sixty-five other persons were borne in a steamer to Rangoon. On the 10th of December he left for Madras whence he was sent to live at Ranifet. He is now at Rutnagherry on the Malabar Coast, South of Bombay. From all that I can learn, Thebaw was never thought insane, but weak and indulgent, the tool of his wife. Derived from the same stock, both seemed to have inherited, though in unequal degrees, some of the worst qualities of their race. Stupid, arrogant, cruel, weak, and cowardly, Thebaw was scarcely a free agent, though nominally a despotic prince. Although the Viceroy, Lord Dufferin, invited General Prendergast to remember "that he was attacking not a hostile nation, but a perverse and impracticable Court," the Burmese had to atone for their tame submission to an incapable tyrant with the loss of their national independence. Had it not been for the fear of a French embroilment, the British Government would probably have been content with establishing a protectorate over Upper Burma.

www.ingramcontent.com/pod-product-compliance
Lightning Source LLC
Chambersburg PA
CBHW030729230426
43667CB00007B/645